Ferlinghetti

Ferlinghetti: the Artist in His Time

BARRY SILESKY

WARNER BOOKS

A Warner Communications Company

Grateful acknowledgment is made to the following for permission to reprint passages:

"Clickety Clack" copyright © 1972 by Joan Blackburn. Reprinted by permission of Black Sparrow Press.

Introduction to "Howl." Copyright © 1956 by William Carlos Williams. Reprinted by permission of City Lights.

Printed in the United States of America
First Printing: August 1990
10 9 8 7 6 5 4 3 2 1

LIBRARY OF CONGRESS CATALOGING-IN-PUBLICATION DATA

Silesky, Barry, 1948–
    Ferlinghetti, the artist in his time / by Barry Silesky.
        p.   cm.
    ISBN 0-446-51491-8
    1. Ferlinghetti, Lawrence—Biography.   2. Authors, American—20th
century—Biography.   3. Publishers and publishing—United States—
Biography.   4. Beat generation—Biography.   I. Title.
PS3511.E557Z86   1990
811'.54—dc20
[B]   89-40473
                                                                          CIP

Designed by Giorgetta Bell McRee

For Sharon, Seth & Jesse

Acknowledgments

The first and greatest thanks to Lawrence Ferlinghetti, of course, for the work which is the occasion for this book. Along with that thanks, my sincere apology for the unease I know he feels at my inevitable failure to write the book he might have wanted and imagined when he agreed to help me with the project. No one can construct a picture of another that matches the subject's view of himself; perhaps the subject, and the author, can only hope that the picture that emerges is not too painful to either in its differences.

From the first, this has not been envisioned by either of us as an "authorized" biography, in the sense of Ferlinghetti's approving the text. Though he agreed to cooperate in tracking down sources and information, gave me access to his personal journals and permission to quote from them (in most of the cases I wanted), submitted to extensive interviews in person and by phone, and has read and commented on all drafts, all the interpretive writing—conclusions, inferences, hypotheses, et al—is my own. At the same time, every word in direct quotations in the text is verbatim transcription from tapes (or in one or two cases, from notes) recorded during interviews. I have tried to note the places where he has disagreed specifically with my interpretations.

Secondly, I want to thank Nancy Peters, whose help in suggesting and tracking down sources, in shaping and balancing the picture, especially of the last twenty years, has been incalculable.

Equally, I want to thank Nat Sobel, whose enthusiasm for this book, as much as anyone's, made it happen; and Richard Bray and Paul Hoover, who helped me arrange the initial interview with Ferlinghetti for our magazine *ACM*, which led to this project.

And for critical reading, suggestions, warmth, and comfort, crucial beyond what I can say, thanks especially to my wife, Sharon Solwitz, and to Dan and Gina Hurlbutt, who housed me and my family during my stays in California.

Also vital, the list of others—poets, critics, researchers, translators, correspondents, friends, acquaintances, more—who've given generously of their time to provide crucial information, and whom I want to thank:

From City Lights, Rich Berman, Amy Scholder, Bob Sharrard; from the Bancroft Library at the University of California–Berkeley, Anthony Bliss, Lori Emison, Peter Hanff; from the library at the School of the Art Institute of Chicago, Roland Hansen; poets, writers, and others, Paul Ashley, Robert Bly, Paul Carroll, Neeli Cherkovski, Robert Creeley, Loren DeLorenzo, Charles Depondt, George Drury, Kirby Ferlinghetti, Lorenzo Ferlinghetti, Pablo Armando Fernández, Allen Ginsberg, Ethel Guttman, Robin Hemley, Phyllis Janik, David Michael Kaplan, Pamala Karol, Mike Keller, George Krevsky, Philip Lamantia, Maurice Lapp, Karen Larsen, James Laughlin, Paula Lillevand, Julie Maffie, Michael McClure, James McManus, David Meltzer, Ralph Mills, Shigeyoshi Murao, Gerald Nicosia, Patrick O'Connor, June O'Donahoo, Griselda Ohanessian, Thomas Parkinson, Jim Perlman, Nancy Peters, Charles Richards, Bob Rosenthal, Mary Sherman, Gibbs Smith, Gary Snyder, Vickie Stanbury, Diane Wakoski, Anne Waldman, S. L. Wisenberg, and not least, the School of the Art Institute of Chicago.

My grateful thanks as well to the publishers and publications who've permitted me to quote from various works: Black Sparrow Press, City Lights Books, New Directions.

And to all those I have inevitably forgotten to mention by name, who spoke with me, whose words or ideas I've used, my apologies and no less thanks.

Ferlinghetti

In many ways his beginnings seem straight from a Dickens novel—both parents gone before he was two, abandoned at six, sent away by his caretakers as a teenager after leading his gang into petty crime—and yet, just as in such novels, circumstances so unlikely they could only be a novelist's dream somehow combined to raise him out of the backwash. And raised him not just to salvage some ordinary life—decent job, wife, kids, car, etc.—but to other circumstances as extreme as those beginnings: to become Lawrence Ferlinghetti, publisher, poet, novelist, painter, spokesman of his time.

Genius? Luck? Whatever we call it, the explanation, from one view, is in the writing itself—the poems, the plays, the novels evidencing in their lines, in addition to the passion and the craft, the seeds that led to them. Even the most strictly autobiographical work, however, is at best a palimpsest, full of lies and wishes; and in Ferlinghetti's case, there isn't much that's strictly autobiographical. Above all, he is a private person. He has friends, he has a family, keeps in close touch with his two children, with his ex-wife, even with women to whom he's been romantically connected in the past, and is no longer. But his temper is reserved, in a sense old-fashioned, declining the religion of personal revelation that suffuses so much late-twentieth-century art and celebrity.

"Lawrence is just not interested in people," one longtime friend said, not as criticism, but as explanation for the detachment with which he regards the lives around him. It isn't really that he's not interested, as the friend went on to elaborate, but his interest is from a greater distance, through a different lens than for most. "It enables him to have the kind of vision he has; to see things without getting emotionally involved in the ordinary way." It is perhaps the essential difference that makes the artist. How did it happen? Though the writing is better known, the painting he's been doing with equal passion for the last decade offers its own images, and in them, perhaps even more fertile clues to who he is, who he was, how he came to be.

In the lower left corner of a canvas Ferlinghetti painted in 1987, a long, slender, red-tinted figure holds his arms up and out in a "V." The figure is standing in a slight depression on what seems to be the blue-black peak of something. The surface is uneven, blurred at the edges, as if roiling or cloudy. It may be the sea or a mountain, swept by fog. But it seems to be in motion: something is bubbling up from below, sweeping about the body, which is extending toward the brighter red and yellow above it. Two or three orange pools spot the blue-gray ground, as if reflecting the space overhead. There are faint lines running from the arms into those bright colors, and as the eye moves right, the red becomes yellow, then gray.

Earth First (The Dark Strand), the painting is titled. It's the name of a militant environmental group Ferlinghetti supports, and the primary colors, the sensational, vibrant, but undefined energies, suggest some sort of gloss on the group and its concerns.

In a 1988 interview he explained, "According to Earth First and the people on the radical left of the ecology movement, the situation is much too critical today and has reached such a point of crisis ecologically that the conservative measures taken by the Sierra Club are much too timid and don't go anywhere near far enough. So they will come out at night and push huge earth movers that were going to be used to destroy some wilderness area over a cliff into a deep canyon. They've been attacked for their wild tactics and are sometimes called the crazies of the ecology movement. But this is the kind of action that's really needed."

Ferlinghetti's interest in the current headlines goes back a long way, but his sympathy for radical action, for the outlaw acting against faceless, destructive institutions, is really founded in his very beginnings—as an orphan, alone in the world. The image of the painting seems to have much more to do with that than with politics. Or more accurately, whatever is political is always personal as well, if it has any real meaning.

The outspread arms of the figure don't hint at any conflict, however, political or personal. Rather, they suggest celebration, the colors, something extraordinary. The eye keeps coming back to the bright red sky, the figure. It is not a picture of peace, not the pastoral morning of a tranquil sun spreading ease over some idyllic landscape. The lone figure standing on "the dark strand" is the only recognizable object. The rest, alive with light, color, energy, the power of something coming to be, is still unformed. The sharp contrast of the dark lower surface with the red and yellow, those lines moving out from the figure, the way the color seems blotched in pools, layered, the outlines shifting—all tell us this power is not controlled. It is primeval, a drama whose outcome we can't predict. The figure just born, rising to the light, calling it up, is caught in something huge, hopeful, but at the same time ominous; something which could in the next instant overwhelm it.

Clearly Ferlinghetti did not intend the painting to be a backward look. But just as a poem reveals sides its author never expected, so the elements of Ferlinghetti's own beginning, the forces that brought him to the poetry, the painting, and the political stance, are all here: the sea, the bright colors; the turmoil, the drama, the threat. The lone figure. As in his own poems, the image and the design are simple. But meanings gather with a force that is undeniable.

At the very beginning, his prospects seemed rosy. Sometime at the end of the 1890s, his mother, Clemence Mendes-Monsanto, met her husband at Coney Island, where many French families operated boardinghouses. Charles Ferlinghetti was living at nearby Bath Beach in Brooklyn, and had caught her attention initially because of his fluency in French, which she had also grown up speaking. Her French mother, wanting to retain that heritage, saw to it that her daughter was as fluent in French as she was in English. But besides the knowledge of French, Clemence also had in her background wide education. Her father, Herman Mendes-Monsanto, was the son of a wealthy broker on St. Thomas, where his family had come from Portugal, via the Netherlands Antilles. He had attended a private school and a European university, moving to the United States in the late nineteenth century, where he met his future wife, who had come to America with a daughter by a previous marriage. Having grown up in a wealthy household, with plenty of books and servants, he became a professor of language at the Naval Academy at Annapolis, then at a small college in New York City, and authored several textbooks.

Lawrence's father had come from northern Italy, and like so many immigrants, changed his name from Ferlinghetti to the simpler, less identifiably ethnic "Ferling." He had been an auctioneer in Italy and was able to use that talent to make a living in America. And again, like so many enterprising immigrants, he had parlayed his skill into a successful business, helped by a knowledge of several languages. By the time

Lawrence was conceived in 1918, Charles had a real estate office on Forty-second Street in Manhattan and had moved his family to a new house on Saratoga Avenue in Yonkers. Thus prospering in the New World, with the economy flourishing and World War I almost over, Charles and his family seemed in every respect the successful-immigrant dream.

Beyond Yonkers, however, the postwar optimism of which the Ferlings were part was tempered by other facets, some of which would reflect directly, some indirectly, on the future of Lawrence, their fifth son, who was born in a small white clapboard house on Saratoga Avenue on March 24, 1919.

That day, twenty-year-old Ernest Hemingway was home in Oak Park, Illinois, restlessly convalescing from the wound he had received in Italy, which had ended World War I for him; ten days before, he'd regaled a high school class in his suburb with tales of death and heroism on the front.

And about the same time, Naomi Ginsberg, who would become Allen Ginsberg's mother seven years later, lay for some three weeks in a darkened room in Woodbine, New Jersey, suffering from a condition where light and sound were actually painful to her. Though she wasn't hospitalized, it was the first of several increasingly serious breakdowns that would culminate in the schizophrenic symptoms Ginsberg recounted in "Kaddish," the major poem Ferlinghetti's City Lights Books would publish more than forty years later.

In March 1919 in Paris, the city where Hemingway would spend several notable years in the next decade, Woodrow Wilson was negotiating the terms of the Versailles Treaty, which would disarm Germany and lead ultimately to World War II. And the same year, Sylvia Beach opened Shakespeare & Co. at 8 rue Dupuytren. The small bookstore would move in 1921 to 12 rue de l'Odéon, where, with its rental library for the use of indigent writers, its big stove, its pictures of famous writers on the walls, it would become an international literary center and a model for some of the most important bookstores to come in both Europe and America.

Beach's store would also provide one of the first public audiences for the reading of the newest experimental novel that Ezra Pound knew would change the face of the world's literary landscape. When the novel arrived in America in 1934, James Joyce's *Ulysses* was banned for its "obscenity," which would again justify Pound's assessments of the backward philistinism ruling his native country. Still, the court case that followed would establish the landmark precedent which would be used to defend future attacks on some of the most important American literature of the century. And despite whatever philistinism, Frances Steloff created at least an outpost of culture in midtown Manhattan when she opened the Gotham Book Mart in 1919, which would itself become a literary center.

The Poetry Society in 1919 turned its attention to the Midwest, awarding half its prize to a volume titled *Cornhuskers*, by the motion picture reviewer for the *Chicago Daily News*, Carl Sandburg. Sandburg's populist sympathies and his disdain for the conventions of more refined, "intellectual" verse, however, drew vitriolic reviews from the competing *Chicago Tribune*. Sandburg and his populism, the American expatriate writers in Paris, the Shakespeare & Co. store, the political complications and upheavals in both Europe and America, would all be important foundation pieces in Ferlinghetti's development, but his father would never know.

By the time Lawrence was born, the Ferlings' promising rise had been cut off by Charles's sudden death, of either heart attack or stroke, the previous October. Clemence was desolated, and like most women of the time, was ill equipped to support herself, let alone a family. She continued to collect royalties from one of Charles's textbooks, a Spanish grammar, until her death, but the money was nowhere near enough. Soon after Lawrence's birth, she was forced to move from the new house on Saratoga Avenue to a smaller place. Then, with four young children to support (Arthur, the oldest, was nineteen), no way to make a living, and no one to provide for them, she had to move several more times over the next months, to increasingly cheaper housing, while her physical and emotional condition worsened. She was still in touch with some relatives, but they couldn't help her financially, and she simply couldn't manage. Finally it became clear that she would have to be taken to a hospital. With Lawrence still less than two years old, she was admitted to the state hospital in Poughkeepsie, New York.

The older boys—eight, twelve, and sixteen, in addition to Arthur— were sent to live at a boarding home in Ossining, but the family decided the baby should be cared for by a relative if at all possible. Clemence's uncle Ludovic Monsanto—also called Ludwig—had a home on Riverside Drive, but he and his second wife, Emily, had no children of their own; Emily was pleased to have Lawrence come to live with them. It seemed to be a fine solution to the problems of the trauma that had split the Ferling family. Ludwig and Emily had their own marital problems, however, and soon after Lawrence was moved in, they reached a crisis. Packing up herself and the toddler, she left Ludwig to move back home—to the city of Strasbourg in Alsace, on the Ill River near its junction with the Rhine on the French-German border.

While Gertrude Stein was telling Hemingway that he was not a good enough writer to be published in *The Atlantic* or *The Saturday Evening Post*, Emily was living with her young charge some 120 miles east of Paris in the beautiful old Alsatian capital, where Gutenberg may have been when he invented the printing press, and whose university Goethe had attended. With its centuries-old buildings, Strasbourg had much of the charm of Paris, though it was much smaller; and it suited Emily's own eccentric temperament. In a 1983 poem Ferlinghetti remembers her "mad" Catholicism, "as if she had some special connection with the Pope." But at the same time, she had a certain elegance and liked to think of herself as a writer—as having "something important to say." She made sure Lawrence knew that he came from a well-educated, well-cultivated family; Clemence had played the piano and given lessons, and had a half-sister who was an opera singer. She read him stories, made others up, and introduced him to music by playing the piano herself. As a result of those early years in France, he learned to speak French before English, forming the basis for a lifelong attachment to the French language and culture. Things certainly could have been worse; despite the separation from his parents, and his caretaker's own separation from her husband, he was fortunate to begin at least amid the advantages of an educated background. For a few brief years, his childhood seems in some ways almost enviable. It was not to remain so.

While in Strasbourg, Emily exchanged letters with Ludwig. After four years he convinced her that a reconciliation was possible, and she returned with Lawrence to New York. Ludwig was working as a language instructor at City College, and from him Lawrence finally began to learn English. But soon after the family was reunited, Ludwig lost his job, and financial problems reawakened difficulties between him and Emily. As the money strain worsened, the arguments did too, and at one point, Lawrence developed a case of rickets when there was too little money even to buy milk for him.

Apparently Ludwig, who was much older than his second wife, did not seem to be able to find work to support the family, and Emily realized she would have to do something. She tried various financial schemes, but nothing really worked. Though women's suffrage and the invention of labor-saving household devices had begun to open the door to greater opportunity in the larger world, like Clemence, she had no training for any real job, and no way to take care of the baby while she worked. The only choice was to find somewhere else for her charge to live while she earned some money and maybe saved enough to get him back. In Chappaqua, a town only a few miles from Ossining, where Lawrence's brothers lived, and near Poughkeepsie, where his mother was still hospitalized, Emily found an orphanage to take him. Despite his family's proximity, however, the six-year-old child had no knowledge of their existence. Instead, he was left to fend for himself among strangers.

The time there must have been difficult at best; more than half a century later Ferlinghetti has no memory of the experience besides the undercooked tapioca pudding he was served. Meantime, Emily left Ludwig for good, and after seven or eight months, found a position doing what she was probably best qualified to do. Being educated and well bred, she must have seemed just right to be a governess for the wealthy Bisland family, caring for and tutoring their daughter. The job meant at least a place to live, food to eat, and luxurious surroundings, not only for herself but for the child she could now take back.

Presley and Anna Lawrence Bisland lived in Lawrence Park West, an exclusive Bronxville neighborhood, in a genuine mansion. When young Lawrence was suddenly transported there, he must have been awed at the change in his fortunes. Though he and Emily were consigned to a small room in the third-floor servants' quarters, the surroundings at Plashbourne, as the mansion was named, were far more opulent than anything he had known. Still, the luxury was likely small comfort to the child who had been shunted between houses and countries and circumstances without any real stability, as he was left as much to his own devices there as at the orphanage. The Bislands themselves were in their sixties, their daughter, Sally, was a good deal older than Lawrence, and there were no other children at all around to play with.

Emily continued reading to him, though, and taught him to read, presenting him with the first book he read all the way through: *Little Lord Fauntleroy*, the classic tale of the poor American boy who inherits a fortune and goes to live in style in England. Emily had made sure he was aware of his French origins, and certainly Lawrence, like millions of young boys at the time, must have found the book rich fruit for his imagination, especially given the parallels with his own life. But the book obviously portended more than stimulus for his imagination. Almost as soon as she gave it to him, she gave him even greater reason to identify with Fauntleroy's origins.

Only a week after the gift, Emily went out as she did each Sunday for her day off. This time she never came back. Neither the Bislands nor

Lawrence ever learned what became of her until years later. Then, in the Navy, he received notice from Central Islip State Hospital in Long Island that Emily Monsanto had died at the age of fifty-six. On the hospital form she had listed him as her only living relative; apparently she had kept track of his whereabouts, though he never knew.

Though he had already been moved several times and been left completely on his own at the orphanage, Emily had been the most stable element in his early life. Now that was gone, too. Certainly the abandonment must have been devastating. Such dislocations no doubt contributed to the formation of a certain shell, the distance from others that all who know him remark, to protect against future damage.

The damage was lessened to some degree when the Bislands assumed his care, apparently without hesitation. It was a decision that seemed to come from values rooted deep in both their backgrounds. Anna Bisland's maiden name was Lawrence, and she had lost a son in early childhood whose name was also Lawrence. But it was almost certainly not just the sentimentality of coincidence that led her to take on the burden of raising an orphan. For she was much more than a wealthy socialite. Her father, William Van Duzer Lawrence, the Lawrence after whom their neighborhood was named, had founded Sarah Lawrence College near Bronxville and named it after his wife. Like him, Anna contributed actively in various community affairs, and as heiress to a great deal of the family wealth, superintended an array of real estate holdings and businesses. Further, she had some literary interest, and later in her life wrote a history of the Lawrence family. With the values of education and, especially, commitment to community service so much a part of her background, it was not surprising that she should take up Lawrence's care. Emily herself must have believed the Bislands would, and probably do better for him than she ever could.

Still, however pleased Anna might have been to have Lawrence there, he could not take the place of her own lost son, nor did she try to make him. The adoption had come, it seemed, more from obligation than from affection. And neither she nor her husband was by nature affectionate, anyway, imbued as they were with the aristocratic, Protestant reserve of their social class. Thus, Lawrence's isolation deepened. When he would crouch by their bedroom door hoping for some attention, rather than any hugs or caresses, he would get cheerful encouragement to go downstairs and play, though there were no real playmates there. Instead, Lawrence made friends with the chauffeur, Gerhard Rulof, and the cook, Delia Devine.

Besides spending hours in the garage with Rulof, he spent a summer working with him, painting some of the family's rental houses. And Ferlinghetti remembers especially the summer trips to the family's lodge on Big Wolf Lake in the Adirondacks, when he would ride in the front of the big touring car while Presley drove separately by himself. Rulof, an avid fisherman, would sometimes take Lawrence fishing with him. Sadly that childhood ally was also lost when the chauffeur drowned in a fishing accident, though it happened some years later while Ferlinghetti was away at college.

Still, though he was not showered with a great deal of human warmth by the Bislands, he did receive other benefits which were crucial in the formation of his character. Presley was also from an aristocratic family whose Scottish forebears settled in Mississippi and Louisiana in the late eighteenth century. The son of a wealthy southern gentleman and raised in Natchez, Mississippi, he was the youngest son, however, and so didn't share in the family inheritance. Knowing he would have to make his own fortune, he became something of an adventurer as a young man, and prided himself on having been on the last great cattle drive up the Chisolm Trail. Young Lawrence spent many hours playing among the saddle and western gear Bisland still kept up in the attic.

Though Presley never had anything of their wealth, his family knew the Vanderbilts, the Whitneys, and other very wealthy families, and traveled in their social circles. It was through those connections that he had met Anna, who had much more money in her background than he did.

Distinctly straightforward and unpretentious, Presley modeled himself after his hero, Mark Twain, dressing like Twain and evincing Twain's sense of humor. Later, when he became president of the Abbot Coin Counting Company in 1912, he began a newsletter for employees that included poetry and short prose sketches. And he was selective about what he published there, sending sometimes biting rejections to potential contributors whose attempts he thought too pompous. He also wrote a number of short stories himself, though never published, which imitated Twain's brand of down-home clarity and humor.

Further, Presley was schooled in Greek and Latin classics, which he still read, and was interested in nineteenth-century American literature—William Cullen Bryant, Henry Wadsworth Longfellow, John Greenleaf Whittier. His huge library of leather-bound volumes fascinated Lawrence, and Presley encouraged him to read. As Lawrence grew older, Bisland drilled him on the ancient classics, until Lawrence had a better working knowledge of them than most students his age, and paid Lawrence silver dollars to memorize long English poems like "The Burial of Sir John Moore."

One of the family businesses was a chain of automobile garages, the Kensington Plaza Garages, which Presley also managed. Lawrence worked there one summer, though he didn't like it much; but he did enjoy his first literary success, writing a simple rhyme that, thanks to a little nepotism, won a contest the garage sponsored: "Kensington Plaza Garages," he wrote, "make car troubles fade like mirages!"

By the time Lawrence was eight, and the Bislands sent him to Riverdale Country School, a private school for the children of Bronxville and surrounding elite, he already had solid intellectual beginnings. And at Riverdale the daily contact with children his own age began to bring him out of the shell of isolation that had surrounded him since Emily left. He learned sports, went to summer camp, and did well enough at school to earn some praise from the Bislands. On the other hand, back at Plashbourne, he was moved to an upstairs room, which, though well appointed, was also a bit sterile, and reinforced the isolation he was just beginning to come out of at school. There was a huge four-poster bed with fancy coverings, and cleanliness and order were the rules of the house. He wasn't allowed to put anything up on the walls and was discouraged from making any mess. Altogether, they were not the kind of surroundings to put a young boy at ease. But the view out the windows of the huge old oak trees climbing up the walls of the house offered substance for poetic meditation, and just below was a music room with a grand piano on the marble floor, and French doors that opened onto a patio which looked out on a private stream.

Despite his rocky start, the orphan boy seemed to have landed pretty well. If he didn't get the kind of emotional support a real family gives, his material circumstances were virtually royal, and the intellectual encouragement was exceptional. But the parallels with the Victorian saga that his life had so far assumed were not through.

One Sunday when Lawrence was ten and a half, an old car drove up to the mansion and an older woman and two younger men emerged. The older woman was his mother, Clemence; the men, Lawrence's brothers Harry and Clement. Clement had arranged Clemence's release from Poughkeepsie five years earlier and moved her into an apartment with three of her sons in Ossining, where he worked as a warden at the state prison. Charles, Jr., the oldest, had already married by then and lived with his own family while Lawrence was still in France with Emily. Clement remembered that their mother seemed "very vague" and "sort of mixed up" about her baby, and given her delicate state, the responsibility of taking care of him apparently would have been more than she could manage. But she continued to recover well, and by now apparently felt that she could assume his care. Her other sons, who bore the financial burden, no doubt agreed that it wasn't right to leave his upbringing to strangers, no matter how wealthy. Her youngest son, they decided, should be reunited with the family; or at least given the chance to be.

Ferlinghetti remembers he found it odd that the Bislands did not invite his family into the house during their visit, emphasizing the gap of wealth and social class between them. Instead, all stood on the front lawn for a short time. Though the Bislands were distant emotionally, their affection for their charge was genuine, and they apparently assured the Ferlings that it was more than obligation that made them keep him. For the Ferlings' part, how much they really wanted their relative—whom they'd never known—is impossible to determine, but after continuing the discussion for a time, they decided the child was old enough to make up his own mind.

They turned to Lawrence and asked him whether he wanted to go and live with his "real" family or remain at Plashbourne. Twice abandoned, uprooted from New York to France to New York to an orphanage and finally to Plashbourne, there was no real choice. By then, the Bislands were the only family he knew and Plashbourne the only home. Though afterward he was haunted by that day, and the unfairness of forcing him to make such a choice in those conditions, of course he wanted to stay.

That October of 1929 the stock market crashed, beginning the Great Depression. Though the Bislands were not one of the thousands, even millions, of families who were wiped out financially, they did lose a good deal of money, and the loss led to yet another dislocation for their ward. The expense of Riverdale for Lawrence seemed an extravagance they could no longer afford. Clearly their own commitments to community dictated that they act in Lawrence's best interests as far as they saw them, and that meant assuring the continuation of his education in an environment which would be healthy and constructive.

They found another family who would open its doors to him, where he could attend the Bronxville public schools. The Bislands arranged his move there, at the same time agreeing to continue paying his board. Zilla Larned Wilson, who had come to New York from Ohio five years earlier, had no husband, but her son, Bill, was five years older than Lawrence. The move seemed to work out well for the young orphan, despite the readjustment, as Bill became a real big brother to Lawrence, taking the younger boy to baseball and football games, playing basketball with him, and coaching him so that when Lawrence reached junior high, he was good enough to play on the basketball team.

Lawrence also had a newspaper route, which, like the books at Plashbourne, helped feed his interest in writing. He became fascinated with print and the whole process behind the newspaper, and for the first time imagined a career as a journalist. That interest was fed further by his basketball coach, who also ran the school print shop. It was the only subject in junior high that Lawrence was really interested in, and he excelled in it.

The years with the Wilsons turned out to be the happiest he had yet known. There were other children at school and in the neighborhood, there was an older brother, there were athletics: all the activities that "normal" adolescent boys are so involved in. And as if to complete the portrait of the all-American boyhood that life there supplied, he even became a Boy Scout.

At the same time, however, he became a member of the "Parkway Road Pirates." At first this adolescent "gang" played imaginary pirate games; unfortunately they soon grew bored with that and needed to make it real. Lawrence became one of the ringleaders, heading up forays into petty thievery and shoplifting, after which they stashed their booty in an abandoned storefront. They didn't take anything of much value; as with most adolescents, the excitement was the point. The same month that Lawrence made Eagle Scout, he was arrested for shoplifting—a deeply ironic but true episode that he relates in his early poem "Autobiography." His scoutmaster bailed him out.

Such adolescent escapades into the outlaw side are common enough for many teens, symptomatic of the alienation and the frustrated desire for power that is a part of that age. For Lawrence, more than most, the outsider was an inextricable part of his identity. The coupling of such delinquency with the high social approval the achievement of the Eagle Scout rank represented gives a clear, tangible sign of the two forces whose mixture would always be central to Ferlinghetti: the eternal outsider, the "Charlie Chaplin," always sympathetic with the everyman in all of us who feels the pain of that alienation; and the public high achiever whose work as poet and publisher has made such a mark.

After this incident, a sort of climax to the growing restlessness of which Mrs. Wilson was certainly aware, she felt she couldn't continue taking care of him. She discussed the problem with the Bislands, and they agreed.

Lawrence would have to be relocated yet again. They decided to place him in Mount Hermon, a private boys' high school near Greenfield, Massachusetts. Founded by Dwight L. Moody, who also founded the Moody Bible Institute in Chicago, it was mainly attended by the sons of missionaries. The point, however, was not so much to give Lawrence religious training, but to give him discipline. The regime there was rigorous, to say the least. The day began at 5 A.M., when students headed out to the barns and fields to work the farm, which supported a herd of some five hundred cows. At seven they returned for chapel, then attended class from eight until one. After dinner and a short break, they went to class again from four until six. And this regime went on every day except Sunday.

The school also had high academic standards and a good record of success with its students. The long days and close supervision meant there was no opportunity to cut class, as Lawrence had often done at Bronxville, or to waste time and get into trouble. For this budding troublemaker at least, it worked.

And some of the people he met made impressions that would help shape lifelong interests. His first roommate, Jim Alter (who went on to Yale), wrestled him to the ground on meeting him, swearing he wouldn't let him up until he could prove his own existence. Such a shock caught and intrigued Lawrence, and Alter's interest in philosophy apparently became one of the things that helped turn Ferlinghetti toward more academic pursuits. Another student, Alden Monroe, fanned those intellectual sparks, becoming Lawrence's best friend there and ultimately his roommate. Monroe, who was known as "Rube," carried everywhere tattered copies of Hemingway's *The Sun Also Rises* and Thomas Wolfe's *Look Homeward, Angel.* When Lawrence read Wolfe's novel, he was, like so many adolescents and young men, struck by the poetic romanticism of both the language and the stance. In Lawrence's case, however, the correspondences with the obsessive sense of exile, of "dispossession," at the heart of Wolfe's novel weren't poetic imaginings but vivid facts of his life. Reading Wolfe's novel, the young Ferlinghetti discovered that he was not completely alone in his isolation; others shared these feelings, and they could be expressed, transformed through literature, and so comfort, justify, enhance the lives of both the reader and the writer.

He worked hard and read as well several other books that stayed with him. Henry David Thoreau's *Walden* particularly impressed him with its lessons on self-reliance that reinforced values Presley Bisland had been trying to impart. He also read *Don Quixote* from beginning to end, and

Nathaniel Hawthorne's *The Scarlet Letter* and *The House of the Seven Gables*. And on his sixteenth birthday he received the first poetry book he read from cover to cover. Sally Bisland gave him a French-English edition of Charles Baudelaire; he was pleased that he could read it in both languages, and for the first time began writing poems himself. Like so many, he discovered through writing a way to unlock his buried emotions, and the feeling of freedom that came from being able to invent his own rules, or dispense with them completely.

As with most people, however, the young Ferlinghetti's conversion—in his case to more accepted, intellectual tastes—was not absolute. He was still an outsider, and an adolescent with a taste for adventure and an attraction for the forbidden. Along with Rube, he would escape down a rope used as a fire escape and make nighttime visits to Northfield Academy, the nearby "sister" school. They never actually saw any girls, and they never got caught, but as with the Parkway Road Pirates, the excitement was the thing. He was also caught smoking and as punishment was sent to work on a nearby farm in Colrain, Massachusetts, where under the supervision of farmer Calvin Call, he learned to milk cows, to plow, and to drive the hay wagon.

In his final year at Mount Hermon, the Bislands began taking him to visit his mother and brothers in Ossining. This time the initial awkwardness gave way to genuine familial warmth, as they finally began to know each other. When Lawrence graduated from Mount Hermon in 1937, he changed his name from Lawrence Ferling Monsanto, the name with which he'd grown up, to Lawrence Monsanto Ferling. It was a step toward reclaiming the lineage and the sense of connection it gave, whose absence he felt with increasing sharpness.

In the fall his interest in Thomas Wolfe took him to Chapel Hill to attend the University of North Carolina. Still a small, southern college town of nine thousand, it was one of the more liberal in the South. Ferlinghetti joined the Kappa Sigma fraternity and followed up his interest in journalism by becoming circulation manager of *The Daily Tar Heel*, the campus newspaper. He paid his tuition and expenses by rising at 5 A.M. every day to deliver the *Tar Heel* and the *New York Times*, and he also began writing on the sports staff of *Carolina Magazine*, for which Wolfe himself had written when he was at the university. At the same time, he began writing short stories, and during his tenure at North Carolina, tried to write his first novel. Not surprisingly his prose came out heavily under the spell of Wolfe.

After the rigor of Mount Hermon, however, college seemed almost a vacation. "When I got to Chapel Hill," he remembers, "I was so far ahead of everyone else in my class, it was a breeze. I don't think I did any work for the first couple years."

After his second year he and two friends adventured to Mexico. One of them was a nephew of Josephus Daniels, at the time the U.S. ambassador to Mexico. They assumed that once they got there, Daniels would put them up at the embassy. They hitchhiked and hopped freight trains and finally arrived, but were disappointed to find that Daniels in fact would not let them stay. They found an inexpensive *pensión*, and Ferlinghetti wrote dispatches on the Mexican political scene as a foreign correspondent, which he sent off to *Time* magazine and other magazines of similar prominence. Not surprisingly there was no sign of interest; but his ambition was clear, and the determination which would be necessary was clearly taking shape.

When school began again in the fall, he took a creative writing class from Phillips Russell (to whom he eventually dedicated his third book of poetry, *Starting from San Francisco*). Russell introduced him to Carl Sandburg, Edgar Lee Masters, Vachel Lindsay, and other populist writers whose accessibility and political-social values he found immediately attractive. Russell's interest wasn't limited, however; he introduced a wide range of contemporary writers, emphasizing as well the importance of humor in poetry, and urging his students not to take themselves and their writing too seriously.

In the spring of 1941 Ferlinghetti received his B.A. and listened to Carl Sandburg give the commencement speech. He noted in his journal Sandburg's remark that theirs was a "bridged generation," with "one foot in one war, the other in the second one." It had been a year and a half since Hitler overran Poland, and though the United States was not yet directly involved, everyone felt the threat.

After graduation Ferlinghetti and some friends rented a small island off the coast of Maine. Only a couple of hundred yards long, it came with a small cabin and a little boat, all for thirty-five dollars for the entire summer. They met expenses by collecting the native Irish moss with long rakes and hauling it down Casco Bay to Portland, where a chemical company bought it for use in explosives. It was an idyllic time, spent mostly hanging about in the sun and water, enjoying the big Maine lobsters. But the war was on its way to America. Very much a part of Sandburg's "bridged generation," before Ferlinghetti left for Maine, like thousands of others, he had decided what his next step must be. On June 16 he had gone down to New Rochelle and enlisted in the Navy.

On October 15, 1941, a Nazi submarine "wolf pack" attacked a British convoy, and the U.S.S. *Kearney*, one of five U.S. ships that came to the rescue, was hit by a torpedo. The eleven sailors listed as missing, presumed dead, became the first American casualties of World War II. The following day, after a month of instruction in "deck training," Lawrence Ferling was sworn in as a midshipman at Abbott Hall, home of the U.S. Naval Reserve Midshipmen's School in Chicago, and began the three-month training program at Great Lakes Naval Base, just north of the city, that would make him one of the Navy's thousands of "ninety-day wonders."

In the next four years he certainly saw his share of combat, but as for so many who fought in that war, the overwhelming majority of his time was spent preparing to fight, waiting to fight, and sometimes simply waiting. And it was some of these noncombat experiences that proved to be the most important in their later influence.

At the same time, his years in the Navy could almost be used as advertising for military service, as his work there did help to bring out that "man" the ads promise the military will make of its enlistees. Though his longtime stance outside the American mainstream and in opposition to its authority and institutions makes him seem so far from the exemplary soldier that many are surprised when they learn of his service, those oppositional values hadn't emerged yet. And the proverbial qualities of leadership—the quickness of intelligence, the ability to make good decisions, to attract others through sheer competence—that were brought out and developed became part of the basis for real success in the postwar, material world.

When he graduated in January, he was commissioned as an ensign—an officer—appropriately, given his education and background and performance in training. It was a position that of course set him apart from the enlisted men he would command, and not incidentally served to reinforce that distance from others that the dislocations of his past and his life with the Bislands had already established.

His first assignment was to the Third Naval District in New York City, a welcome stroke, as it meant he would be near home. There, aboard J. P. Morgan III's private yacht, which had been given a coat of regulation gray paint and converted to use as a subchaser with sticks of dynamite to use as depth charges, he had his first glimpse of the war. The boat spent twenty-one days on patrol along the East Coast where German submarines were trying to stop shipments of arms to Europe, then five days in port. Though they were never in direct engagment during the five-month tour, Ferlinghetti got his first brush with combat when he was out on deck one day near Atlantic City, with the wind blowing and ice on the rigging, and a German submarine blew up an empty tanker nearby.

He found his commanding officer, thirty-year-old First Lieutenant Morgan, the grandson of the first financier, friendly and easygoing, though somewhat stiff and formal at times. During one shore leave, Ferlinghetti accompanied him to the family mansion on Fifth Avenue across from Central Park where Morgan offered him use of its "conveniences." Ensign Ferling, however, a bit in awe of his commanding officer, and familiar enough with prodigious wealth because of his own background to prefer the urban adventures of New York City streets, declined, pleading another pressing engagement.

During his time off, he stayed with the Bislands in Bronxville and got to know New York and Greenwich Village. For the first time he looked seriously, firsthand, at paintings, at the Museum of Modern Art, sparking an interest that grew to be central to all his work. And early in his tour he called up a girl from Northfield Academy who had also lived in Bronxville. She in turn introduced him to a classmate of hers, leading to another, equally significant dimension in his education.

Laura Lou Lyon had gone to Swarthmore and was attending Columbia Law School. Ferlinghetti began dating her, and eventually she brought the young officer home to meet her brother, who was an avowed sympathizer with the political left. Ferlinghetti was completely surprised at the welcome he got.

"I would go up to their house with my Navy officer's uniform," he remembers, "and I couldn't imagine why he gave me such a cold reception. I looked like something out of Gilbert and Sullivan. I looked on the table and there were these strange magazines like *The Nation* and *The New Republic* and I thought, what's that?" Ferlinghetti calls those experiences the beginning of his political education.

His second assignment kept him in New York, on the U.S.S. *Fire Island*, which was stationed in the Ambrose Channel off Long Island. Its job was to protect the harbor, challenging every ship that came in order to ascertain its identity and cargo. The information would be given by signal and in coded messages, and Ferlinghetti, besides decoding, had become a fast and expert signalman, so he did his own signaling even though he was one of the ship's officers. This assignment lasted until April 1943, during which time his diligence earned him promotion to lieutenant. And while they were there, the crew would get a week off in town after every few weeks on duty; thus, he could continue to hang around the Village and see Laura Lou.

That spring, however, the easy days in New York came to an end, and his Navy duty became more serious. After a month's instruction in Miami, Ferlinghetti was assigned to a new subchaser patrolling in the Atlantic, one of the hundreds of 110-foot wooden "SC"-class boats the Navy built for these patrols. There were thirty sailors under the three officers, and the junior officer assigned under Ferlinghetti was Chuck Feeney, later known as "Chub" Feeney, who became an executive of the San Francisco Giants baseball team and then president of the National League.

The conditions on this tour were harsh. "It was rough out there and the food wasn't much. Hardtack and things like that," he recalls. The crew, most with beards and earrings, were a rough-looking bunch. When a new man came on, he was wrestled to the deck and his ear was pierced. But the very harshness bred a toughness, and an atmosphere that suited Ferlinghetti well. He liked the informality, the relative absence of regulations, and he liked being on the sea. Despite the informality, "there was a certain amount of discipline. I would climb up the mast to the crow's nest when it was real foggy and shout out orders to the helmsman down below. It was a great experience for people who loved ships. Everyone on board was under thirty years old except the chief machinist's mate. It was too damn rough for older sailors."

Sailing on convoys up and down the East Coast, Ferlinghetti remembers that the merchant ships would sometimes turn back, but the SC "could go through anything."

Finally the boat was sent across the Atlantic, loaded on a big Liberty ship. They were unloaded in Liverpool, then sailed up to Belfast and Scotland's Firth of Forth. There they were assigned to train a Norwegian crew who would take over the boat.

"The Norwegian underground was sending escapees out of Nazi-occupied Norway," he remembers. "Sometimes they would arrive by open boat, sometimes they'd go out in fishing boats off the coast of Norway and never return. They'd take off for Scotland and spend many days in the open boat, getting to Scotland. So gradually we accumulated a crew. Every week or so, more guys would show up from the Norwegian underground, and we trained them to run this ship."

After the hard weeks patrolling the Atlantic coast, this duty was really a pleasure. "I was having a great time," Ferlinghetti says, "going to dances and chasing the Scottish lassies up and down the moors. We had bicycles and cycled all up and down Loch Lomond. It was 'oh what a lovely war' as far as I was concerned."

When the ship was finally turned over to the Norwegians, he became an officer messenger and for a few weeks traveled first-class on trains between Glasgow, Edinburgh, London, and Plymouth, "guarded" by an armed sailor. He remembers that sometimes his "message" was nothing more than a bottle of whiskey; but he had plenty of free time again and managed to see the countryside, bicycling all over. Finally in late 1943, he was sent back to Florida for more instruction, then to Norfolk, where in January he assumed his first command. The ship was a larger, newly commissioned subchaser, also with a crew of three officers including Ferlinghetti and thirty-three sailors. The previous commander assigned to it had run into trouble just trying to get it out of the harbor, hitting some buoys and getting tangled in antisubmarine nets, and had been immediately relieved of the command. Now Ferlinghetti reported to the admiral in charge, and the veteran officer regarded the skinny kid with more than a little skepticism.

"He was a hard-bitten old admiral," Ferlinghetti remembers, "a real sea dog, too old for the sea anymore, and I'm standing at attention and he's looking over my orders. And he looks up and sees this beardless stripling standing in front of him there, and he growls, 'And what gives you the idea you're qualified to take this ship out of this harbor?' He's probably saying to himself, good God, another ninety-day wonder."

But Ferlinghetti told him he had been at sea for three years, on North Atlantic patrol, and the admiral said he could give it a try. That night Ferlinghetti guided the boat smoothly out of the harbor and joined a convoy forming to travel up the coast.

The duty of escorting convoys along the coast continued until spring, when he got orders to go to England. Again the boat traveled across the Atlantic on the deck of a Liberty ship, landing again in Liverpool. During May the boat was sent once up to Amsterdam harbor, then was stationed in Plymouth, escorting convoys along the southern coast around Dartmouth. The duty there gave him time to explore southern England by bicycle and visit the resort towns of Dartmoor, Torquay, and others.

But those pleasures came to an end at the beginning of June. On the night of June 5 Ferlinghetti's SC joined the hundreds of boats sailing across the English Channel in the predawn hours of June 6, on the way to D day. Like the thousands of others who participated in the historic Allied invasion of France, Ferlinghetti remembers it vividly:

"The night before the invasion started we were in Plymouth, and the side lanes leading up to the harbor were choked with transport—weapons, wagons, lorries jammed with troops—American, French, British, all lined up silent. And there was a blackout, so you'd go along these roads just packed with troops and all kinds of equipment and everything was in the dark. It was like the night before Agincourt—small campfires and men huddled around them and everything very silent, like the description in *Henry V*.

"We started off about 3 A.M., and we were already a few leagues out of the harbor, then Eisenhower called it off because of the weather. Then the next night it went. We went to this rendezvous point, and it was starting to get light, and I looked behind me, and practically all 180 degrees along the horizon ships were rising out of the sea, converging on this one point. All along the British coast the whole invasion armada was coming up above the horizon. Gradually you'd see the masts, then the hulls, and the whole works converging on some beachhead just as it was getting light. It was quite a dramatic sight."

Ferlinghetti's boat was assigned to patrol outside the breakwater that was formed by the deliberate sinking of old Liberty ships after they had discharged their cargo. When they weren't out patrolling as an antisubmarine screen, they were anchored behind the breakwater. The third night a storm blew up, and the debris the invasion had left started breaking loose, threatening the boats on the beach. Ferlinghetti's SC was anchored about a hundred yards offshore and lost its anchor trying to keep from being washed onto the beach. Then some cables got wound around a propeller so the boat couldn't get away, either. With the storm blowing them broadside out of control toward the beach, and debris ramming into them, their situation grew perilous.

A brave sailor went overboard on a breeches buoy and went to work on the propeller, eventually managing to loosen the cable and free it so they could start the engine. But they were still stuck behind the breakwater of sunken ships, a long way from the entrance, with the wind howling in the pitch-dark of the storm. Ferlinghetti, though, thought he saw a way out—a low spot between the bridge and the bow of a sunken Liberty ship in front of them.

"A more experienced old salt probably wouldn't have tried, but 'fools rush in where angels fear to tread,' " he said. "I just took this chance and went over the ship. I don't know how many feet we cleared the ship by. If it hadn't been high tide, we couldn't have made it."

Though they got to the open water of the Channel, and out of the danger of the landing debris, they weren't safe yet. The ship had lost part of the forward rail and sprang a leak. Ferlinghetti radioed the command ship and got permission to take off for Plymouth. The boat managed to limp across the Channel, "and when we finally got to Plymouth harbor," Ferlinghetti said, "the sailors jumped off and kissed the ground. They didn't think they'd ever see land again."

The ship was put in dry dock for repairs, and for the next six weeks Ferlinghetti stayed mainly in London. Buzz bombs were falling regularly, and he remembers that he was going to stay in a hotel next to Green Park, but the only rooms they had vacant were on the top floor, so he decided not to stay. That night the hotel was hit by one of the bombs. But the weeks in England were good ones, spent enjoying the USO clubs and bicycling about the Devon countryside. For Ferlinghetti the European war was about over. He had faced the intense perils of the invasion and had done his job well.

In late summer, when the SC was seaworthy again, he was sent back to France with it and given duty patrolling around the Channel Islands of Guernsey and Jersey, which the Germans had been left to occupy while the Allied infantry fought its way through France. On August 25, the day Paris was liberated, the ship was in Cherbourg and the whole crew got liberty. On that day Ferlinghetti and a junior officer found an abandoned jeep down the coast which they decided to take to Paris. The jeep broke down along the way, however, leading to one of the more fateful discoveries of Ferlinghetti's future.

Stopped in St.-Brieuc in Brittany, the two American officers found a café, where they sat for some wine and refreshment. There, Ferlinghetti noticed a tablecloth with something scrawled on it; he looked closer and saw that it was a poem. The lines were signed by Jacques Prévert, a French poet who had become popular in the thirties for his plain, concrete images and observations about the ordinary life of common working people, and his irreverent, satirical view of established authorities. Two years later, in 1946, that popularity burgeoned, especially among young people, with the publication of his collection, *Paroles*, though many more formal, academically oriented poets disparaged the work.

When Ferlinghetti left with his companion, he took the paper table-cloth with him. After the war he would begin to translate Prévert's poetry, and in 1964 a collection of the translations, *Paroles* (which includes about half the poems in the French collection), was issued from his own City Lights Books. But even more important, Prévert's voice and style would seep into Ferlinghetti's own, modifying the ponderous romanticism of Thomas Wolfe and the portentousness of T. S. Eliot, under whose influences the young Ferlinghetti, like so many aspiring writers, labored at the time.

Now, with Paris liberated, the Allies advanced quickly. The outcome in Europe seemed just a matter of time, and the major effort, especially of the Navy, was shifted toward the Pacific. In December, though he tried to stay in France, Ferlinghetti was sent back to the States, where he was given another four months' instruction, then assigned duty as a navigator on an "attack transport"—the AKA 41. It was "a big regulation ship with everybody saluting," as he described it, and a disappointing assignment after commanding his own ship. However, it did give him the chance to sail the Pacific, down through the Panama Canal to the Far East, where the ship's duty had it supplying American bases on Midway, the Philippines, and other Pacific islands. While in those waters, they ran through a typhoon near Saipan, another dangerous and dramatic experience, and just a few days after the atomic bombing of Nagasaki, they were the first ship into Sasebo harbor, which had been mined against the invaders by the Japanese. Again, Ferlinghetti escaped any damage, and on August 28, 1945, the ship landed in Japan—the first day of the American occupation. As in the D-day landing and the liberation of Paris, Ferlinghetti again managed to be present to witness the historic event. This time, however, there was no celebration; instead, the entire port seemed deserted.

It took several months after the war ended and the treaties were signed for all the many thousands of American troops to return. Stationed in Japan, Ferlinghetti waited his turn with the others. In mid-September, six weeks after the second atomic bomb destroyed Nagasaki, Ferlinghetti took the train there with several of his shipmates. The images he saw were barely believable. "You'd see hands sticking out of the mud," he remembers; "all kinds of broken teacups . . . hair sticking out of the road—a quagmire—people don't realize how total the destruction was." As with so many who saw the ruin, the shock was permanent; its echoes resounded through the rest of his life, adding to the shape of his political convictions.

Finally his ship was sent home, and by Christmas he was back at Plashbourne. While he was trying to settle into civilian life again and figure out what to do next, nineteen-year-old Columbia scholarship student Allen Ginsberg was working as a spot welder in the Brooklyn Navy Yard. He had been suspended from classes for writing obscene epithets on his grimy dorm window, to call attention to the cleaning lady's omission, and for permitting his friend Jack Kerouac to spend the night after a long evening's talk. In his spare time, Ginsberg was exploring the city's underside, led by his friend Bill Burroughs. While Burroughs made his own systematic study of Eighth Avenue bars, with characteristic diligence Ginsberg was keeping lists of those around Times Square according to types of clientele, and along with Burroughs, hanging out with whatever small-time hustlers, pimps, junkies, and other characters were around. But Ginsberg's poetry had already been noticed and praised by students and teachers alike.

Though Ferlinghetti had been writing poems sporadically all through school, the results were undistinctive by his own standards, and none have been collected. During his years in the Navy, though he could have found time, the immediacy of the new world in which he found himself mostly overwhelmed any literary urges, and besides letters home, he wrote little. He did, however, read in his spare time, slowly, as always, underlining and noting striking passages. He became interested especially in the poetry of T. S. Eliot and Ezra Pound, both of whose styles he imitated in what writing he did. In 1943 Laura Lou Lyon had given him a copy of Eliot's *Four Quartets*, and though he didn't think of himself as particularly religious, the long poem's lyric evocation of Christian mysticism gripped him profoundly and exerted a hold that extended for years.

"I had it at sea, and one of the *Four Quartets* is about the sea, the one called 'The Dry Salvages.' It comes from Trois Sauvages—they're a group of little islands off of Cape Ann, Gloucester, Massachusetts."

More than thirty years later, in 1977, he "finally succeeded in writing this poem that I had been wanting to write for many years," he said about "The Sea and Ourselves at Cape Ann," which was inspired by that quartet.

And nearly forty years after first reading Eliot's poem, he still called it "the greatest modern prose, the most beautiful modern prose there is. It's called poetry, but it's essentially prose. It's beautiful; it's the greatest work Eliot wrote, I think."

But the pervasive Eliot influence was something he knew he had to overcome. After the war Ferlinghetti came to the point where he actually took all of Eliot's books out of his house, to try to escape from the echoes of his voice.

"Everything I wrote sounded like him," he explained. "I was a complete clone. It was quite common for poets of that day to be affected like that by Eliot. Even people like Robert Lowell, Allen Tate. The influence was very pervasive. Everyone was doing Eliotesque poetry. His influence was absolutely dominant."

As he looked beyond Eliot during those years, he was struck also by the work of Kenneth Patchen and e. e. cummings. The last two impressed him with the political emphasis in their work as well as by the power and invention in their straightforward "American" language. Soon after he got back he began reading William Carlos Williams and Marianne Moore as well. The 1946 publication of Williams's *Collected Poems* had finally begun to establish his reputation as a great American poet for his plain language, though he was still not much regarded by most serious critics. Though he read the work with interest, Ferlinghetti himself was never particularly drawn to Williams, finding both Cummings and Patchen more colloquial, more inventive, and more attractive.

Like the other returned veterans, Ferlinghetti's first order of business was to find a job. The booming war economy continued in spite of doomsayers' predictions of a return to depression, but he quickly found that his journalism degree from the University of North Carolina wasn't going to help him much.

"I wanted to get on a newspaper," he said, "but there were two people for every newspaper job—the guy who had it before the war and the guy who took his place when he went off to the war. And then there was me. I didn't stand a chance."

He scaled down his ambitions and looked into working for a few advertising agencies, but he quickly decided against that world. Finally he was offered a job by *Time* magazine—in the mail room. He commuted from Bronxville to *Time*'s Manhattan offices until he found an apartment in Greenwich Village at 235 West Thirteenth Street with Ivan Cousins. Cousins was a Navy buddy he had met in midshipman school who had also become a commander of a subchaser, an even bigger one than Ferlinghetti's.

Ferlinghetti well knew that Cummings and Patchen were also living in the Village then, though he never saw them, but like the writers haunting the Paris cafés, such presences added an attractive mystique to the neighborhood. Ferlinghetti began writing news stories every evening when he came home from work, hoping that *Time* might eventually publish one, and he did finally give one about the Bowery Mission to an acquaintance who worked upstairs in the editorial department. It was the last he saw of it.

Later that summer of 1946, he and Cousins moved to another apartment on far East Twenty-sixth Street, near Bellevue Hospital, but after eight months in the basement of the Time-Life Building, the tedious, apparently dead-end job became unbearable. Ferlinghetti decided to make use of the GI Bill and enroll in Columbia University to work on a master's degree. There his ambition to write and be a part of the literary world was fed by both teachers and the environment around him. He began reading Dylan Thomas, already Great Britain's most singular poet, for the strange, compelling music of his native Welsh diction, though it would be five more years until he came to the United States to draw huge crowds with his public readings. At the same time, in his first year at Columbia, acquaintances in the Village pointed out the building that housed New Directions, the avant-garde publishing company that steel heir James Laughlin had started at the suggestion of Ezra Pound after Laughlin had sought him out in Rapallo, Italy. Thomas was one of the poets New Directions published, along with such other "radicals" as William Carlos Williams, Kenneth Rexroth, and Pound himself. The building was "the tower of gold as far as I was concerned," Ferlinghetti recalls; a dozen years later it would begin publishing Ferlinghetti's own work.

The teachers the young poet had at Columbia were among the major literary lights of the time, and he was already clear enough in his own direction to take advantage of them. Besides keeping up in the classes where he was enrolled, he consistently went to other lectures to hear some of these noted faculty speak. Lionel Trilling talked about Alfred Kazin's *On Native Grounds* with its section on Ferlinghetti's earlier hero, Thomas Wolfe. Mark Van Doren, who was literary editor of *The Nation* in the twenties and won the Pulitzer Prize for poetry in 1939, gave a course in tragedy and comedy that Ferlinghetti frequently attended. He also took critic William York Tyndall's class on James Joyce; Ferlinghetti had discovered Joyce on his own at Chapel Hill. He attended other lectures by poet and critic Babette Deutsch, by thinker Joseph Wood Krutch, and by Marjorie Nicholson. Nicholson's lectures on seventeenth-century literature were so engaging she made the subject nearly as alive for Ferlinghetti as the contemporary literature closest to his heart. He also heard historian and writer Jacques Barzun lecture, and he was particularly impressed with Gilbert Highet's course, "Classical Influences in Modern Literature."

At the same time, he continued reading on his own. Though war novels were tremendously popular, Ferlinghetti wasn't particularly interested. He found a copy of Yeats's poetry on the Third Avenue El—an event he remembers in poem 26 of *Pictures of the Gone World*—and became acquainted with the great Irish poet, who had died only six years earlier, in 1939. He also read Henry Miller, Gertrude Stein's *The Autobiography of Alice B. Toklas*, and Elliot Paul's popular novel *The Last Time I Saw Paris*. These last three in particular affected him with their romantic portraits of Paris life amid its cafés, its ancient streets and cathedrals. Though he didn't know much about his past, he knew he had spent some of his first years in France, and he still knew some French. He'd liked what he saw of it during his leave time in 1944, and now he began to think seriously about going back there after he finished his degree.

All through his two years at Columbia, he kept writing, still largely under the spell of Eliot and Pound. But he was specializing in Victorian literature, an important and necessary foundation, he believed, for further studies in modern literature. That concentration on the Victorians led to his first serious involvement in art. In the Columbia graduate library he began reading nineteenth-century critic John Ruskin, whose reputation was founded on his extensive writing about art. The stacks of the library housed the enormous Kelmscott edition of Ruskin's five-volume *Modern Painters*, which was famous among scholars and artists for the high-quality reproductions of paintings Ruskin discussed. Looking through them in the library, Ferlinghetti was particularly entranced with the reproductions of J. M. W. Turner's paintings.

"These volumes were nearly two feet by three feet," he remembers, "great big beautifully bound volumes by Kelmscott Press, letterpress with very fine paper and very fine reproductions of all the paintings by Turner that Ruskin was discussing in the text. I spent months poring over these illustrations of Turner."

He wrote his M.A. thesis on Ruskin and his relationship with Turner, calling it "Ruskin's Turner, Child of Light."

Ferlinghetti smiles as he thinks about it now. "It's a very romantic title. Ruskin had undertaken the whole writing of modern painters to extol Turner. He traced painting from its very beginnings through the Middle Ages and into the Renaissance, and he showed how everything was darkness, and then with the Renaissance the light started breaking through, and then with Turner the light really broke through into the sky.

"He was obsessed with light, and I linked it in my paper to fertility symbols, light as a fertility symbol, and the symbolism of *The Golden Bough*. That was one of Turner's great paintings showing the sibyl holding up the branch. It was a great fertility trip.

"Then years later we find out in Ruskin's letters, that couldn't be published until about the 1960s, that Ruskin evidently was impotent. I didn't know that, of course, when I wrote that master's paper. It was almost like an intuition of Ruskin's makeup that I should have happened on this thesis."

When he finished the thesis and got his degree in 1948, he still had three years left of benefits on his GI Bill. He had been thoroughly involved in the worlds his studies opened for him at Columbia, and he wanted to go on. But at the same time, he remembers, "the requirements for an American Ph.D. were so academic. You couldn't do your dissertation on a living author. And you had to do all these courses that I wasn't interested in."

Perhaps even more significant was his own war experience, and the poems and novels and stories he'd read, by and about Hemingway, Elliot Paul, Pound, and Eliot, "that whole tradition of the American expatriate in Paris."

Either way, the next step became clear. He would go there and become part of that tradition.

3

In January 1948, Ferlinghetti sailed again across the Atlantic, and as he put it a decade later in his novel *Her*, "ended that year where all the trains end, fell out into . . . a *pension de famille* on the far side of the Bastille."

The family was that of Edgar Letellier, their flat was on the Place Voltaire, and Ferlinghetti had been told they rented out rooms. He arrived with his seabag, having ridden there in the open back of a bus in the snow, and Madame Letellier's warm welcome immediately made him feel at home. Her morning ritual of greeting him at breakfast with a cup of *café au lait* and slices of French bread covered with butter and jam (a *tartine*) deepened the welcome, and he was delighted also with the opportunity to recover and improve his French in conversations with the family. Mr. Letellier was an old leftist and a classical music instructor who gave lessons at home, and they had two daughters not yet in their teens, all of which added up to an inviting family scene that put Ferlinghetti at ease.

He enrolled at the Sorbonne, and as he had hoped, found the French university graduate school system perfectly suited to his taste. There were no classes where attendance was required, and doctoral candidates were only required to report to their thesis director twice a year. Once a month he had to go and sign a form to continue receiving the sixty-five-dollar check from his GI Bill which he lived on, but the rest of the time he was free to explore the city and to do what he had come mainly to do—to write.

"I considered myself first a Symbolist poet, then a surrealist poet," he wrote for a 1987 lecture ("a 'Nadja' surrealist, not a 'manifesto' surrealist," he explained later to clarify the point). "I was Baudelaire. I was Rimbaud. I was Apollinaire and Cendrars, and of course I was Stephen Dedalus, Joyce's eternal young hero who sets forth to forge in the smithy of his soul the uncreated conscience of his race, and also to do battle with the world, in the classic tradition of young heroes since the beginning of time, or at least since the beginning of literature. I used to walk the streets reciting Blaise Cendrars:

" 'And all the days and all the nights and all the women in cafés and all the glasses, I wanted to drink them all and break them—And all the windows and all the lives and all the wheels of carriages turning and turning on the *mauvais pavés*—And I wanted to plunge them all into a furnace of swords!' "

He began a novel almost immediately upon settling in. As with many first novels, it was autobiographical, and his passion for Thomas Wolfe's work, with its themes of alienation and loss, heavily influenced the writing. He worked at it steadily, having heard from a friend in Bronxville about a novel contest sponsored by the publisher Doubleday, Doran & Co. The contest called for submission of twenty thousand words and a summary of the rest. Three months after he arrived in Paris, Ferlinghetti had finished half that much—about forty pages—and titled it *The Way of Dispossession*, a phrase taken from "East Coker," the second of Eliot's *Four Quartets*, in a passage Eliot had borrowed from *The Ascent of Mount Carmel*, by Catholic mystic St. John of the Cross:

> *In order to arrive at what you do not know*
> *You must go by a way which is the way of ignorance.*
> *In order to possess what you do not possess*
> *You must go by the way of dispossession.*
> *In order to arrive at what you are not*
> *You must go through the way in which you are not.*

As they did for so many, the romantically paradoxical lines struck an obvious chord in Ferlinghetti, who was in Paris, partly at least, to recover his own lost beginnings and to live out the expatriate myth.

He continued working on the novel through the winter, relearning his French at the Letelliers', spending time at cafés, and reading poetry. Alone in Paris except for his contact with the Letelliers, he looked up the brother of a girlfriend he had known at Columbia, Mary Whitman, who had been working on a Ph.D. in philosophy. Like Ferlinghetti,

George Whitman was living on the GI Bill, in a small windowless room in the Hôtel Suez, a poor-class hotel on the boulevard San Michel. He had left Boston and come to Paris in 1946 to work for the summer as a volunteer in a camp for war orphans, and had remained in Paris. The book allowance from the Bill was unlimited, and Whitman had decided to go into business, selling books from his room to GI students.

"The room was about eight or nine feet square," Ferlinghetti remembers. "George was sitting in an armchair in the middle of the room, with books stacked up to the ceiling along all the walls, and he was cooking his dinner over a can of Sterno." When he ran out of room completely, Whitman supplied his library by selling and trading books at the Sorbonne.

This sensibility appealed immediately to Ferlinghetti, and the two became lifelong friends. Three years later, in 1951, Whitman would use the funds from a small inheritance to open the Mistral Bookshop at 37 rue de la Bûcherie in Paris, looking out on the Seine and Notre Dame. Patterned after Sylvia Beach's Shakespeare & Co., which was a major literary center for American writers between the wars, Whitman's likewise became a center. Ginsberg, Gregory Corso, Burroughs, Lawrence Durrell, Henry Miller, Harold Norse, Ferlinghetti, and many more dropped in during the following decades when they visited Paris. And in the 1960s he renamed the Mistral "Shakespeare & Co.," when, he claimed, he came upon an original nameplate from Beach's store. Whitman also published a few books and, sporadically, a literary review as well.

In the spring of 1948 Whitman and Ferlinghetti decided to see the country with several other friends, traveling to Le Touquet, a coastal town near Bologne, and to Amiens, Baume, and other small villages and towns along the way. In Poix he met the Rameau family, who invited him to remain. Finding them "charming," he decided to take advantage of their hospitality and let the others go on without him. As he wrote to Mrs. Bisland, "M. Rameau is a kind of squire who seems to spend most of his time riding to hounds, as they say in England, while Madame Rameau seems very much a lady. They plied me with hospitality and champagne and sent me off to Paris with preserves and butter (unobtainable in Paris)."

During that trip he kept what he judged some years later were "the first journals with potential." And indeed, they evidence the concrete, image-rooted descriptions that mark his mature style, coupled with the occasional trace of irony that also came to be characteristic. In notes toward a poem, he describes Arles with its "low red tile roofs / and the tin charley on the Mairie with / a rusty tin flag and a sword. . . . Its burnt steeples are a part / of the sky and do not hold it up."

A little later he recorded his arrival in Aix at the same time Winston Churchill visited: "As I was passing the Hôtel du Roy Rêve 3 black taxis pulled up to the door and Churchill climbed out first. I was across the street, and as he lumbered up the steps I could see only the back of his head, and I said to an old French dame next to me (who was looking through opera glasses), 'Qui est il?' and she said, 'Meester Chursheel.' I think I could see his cigar through the back of his head but I'm not sure."

That spring he had also finished *The Way of Dispossession* and sent it off to Doubleday. "It is just 50,000 words," he wrote to Mrs. Bisland, "but being (as it is) an 'interior monologue,' it is necessarily limited in length. However, this is just long enough for the new genre of novel which I am writing." It didn't win the contest, but an agent became interested and sent it to Simon & Schuster. In June they too rejected the book, but sent Ferlinghetti strong encouragement: "We all agree that here is a writer, perceptive, sensitive, and a weaver of tales. We want to see anything else that he does, even if it is only a few pages." Though he was disappointed at the rejection, the encouragement was heartening, and he soon began making notes toward a new novel, which would also be an interior monologue.

Though he enjoyed living with the Letelliers, particularly for their warmth when he first arrived and for the opportunity they gave him to speak French, as he became more settled he outgrew their hospitality and wanted his own apartment. Even after three months there he had written Mrs. Bisland that he had begun to look for a place of his own, "since living with a French family costs too much in proportion to living independently. If one actually finds an apartment at non-black-market rates, it is much much cheaper than hotels or pensions . . . about 8 dollars, while I am spending $50 a month for my present lodgings and 2 meals a day. (This 2 meals a day is deceiving, however, since one of them is breakfast, consisting solely of coffee and a piece of bread, so that it is necessary to spend more money for extra food.)"

That spring Mrs. Bisland had also written with the sad news that Presley was in very poor health and was not expected to live much longer. Ferlinghetti decided he would return to Bronxville for a visit. He made the trip in summer, very happy to see them, and asked Bisland's doctor if he ought to remain, but the doctor recommended against it.

"He said it'd be much better if you went back to France," Ferlinghetti recalls, "because if you stuck around it would make him feel that you realized he didn't have long to live, and he wouldn't appreciate your sticking around. So I went back to France."

On the way back he met two young women, Mary Louise Barrett and Marie Birmingham. Birmingham was on her way to live in Paris, and like Ferlinghetti, she had literary ambitions. "I guess Laura Lou Lyon was the first woman intellectual I met," he recalls, "and I guess they were the next. And I learned a lot from them. Marie was a Jesuit-educated Catholic, and extremely sharp with a high IQ." She soon married a French painter from Morocco, Claude Ponsot, and later became an accomplished and recognized poet, a mother of five children, then a professor at Queen's College.

The two women lived on the same street where the women in Djuna Barnes's *Nightwood* lived, and Birmingham and Barrett gave him a copy of that novel, which would become very influential both as part of his dissertation and, even more important, in the writing of his own novel *Her*. And ten years later Ferlinghetti would go on to publish Ponsot's first collection of poems, *True Minds*.

Ferlinghetti spent the end of that summer with the Letelliers at their thatched-roof cottage on an island in Brittany. When he returned to Paris, he finally found his own apartment at 89 rue de Vaugirard in Montparnasse. Only ten blocks from the boulevard St.-Germain, close to the Sorbonne, and just a few blocks from the Café Dôme, Ferlinghetti felt himself in the heart of "Hemingway Country," as he described it later, where the bohemian café life of so many famous expatriate writers had flourished between the wars.

That bohemian feeling was emphasized by the apartment itself, as well as by the way he came to find it: "It was absolutely impossible to find any apartments in Paris. Even today you have to buy the key and it costs an enormous amount. I met a worker in a bar, through George Whitman, I think, and he was tubercular and his wife and children were tubercular. He had three children and they were all living in this dank two-room apartment and it was very damp and the kids were coughing and they were all sick, and he owed everyone in the neighborhood. We agreed that I would pay up all his debts in the neighborhood so he could leave, and he would move me in at night, and when the concierge came the next day, I would tell her that I was a friend of his and that he was away in the country. So the whole thing cost me a hundred dollars to pay off all his debts. It went on like that for three years. I had this place and kept telling the concierge that he was coming back."

Years later he described the place as "a cellar with two rooms and a little tiny air-shaft kitchen with a sink hollowed out of solid stone, which must have been there since the Middle Ages." The cold-water spigot over the sink was the only source of water, and there was only "a broken-down gas stove" for cooking. The bathroom had no windows at all and was very damp. The front room was the only one with any light, from a French window that looked out on a cobblestone courtyard. But Ferlinghetti did some decorating in that front room.

"I painted the walls white, and I put a big mural on the wall, a line drawing of a head of a great classical nude woman, sort of Greek style. Then I wrote the quotation from Edgar Allan Poe's poem ('To Helen'). It said, 'Thy hyacinth hair, thy classic face, / Thy Naiad airs have brought me home.' This was our living room. As I say, it was something out of the thirties."

The rent there was only twenty-six dollars a month, and at that rate, its inconveniences were trifling. As far as Ferlinghetti was concerned, he could stay there indefinitely.

Since leaving New York, he'd been writing steadily to Ivan Cousins about the magic of Paris, and now he urged Cousins to come and stay with him. Cousins had left New York and gone in the opposite direction, winding up in Alaska. That fall, however, he had no particular plans and decided he could use his GI Bill money to take Ferlinghetti up on the offer, at least for a while.

In October Cousins pulled in on the train at the Gare St.-Lazare, where Ferlinghetti met him, and the two went straight to the Left Bank and the Deux Magots, the café which Jean-Paul Sartre and Simone de Beauvoir, among other writers, were known to frequent. Ferlinghetti's own "two-room cave," however, didn't have the same charm for Cousins. "Our rooms were very cold," he remembered, "and we kept a continuous pot-au-feu going on the stove. . . . Our concierge looked upon us as Communists and treated us very badly." It was true that if they arrived home after 10 P.M., the concierge often wouldn't respond to their calls and kept them waiting sometimes for hours. But Cousins did remain as Ferlinghetti's roommate for the next year.

Though he had done almost no real schoolwork at all, as there were no required classes or exams and attendance wasn't required even when he did sign up, Ferlinghetti kept reading steadily. Now he began thinking about writing a dissertation about some of the poets he'd been reading— René Char, Eliot, Pound, and some other urban poets. Gradually his thesis began to take form around the relationship between poetry and the city.

"One of the first books I read was *La Ville Tentaculaire* [*The Tentacular City*], by the French-Belgian poet [Émile] Verhaeren," he recalls. "It was an early, nineteenth-century attempt to realize and embrace the new cities, the cities that had been growing up, the industrial cities of the world. It was a definite precursor of Eliot's 'The Waste Land.'

"And I guess 'The Waste Land' probably had a lot to do with my choice of subject. I was really very much influenced by Eliot in those days. Everything I wrote sounded like Eliot."

Eventually he titled the dissertation "La Cité: Symbole dans le poésie moderne: À la recherche d'une Tradition Métropolitaine" ("The City: Symbol in Modern Poetry: In Search of a Metropolitan Tradition"). Besides Eliot and Verhaeren, his reading for it included dozens of poets in French and English: Walt Whitman; Hart Crane's "The Bridge"; V. Mayakovsky's poem on the Brooklyn Bridge; Federico García Lorca's *The Poet in New York; City of Dreadful Night*, by Francis Thompson; as well as the avant-garde works *Nadja*, by André Breton, and *Nightwood*, by Djuna Barnes.

"Generally it's a pretty simple thesis," he says. "It just goes through all the poets and summarizes what they had to say about the city, what works of each poet embody the city. It was very easily written. I did a lot of the reading for it in the old American Library in Paris. And of course, I had the background from what I had read at Columbia."

Though he was also working more seriously on the new novel, to be titled *Uncertain Spring*, in truth, he says, "I wasn't really working too hard. I'd work a few hours a day, but I was out in the cafés a lot, I was out late at night every night in St.-Germain. It was like old bohemian days, really. I was living out this Hemingway myth in Montparnasse. I'd go and sit on the terrace of the Dôme, or the Select, which is across the street, or the Coupole."

Particularly he remembers spending many nights at the Pergola, "a café where a lot of pimps and whores and small-time drug dealers hung out. The Pergola stayed open all night, it's where all the action was. Some people I used to hang out with, we used to meet at the Pergola. I drank a lot of Pernod."

And if he woke early, he would go to sit "on the sunny terrace of the Select, which was on the opposite side of the street from the Coupole, because it was cold and damp in my apartment."

At the same time, he began writing another new novel, an interior monologue based closely on *Nightwood* and on his own daily experiences hanging out in the streets and the cafés. He finished a draft of it that year, but realized it was still in need of much work, and so set it aside. Unlike other early work which was simply abandoned, however, this one remained incubating, to grow to life a full decade later as the novel *Her*.

Besides the hours in cafés, Ferlinghetti also took time to pursue other interests Paris presented to him. The Académie Julien, an art school, had the traditional *atelier libre* (free studio) for use by anyone who wanted to come in and paint or draw from models who posed there. Ferlinghetti decided to take advantage, bought some drawing materials, and began to teach himself to draw. He also went to draw models at La Grande Chaumière, the other major art school in Paris (besides Beaux Arts), which was only some four blocks from his apartment.

His student pass from the Sorbonne got him into most of the city's theaters, symphonies, and opera for a greatly reduced price, and all museums for free, and he took advantage of that as well. And he began to study Catholicism, his interest stirred by the cathedrals and churches he saw everywhere in the city.

"If you live in Paris," he explained, "you can become completely entranced by the aesthetic of the Gothic, the aesthetic of Catholicism, and the Gothic churches. I'd been reading Ruskin, and one of his other great works besides *Modern Painters* was *The Stones of Venice*. Part of it was a section called 'The Nature of Gothic,' which was an enormous dithyramb, an enormous description, eulogizing the Gothic. The whole aesthetic of the Gothic church has a very powerful effect, even if you're not interested in theology. The Catholics weren't dumb when they used incense and the Latin mass and organ music. It's like an ancient magic. You can become completely wrapped up in the aesthetic without being persuaded by the theology of it at all."

Moved by that aesthetic, he read Thomas Aquinas and other Catholic thinkers, and got to know a Jesuit priest with whom he regularly discussed and argued Catholic doctrine.

He also discovered Pablo Picasso, La Comédie Française, and the mimes of Paris; and his reading deepened further his interest in European avant-garde literature—the French symbolists, the dadaists, surrealists, and what was current in magazines and bookstores. At the same time, as the second year went on, he worked steadily toward finishing his dissertation and spent more time in various libraries, especially the Bibliothèque Nationale, and at his apartment, concentrating more intently on getting it done.

In the summer of 1949 he made another journey that seems to emphasize the end of one phase of his life and the beginning of another.

During the first part of that year Mrs. Bisland, whom Ferlinghetti had begun addressing as "Mother Bisland," reflecting the familial affection he felt, wrote him that Presley had died; and that summer Ferlinghetti returned again to Bronxville. During the two-week stay he and Mrs. Bisland drove out to Presley's grave at Mount Kisco Cemetery, about an hour north of Bronxville. He also visited his natural mother, Clemence, briefly, but felt no real connection to her, as he'd seen her only once since she left him to Emily. Though nothing of Mrs. Bisland's patrician reserve had changed, the visit confirmed to him that she was indeed his real family. Altogether, the trip seems to have provided another affirmation of his position in the world—his childhood and early life over, he was a man on his own.

Then on the voyage back to Paris in September, a chance meeting opened another dimension of that new phase. In the ship's lounge one day, he saw a familiar face, and though he was generally shy, he overcame that quality enough to go up to the slender, dark-haired young woman.

"I've seen you before somewhere," he said.

"Yes, you have," she told him.

Selden Kirby-Smith, or "Kirby," as she was known, went on to tell him she had got her undergraduate degree at Swarthmore. Ferlinghetti had dated Laura Lou, who had been there; but it was at Columbia that they had seen each other. Kirby had also gone there for an M.A. and was still finishing her thesis on D. H. Lawrence in America. She remembered Ferlinghetti from Lionel Trilling's class and from seeing him in the library. In particular, she remembered the tweed jacket he had worn and the way his clear blue eyes focused intently on Trilling and followed him around the room.

Kirby was traveling to Paris with her friend Arlie Jones Capps, a young painter from Milwaukee. And like Ferlinghetti, Kirby was on her way to the Sorbonne to study for the certificat d'études (le cours de civilization Française). The friendship Kirby and Ferlinghetti struck up through their common interests and experiences continued when they both reached Paris, where Kirby and her friend got a room in the Hôtel Bonaparte on the Left Bank.

Ferlinghetti took Kirby to visit his friend Marie Birmingham—now Ponsot—at their apartment in Châtou, a suburb of Paris. Marie already had two babies, and Kirby was aghast at the small apartment with its stopped-up sink and its clutter of diapers everywhere amid the paints and easel. Arlie had come with Kirby and Ferlinghetti, but left, and Kirby was shocked further when Claude made an obvious pass at her. But she remained and agreed to sit for a portrait Claude wanted to paint, and after two or three sittings the painting was finished with no further "incidents."

Ferlinghetti also introduced her to the Left Bank, the Café Mabillon, and other haunts along the St.-Germain that had become familiar to him, and took her to the opera (where they sat in the balcony for thirty cents) and other Paris attractions.

In 1950 Ferlinghetti finally finished the thesis, 224 pages, written in French. But before he was through, he had to present an oral defense, also in French, to an examining panel of three professors in a public lecture hall. That was scheduled for the fall, as one of the professors directing his thesis had left the country. In the meantime he planned a vacation into the countryside.

Having been impressed with Henry Miller's depictions of Greece and the life there in *The Colossus of Maroussi*, he wanted to see for himself. He traveled down through Spain to Majorca, stopping in Madrid to visit the Prado and the Joaquín Sorolla museum, where he was struck by the work of the Spanish impressionist and went on to write the poem that became number 8 of *Pictures of the Gone World*:

> Sorolla's women in their picture hats
> stretched upon his canvas beaches
> > > beguiled the Spanish
> > Impressionists
> > > And were they fraudulent pictures
> of the world
> > the way the light played on them
> > > creating illusions
> of love?

It was a serious issue for him at the time. Kirby was only one of several women he had been seeing, and for him the time was thick with the fabled romance of Paris and of the Mediterranean. He had invited her to come and visit him at Majorca, where he planned to stay before going down to Greece; and when Kirby's mother came from America to see what her daughter was up to, Kirby, very interested in Ferlinghetti, decided to take up his invitation. She and her mother bought one of the first Renaults off the assembly line and toured Europe on the way down to Puerto de Andraitx, the small Majorcan fishing village where Ferlinghetti was staying.

He was living in a large house he had rented (his share was thirty-five dollars a month) with three friends—two men and a Belgian woman—on the water across the bay from the village, and was also working on a major new poem, "Palimpsest." He'd begun it the year before, sometime after picking up a book (in prose) by that title in a Paris bookshop, a book written by Hilda Doolittle, known as H.D. She was a former companion and disciple of Ezra Pound and had continued working in the "imagist" aesthetic that Pound had been instrumental in creating before World War I. The idea of imagism involved the making of relatively short poems, based on a single image, in clear, economical, concrete language. Though the movement eventually had many adherents who did a good deal of writing for a few years, its theoretical principles were never clearly worked out, and its energy dissipated, especially as Pound himself went on to a more ambitious project, *The Cantos*. The book by H. D. was a limited edition, one of seven hundred copies published in 1926.

Ferlinghetti's own poem "had been heavily influenced by Eliot and Pound," in his words, "and was particularly imitative of *The Cantos*." He'd sent it to his agent over the winter, but she had been curtly discouraging, writing, "Personally I do not like this sort of thing and as your agent I regret the time spent on it." Still she said she would show it to publisher John Farrar. Though Ferlinghetti never heard from him, he was not discouraged, and worked steadily on the poem during the weeks in Majorca.

Kirby stayed in the house with Ferlinghetti, though her mother, acting out the form of the proper southern lady chaperone, stayed the week at a nearby *pension*. She found the food at the *pension* nearly inedible, however, the toilets never flushed, and donkeys kept sticking their heads through her window. All of this contributed to making Kirby's mother ill, and after a week they left.

Kirby had been hoping for a marriage proposal, and though Ferlinghetti's interest had grown more serious, he wasn't ready yet. Instead of a ring, he gave her a fan, and "I cried all the way through Italy," she remembered. "We went to Venice, and I cried all through Venice, and I cried through Florence. Then finally in Florence there came a telegram which said, 'Will you marry me?' Then everything was wonderful, and I wired back 'yes,' in fourteen languages. But then he changed his mind a couple of times after that. He was the reluctant bridegroom."

After Kirby left, Ferlinghetti's intention was still to get to Greece. As he remembers, "I only had about $150, but that was enough in those days. I thought I could get on some kind of yacht. Be a yacht bum and sail to Greece. But the trouble is I met a woman on the waterfront at Palma, an old British woman who had a Bristol schooner. And her husband had died and she wanted to sail to Italy and Greece. And so she said, I'm gonna get the boat ready and we can sail in a couple of weeks. Well, it turned out that she was very old and she lived on this Bristol schooner with a whole mass of cats and dogs, but the Port Authority wouldn't let her out of port. They said the ship was unseaworthy. She kept trying to fix it and saying she was going to get it fixed and get the permit to sail, and so I ended up hanging out there all summer waiting for her to get the boat ready to sail."

When he returned to Paris in the fall for the oral defense of his dissertation, several of Ferlinghetti's friends, including Kirby and George Whitman, came to the public forum to show their support. Ferlinghetti described the scene:

"The three professors who are judging your thesis are up there on the stage facing you, and you're facing them with the audience behind you. And theses are announced in advance on the board at the Sorbonne, so anyone can see what theses are going to be defended that week. For mine there was quite a crowd, though I was completely unknown. I think the subject matter interested people."

Ferlinghetti did well, but when he gave a translation of some lines from "The Waste Land" that seemed in error, one of the professors asked him to account for the mistake. Ferlinghetti marshaled his wits, and with the ironic flair that even then was characteristic, quoted from a French adage comparing a translation to a woman. The audience burst out laughing, and Lawrence Monsanto Ferling was awarded the Ph.D.

He still loved Paris, and when he had come two years earlier, he had thought he might stay for good. But now, having finished his degree, he found himself without anything in particular to do. He had become friends with another American student, Miles Payne, who was from Northern California and lived very near Ferlinghetti in Montparnasse. During their conversations Payne had told him about the attractions of Northern California—that it was the only wine-growing region in America, that wine was cheap and good, that there were cafés and coffeehouses and the hills and the waterfront in San Francisco.

"I used to make up all these literary reasons why I came out here," Ferlinghetti says now, "but I realize it was really because it sounded like a European place to come. There was wine, and it just seemed more interesting than New York.

"Footloose and fancy free," he said, laughing, remembering himself then. And so in early December he packed up, boarded a ship, and headed west.

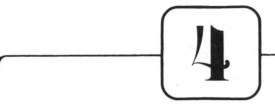

In December of 1950 Wisconsin Senator Joseph McCarthy, who had been in the news much of the year with accusations of Communists in the corners of the highest offices of the nation, which among other things inspired the House of Representatives to hold hearings on links between homosexuality and communism, was pushed off the front pages by the Korean War. The Chinese offensive that had begun at the end of November had pushed back the U.N. forces, and President Harry Truman noted his despair that America seemed to be tipping toward World War III. Still, the economy was flourishing. The budding paperback book industry already had 81,000 titles in print, and though most of it was pop drugstore fare rather than serious literature, increasing numbers of the classics were available for less than half a dollar.

Earlier in the year, on March 2, the first novel of a young French-Canadian, who had changed his first name from "John-Louis" to the more American "Jack," had been published. *The Town and the City* came out to mixed reviews. Though the *New York Times* reviewer, Charles Poore, praised "the depth and breadth of his vision," the reviewer from Jack Kerouac's hometown paper in Lowell, Massachusetts, criticized the "cheap style," finding it an "unpleasant story, with language often profane and vulgar." Kerouac was also disappointed that his publisher gave most of its attention to Thomas Merton's latest book. But he was already at work on what would become *On the Road*, and after visiting William Burroughs in Mexico with Neal Cassady, he began a whirlwind romance with Joan Haverty in New York City. They married on November 15, barely a month since her previous boyfriend, in a misfigured joke, leapt through the window of a subway train and was dragged to his death on the tracks. Best-man honors at the wedding were shared by Kerouac's two close friends, Lucien Carr and Allen Ginsberg.

That December Ginsberg took a job as a market researcher with National Opinion Research Center in Manhattan and was surveying people about their opinions regarding the Korean War. He'd been living with his father and stepmother in nearby Paterson, New Jersey, since his release in February from the Columbia Psychiatric Institute, where he'd spent the previous seven months. He'd agreed to go there rather than to jail after being caught in April with a dissolute friend in a car full of stolen property; the friend had been using Ginsberg's apartment to store the goods he and his girlfriend lifted on their regular forays.

Early in his stay at the institute, Ginsberg had met a brilliant young man who shared Ginsberg's serious interest in literature. Carl Solomon had lived with a prostitute in Paris and become deeply enmeshed in the European avant-garde; he'd been present to witness Antonin Artaud's crazed performance, *Cit-Gi*, just after Artaud's release from an insane asylum. And in his twenty-first year, after disrupting "a critical discussion of Mallarmé, and other neo-Dada clowning" (in his words), Solomon was committed to the Columbia Psychiatric Institute.

It was also in December of 1950 that Ginsberg met twenty-year-old Gregory Corso, just out of Clinton Prison after serving three years for committing a series of robberies. Corso was sitting at the Pony Stable, a lesbian bar on Third Street and Sixth Avenue, a thick sheaf of neatly typed poems in front of him. The typed pages caught Ginsberg's eye, and when Ginsberg heard the poems, he was impressed. They began talking about their pasts and their fantasies, and Corso told him how he would masturbate regularly while watching the woman in the apartment across the street undress in front of her mirror, take a bath, and make love with her boyfriend. As Corso told the story in great detail, saying that his fantasy was to meet the woman, Ginsberg realized, incredibly, that the woman was in fact his—Ginsberg's—girlfriend and that he was the boyfriend. The next day he took Corso over to his girlfriend's apartment and introduced them.

In mid-December thirty-one-year-old Larry Ferling arrived in New York City and met Kirby, who had come a few days earlier. The young Ferling was strikingly good-looking—tall and slender, with high cheekbones setting off the already receding line of his dark hair, and a strong, clean-cut jaw. As Kirby had noticed, recalling her first memory of him, his blue eyes were remarkable in their translucent, watery lightness, so mobile in their quick notice of the world around, and at the same time, so intense in their fixed attention to whatever drew them. He was often quiet, and given to disappearing into some distraction in the middle of a conversation, and he was never too ready to laugh about himself. But along with his ready smile and his dry sense of humor about the world around, both his appearance and his manner made him attractive to women.

On arriving he described New York in his journal as "an uneasy metropolis, featuring the new all-plastic, nylon-reinforced television mentality"; his first impressions confirmed his decision not to live there.

"It was just too tough and avaricious," he remembers. "Everything seemed to be sewn up. So I went west, young man."

Before taking the cross-country train trip, however, he spent a couple of days in the city with Kirby, then traveled with her down to Baltimore to meet his brothers and mother. Kirby went on to Florida to see her family while Lawrence stayed in Baltimore for the holidays. Right after New Year's he got on the train and headed west, arriving in Oakland on January 5, 1951, then taking the ferry across the Bay. He didn't know a soul in San Francisco, and as he would throughout his life, wherever he traveled, he brought along only a single bag that he could carry.

"I had a seabag, I got off the ferry, I put the seabag on my shoulder and started walking up Market Street," he remembers about his arrival. "You could look from the ferry building straight up Market Street then. That was the center of the city, and they had these trolleys riding up and down. I'd heard they had these things called guesthouses where you could stay. So I looked up the yellow pages and sure enough, there was this listing, guesthouses. I found one that said Chateau Bleu, so I thought, this must be run by French people, I'll go there. There was no one French in sight. Just downtown office workers living there. That house was on Pacific Heights. I lived there for about four months. I was trying to write a novel, and I got a job teaching French in the Adult Education Program."

The novel he'd begun in Paris after he completed *The Way of Dispossession* was now called *Uncertain Spring*; and at the same time he worked on translations of Jacques Prévert.

The teaching job was only one French course, but the aspiring writer lived frugally, as much by choice as by necessity, still filled with the prewar expatriate-artist mythos which had been a major reason for his going to Paris. And just as important, he began getting to know and like the city he'd chosen. He took long walks to get acquainted with it, and from the first, he liked what he saw.

"San Francisco had a Mediterranean feeling about it. I felt it was a little like Dublin when Joyce was there. You could walk down Sackville Street and see everyone of any importance on one walk."

It had nothing of the claustrophobia Joyce had felt in Dublin, however. To Ferlinghetti it seemed wide open to ideas and people. It had the waterfront he liked, the cafés and coffeehouses that he had liked in Greenwich Village and in Paris, and the vitality that came from the mix of ethnic communities—Chinese, Italian, and others.

In April, after vacillating again about his relationship with Kirby, he went back east to marry. At the wedding on April 10 in Jacksonville, Florida, his Navy friend Ivan Cousins was Ferlinghetti's only guest. Mrs. Bisland had died, and his own mother was very elderly; both she and his brothers were virtual strangers, and none made the trip. Thus Ferlinghetti began his new life without any family around; it was a circumstance with which he'd long been familiar and the central fact of the man he had become.

Afterward, the couple honeymooned for two weeks at a lake cabin that Kirby's mother owned in Lake Geneva, Florida, then returned together to San Francisco. This time they found an actual French landlord.

Germaine Schmidt was Parisian, a widow, living in a large house on Clay Street. Her husband had been an accomplished pianist, a friend of composer Claude Debussy's, and she also taught piano. In the fall she was forced to move to a smaller house on Divisadero, and the Ferlings moved in with her, to the three-room attic apartment. Kirby loved the gentility of the company and the musicians she met, and she began taking piano lessons from Schmidt. Ferlinghetti enjoyed conversations in French with her, and the reminders of Paris life their lodgings brought. After a while, however, the "bourgeois" atmosphere began to grate on him. In another year, as he began to discover the neighborhood of North Beach and the bohemian life there, he would convince Kirby that they should move.

That summer she got a job teaching at the Catherine Branson School, a private girls' school in the wealthy Pacific Heights district, where Ferlinghetti had first lived. Meanwhile, he continued teaching the one French class, two nights a week, and found another part-time teaching job at the San Francisco Institute of Music and Art, only a block and a half from their apartment.

"It was living on the tuition from GI Bill students," he says of the school. "It really wasn't much of an institution. It didn't really have any set curriculum. They said they wanted me to teach modern American literature. I could define it any way I wanted to. I remember I taught

Thoreau's *Walden*." And the pay "was like starvation wages. It paid about ten dollars an hour, or less—I think I got maybe thirty dollars a week out of that job." But between the two incomes, and their minimal expenses, the newlyweds managed.

Ferlinghetti still hadn't really met any people besides a few perfunctory acquaintances, but Kirby had an old Swarthmore friend living there, Holly Beye, who was, like Ferlinghetti, an aspiring poet and had similar political sympathies. She and her husband had lived in an anarchist community in Woodstock, New York, and through them, Ferlinghetti began to meet some of the people who would influence him most profoundly.

Another couple they met, Charles and Janet Richards, were also part of the San Francisco artistic community. Charles, a jazz trombonist, and Janet, a painter, had lived there for several years, and included among their friends were poets Weldon Kees and Kenneth Rexroth. From their first meetings with the Ferlinghettis, the Richardses had encouraged them to come with them to the weekly literary "soirées" Rexroth had been holding at his various apartments in San Francisco since the mid-forties. There, some of the city's leading writers, artists, and literati—many of the "underground," as yet unrecognized type—would come to hear Rexroth, who had a national, even international, literary reputation, hold forth on an array of literary and political subjects, and to talk among themselves. One night in October 1951 the Ferlinghettis finally went with Beye to Rexroth's book-stuffed Eighth Avenue flat in the Richmond district near Golden Gate Park.

Poet, writer, political-social-cultural critic extraordinaire, translator, teacher, painter, Rexroth had been born in South Bend, Indiana, in 1905 and raised in Chicago. He had quit school at sixteen, attended the School of the Art Institute of Chicago later, and worked variously as a labor organizer, a reporter, a logger, a farmworker, and a factory hand, and finally came to San Francisco with his first wife, Andree, in 1927. Soon after settling, he began to publish his poems widely in little magazines, and won the notable praise of William Carlos Williams. And he was as active politically as he was in literature, joining and leading a John Reed club, an Artists and Writers Union, and a Nurses Union.

After World War II he joined with some others from the Waldport, Oregon, camp for conscientious objectors in helping to organize an anarchist group called the Libertarian Circle, which drew together politically interested writers, artists, dancers, actors, and others for dances and poetry readings as well as political discussions. From this group, KPFA, the first public (as opposed to commercial) radio station, emerged as well as the very political literary magazine *Ark*, which in 1947 included Rexroth, James Laughlin (publisher of New Directions and poet), Richard Eberhart, Robert Duncan, Philip Lamantia, Kenneth Patchen, and E. E. Cummings among its contributors.

Strong-willed, opinionated, and by all accounts brilliant, Rexroth came to be one of the West Coast's leading literary figures, and a sort of father figure for the younger generation of poets. His pacifism, anarchism, and opposition to the conventional materialist order attracted these young writers, and many came eagerly to hear him at his Friday night gatherings.

Ferlinghetti learned much from listening to Rexroth, both at his Friday gatherings and from his broadcasts on KPFA, which, like his informal soirées, covered much more than just books.

"He reviewed everything," Ferlinghetti recalls. "Geology, philosophy, I got a complete education listening to him, particularly political. I didn't have any real political education till I started listening to him and to KPFA. There were people on like Alan Watts, and William Mandel, a Soviet affairs expert who, with other KPFA staffers, told the House Un-American Activities Committee to go to hell. And his knowledge was encyclopedic."

Rexroth seemed to remember everything he'd ever read. Janet Richards wrote in her memoir, "He was everything: conscientious objector, classical scholar, versed in all sciences, political wiseacre, extreme radical, painter, musician, Orientalist, poet, essayist, and the friend of all artists."

Noted for his generosity, he also loved to be the center of attention, and his eccentric personality and didactic views sometimes annoyed others.

"He liked being a daddy to all the little poets," remembers poet and filmmaker James Broughton, an occasional visitor. "But he was just a great noisy Capricorn who knew everything and told everybody who was any good."

Rexroth had been living at the Eighth Avenue flat for some three years with Marthe, his third wife; earlier, they had both been living with his second wife, Marie, on Potrero Hill, and Marie now lived across the street. Marthe invariably adjourned to the bedroom when the guests began arriving to settle into the comfortable, old second- or third-hand chairs that were set before walls lined almost floor to ceiling with old fruit crates filled with books. Some of the dark oak-paneled wall space not covered by books was taken with paintings by Rexroth himself, or Andree, or some other artist he knew. Though Rexroth was making a reasonable living, he hated any scrap of bourgeois trappings, and maintained a deliberately bohemian atmosphere, befitting his anarchist, populist politics.

Ferlinghetti visited the Eighth Avenue flat a few times before Rexroth moved to 250 Scott Street, where he had a spacious, high-ceilinged six-room apartment whose every wall was likewise lined with the book-filled fruit crates, "all his library that he'd accumulated over many years as a reviewer," Ferlinghetti says. "And on every subject conceivable, not just poetry, and in several languages."

There, Ferlinghetti became a regular visitor until well into the 1960s when Rexroth moved to Santa Barbara.

Shy in the extreme, Ferlinghetti said nothing for months. "There was always a big crowd there," Charles Richards remembers, "and he never said anything, just kind of hung back in the shadows, a kind of ghostly figure."

Ferlinghetti's silence, however, was also partly due to his awe of his host.

"Rexroth was the great master, and I was just a kid," he says.

Then again, none of the guests had much opportunity to talk. Rexroth talked nearly constantly, about literature, other arts, politics, whatever interested him at the moment. And his appetite for conversation wasn't limited to his Friday nights. Ferlinghetti recounts that "in the early days of the bookstore, I was super busy, with so much work to do, and he was always calling up, and we'd have these long conversations. I was too much in awe of him to be able to relax."

During the occasional evenings when Rexroth wasn't doing all the talking, he would go around the circle of guests, inviting readings from those who had brought something; then Rexroth would discuss it and pass judgment. The point seemed to be for him to teach, to test his ideas, "to exercise his own genius," as Michael McClure put it. "We would listen, and we'd ask him questions. Kenneth was like Godwin was to early nineteenth-century England—an anarchist, teacher, political figure, litterateur. He was a very brilliant man and put many of us on our feet with a stance we could grow with."

Ferlinghetti may have said little, but he was well aware of Rexroth's influence, and though the younger writer was never pushy, he was certainly ambitious. The day after meeting him for the first time, he called to ask Rexroth about showing him, and getting published, his own translations of Prévert. Though Rexroth initially had no particular fondness for the shy young writer, he came to be one of Ferlinghetti's first and most steadfast supporters in the next decade.

At those evenings Ferlinghetti also met many other writers, artists, and literary figures. Ruth Witt-Diamant, the founder of the San Francisco Poetry Center along with Rexroth and some others from the Libertarian Circle, was a visitor, as was poet Robert Duncan, whom Ferlinghetti liked, though the feeling wasn't necessarily mutual.

"He was a brilliant, nonstop talker," Ferlinghetti remembers about Duncan, "and his voice would go up when he got excited. It was always very entertaining to be around him." He was gifted with "the finest ear of any poet around. I was impressed by his erudition and by how articulate he was."

Duncan, too, had gatherings at his home, only a few blocks from the Ferlinghettis' flat, where he would discuss literature and literary subjects, and Ferlinghetti went there a few times. But the group there was a more flamboyant gay crowd, and Ferlinghetti was less at home.

Poets Thomas Parkinson and Broughton also numbered among the occasional or regular guests at Rexroth's. Parkinson, a poet and professor at the University of California–Berkeley, was another who became a great booster of many young poets of the Bay Area.

In that first year in San Francisco, Ferlinghetti began pursuing his literary career in other directions as well. In late spring he had gone to the *San Francisco Chronicle* offices and asked William Hogan, the book review editor, if he could review books. As in most newspapers, the book reviews occupied a small section of the Sunday feature pages aimed at what was assumed to be a very small audience, and were written mainly by free-lancers. In the case of the *Chronicle*, the reviews paid nothing at all, and Hogan was certainly willing to give Ferlinghetti a try. In July 1951 Lawrence Ferling contributed his first review, of "six of the recent poetry books," and in the fall became a regular contributor, getting valuable exposure as well as sharpening critical discrimination and writing skill.

In June 1952 he also sent a review of poet and storyteller Dylan Thomas's second San Francisco visit to *Counterpoint*, a literary arts magazine, which also paid nothing. Thomas had come with his wife, Caitlin, and easily lived up to his reputation everywhere he stopped, carousing until all hours, battling sometimes publicly with his wife, relentlessly drinking himself across America. A year and a half later, on his fourth tour, he would die in New York after another long night of drinking, his American mistress standing vigil, while his wife had to be restrained by a straitjacket. His appearance in San Francisco during that second tour was portentous. In his review Ferlinghetti noted the tone:

"The poetry he read at the San Francisco Museum of Art constituted, on the whole, one long meditation on dying ... [including] his own 'Ceremony After a Fire Raid' and his poem beginning 'Do not go gentle into that good night, / Rage, rage against the dying of the light.' "

To the young writer, Thomas and his performance were striking. "His reading voice was strange and wild," Ferlinghetti wrote. And in a review of Thomas's *In Country Sleep* that had appeared in the *Chronicle* in March, his praise was unqualified: "There is nothing like Dylan Thomas in poetry today. There is a wholeness, a harmony, a radiance about everything he has written which sets him apart."

While in the city, Thomas gave two readings to large audiences, and one broadcast on KPFA, the Pacifica radio station with substantial arts and political programming. His public readings and presence across the country made Thomas a real celebrity, and the tradition of oral poetry Thomas presented became a model as well for many of the younger poets who were to constitute the heart of the San Francisco Renaissance—the Beat Generation.

Later that same year, in December, Ferlinghetti reviewed another reading at the museum for *Counterpoint*, by Kenneth Patchen, a poet who was also a major force in the Bay Area literary world. Ferlinghetti had liked Patchen's work since he first encountered it in the forties, and his reading was clearly affecting:

"He stood there for a long time, reading his poetry, his voice like the hush of concrete, his only gestures the words themselves. When he stopped reading it was twenty-nine minutes to eleven. The 163 people of San Francisco ... clapped. He read two or three more poems. Then he edged out of the room, looking at the people, not smiling. Outside, Patchen stood still in the dim hallway, against a wall. He had a cigarette. He had a cane. He stood very quietly, very ungiantlike, in the hush of concrete, with his cigarette, with his cane, like a blind man waiting for something.

"But he saw everything."

Like Rexroth, Patchen was originally a midwesterner, born in Ohio, though he'd spent most of his young adulthood in New York's Greenwich Village. After moving to San Francisco in the late forties, he had lived for a while with painter and printer David Ruff and Holly Beye. Patchen painted as well, another similarity with Rexroth, and with Ferlinghetti himself (though Ferlinghetti had no place to paint in his first year in San Francisco), frequently illustrating his poems with drawings. Equally important, Patchen had the kind of anarchist-pacifist political ideas with which Ferlinghetti sympathized.

Also like Rexroth, Patchen himself was often difficult in his relations with other writers, and kept his distance. A spinal illness had crippled him, and "he was always in pain," Kirby remembers. Four years later, when City Lights published Patchen's *Poems of Humor and Protest*, Ferlinghetti arranged the store's first author's autograph party for him; but Patchen never showed.

"He was hard to get along with," Ferlinghetti remembers. "And he always had a young poet as a kind of messenger boy . . . some enthusiast who was in love with his poetry and who was willing to go around running his errands"; though, Ferlinghetti adds, there's "nothing wrong with that."

The links between homosexuality and communism may never have been established during those 1950 congressional hearings, but by mid-1952 McCarthy was at his height, and fresh evidence of the "Communist conspiracy" surfaced almost daily. A housewife who was a member of the Indiana State Textbook Commission deplored the "Communist directive in education to stress the story of Robin Hood. They want to stress it because he robbed the rich and gave to the poor. That's the Communist line." And in San Antonio, Texas, another interested citizen demanded the public library affix a red stamp to any book authored by someone accused or suspected of Communist sympathies.

In December of 1951, when Lippincott rejected *Uncertain Spring*, Ferlinghetti began working on a revision of the novel, taking breaks to work on his Prévert translations. Then in the summer of 1952 he got a job teaching at the University of San Francisco. His tenure, however, was brief, due in part to the social and political climate of the times.

"I was reading a book that had just come out on a homosexual interpretation of Shakespeare's sonnets, so I brought it to class and I was reading from it, and the head of the department walks in. He's a priest. I could see him in the back. He sort of waved at me, and that was the end of my academic career. It only lasted three months."

The University of San Francisco was a Jesuit university; in such a climate the "immoral" theory Ferlinghetti repeated was clearly a danger. He finished the summer session, but wasn't rehired. He wasn't that disappointed, though; he didn't really like teaching, anyway.

"I was only interested in writing. I was too selfish to spend much time on other people," he said later. And write he did, while Kirby's teaching job continued to bring in enough for them to live.

That fall he published the first of his translations of Jacques Prévert and the very first of his own poems. He had sent some of each to *Inferno*, a well-respected local literary magazine which was among the most recent in the line of radical magazines in the Bay Area that defined the leading edge of literature and politics. That most recent tradition had begun with (or been continued by) *Circle* in 1944. Published at Berkeley until 1948, the magazine had begun the synthesis of arts, literature, and politics that came to be called the Berkeley Renaissance. Rexroth, Patchen, Duncan, and Parkinson were among a list of international contributors that also included Lawrence Durrell, Henry Miller, Max Jacob, Weldon Kees, William Carlos Williams, and E. E. Cummings. Leslie Woolf Hedley's *Inferno* followed in its footsteps, and though its list of contributors was not quite as impressive, it was one of the few important radical magazines of the time. When Hedley accepted eight Prévert translations by Larry Ferling for the issue that came out in September 1952, along with the first of his own poems to be published, an early verse titled "Brother, Brother," Ferlinghetti was delighted.

Though he wasn't writing much poetry, over the next year or two his Prévert translations began appearing in more magazines, including the prestigious *Contact* in summer 1953 and *California Quarterly* the following winter. Then, besides continuing work on the Prévert translations and the novel, and doing regular reviews of books and occasional literary events, the interest in painting he had developed as a master's degree student at Columbia, and continued in Paris, led him to begin writing about it.

The connection between poets and painters, which had been very strong in Paris beginning with the dadaists at the time of World War I, had made its impression on him. William Carlos Williams had been interested in painting, and some of the poets Ferlinghetti most admired—Cummings, Patchen, Rexroth—all painted as well. Now in San Francisco, Ferlinghetti was eager to continue the painting he had begun at the Académie Julien. The new wave of abstract expressionism which dominated the contemporary art world had captured his interest with its ideas that deeply felt, subconscious material was being manifest in a new painterly language by focusing on the qualities of its surfaces and the act of painting itself.

In January 1952 *Counterpoint* published an article he had written about "Expressionism in San Francisco painting today," and in the 1953 issue of *Inferno* he had published reproductions of two of his own paintings. Then, beginning in February 1953, with a review of the 72nd Annual Painting and Sculpture Exhibition at the San Francisco Museum of Art, he began writing a monthly column about San Francisco art exhibits and artists for the New York–based *Art Digest* (later *Arts Digest*), eventually earning a listing as one of the "correspondents." These reviews earned him only twenty-five dollars for each, but the work of reviewing exhibits and profiling artists put him in touch with other artists and some of the poets with whom they associated.

One painter, Ronnie Bladen, was a member of the San Francisco Anarchist Society, and in 1953, at Bladen's apartment, Ferlinghetti first met the brilliant young surrealist poet Philip Lamantia, a San Francisco native. When Lamantia was only sixteen, his poetry had impressed André Breton, and Lamantia had gone on to publish in the foremost surrealist magazines. A few years later he went to New York, and there spent some time in Greenwich Village, where he met other painters and poets, including the young Allen Ginsberg. Back in San Francisco for the time being, Lamantia was also interested in painting.

Another group of painters had studios at the Audiffred Building at 9 Mission Street near the waterfront. The building was old, unheated, and had no electricity or running water, but the window light was ample, and rent was cheap. Hassel Smith was one of the artists there, and though Ferlinghetti had little success trying to interview him ("He was very standoffish. He wouldn't talk. He had absolute scorn for journalists"), when Smith left the building, Ferlinghetti took over his studio and resumed the painting he had begun in Paris.

His first *Art Digest* review discussed the "clash of the objective-expressionist and the abstract-expressionist which in recent years has dominated Bay Area art." His own canvases during this period were essentially nonobjective works strongly influenced by Franz Kline. Dominated by geometric forms on dark backgrounds, they were characterized by simple lines and angles, often in muted primaries, set on dark, blue-black fields.

As he continued his reviews over the next three years, the judgments they pronounced couldn't help but reflect an aesthetic inseparable from the social-political views he had been forming since his introduction to politics in Greenwich Village. Though his tone was rarely harsh, his position was clear. In a spring 1954 review of a Raoul Dufy exhibit at the San Francisco Museum of Art, he questioned the values behind the painting, and thus the work itself. In two earlier reviews Ferlinghetti had quoted Joyce to suggest his own standard: "The supreme question about a work of art is out of how deep a life does it spring"; and it is clear that in Dufy's case Ferlinghetti didn't find much depth. Though the artist was popular, Ferlinghetti pointed out that his "racing and boating and balconies and palm trees and paddocks and baccarat tables and orchestras and receptions" were mostly the property of the wealthy, "especially movie people, prominent musicians and great social figures." He concluded by suggesting that an overall judgment of the work must "necessarily involve an evaluation of this kind of society."

It was a pretty strong statement for a rather high-toned magazine whose audience certainly included just those kinds of people. But for Ferlinghetti this kind of criticism wasn't enough. Some kind of action was also needed, some way to integrate work and life that supported and advanced his political and social values. Soon enough, the opportunity for that action would arise.

In the meantime another show he reviewed bore more directly on the development of his own work. Ferlinghetti was familiar with the poetry of Henri Michaux, and was sympathetic with its "audacity" and its "attack on the 'congealed and established,' " but he had no idea that Michaux painted as well. In 1953 the Oakland Art Museum mounted an exhibition of his paintings and drawings, and because of Ferlinghetti's own engagement with both arts, the young writer was very interested in the results. His conclusion, that only three or four of the paintings were strong enough to stand by themselves (the drawings fared better, but there weren't many of them), was less important than the impact of Michaux's own discoveries about painting.

Ferlinghetti quoted from Michaux's explanation of his method: "scrawl unconsciously, there practically always appear faces on the paper . . . ten, fifteen, twenty. And savages for the most part. . . . From what depths do they come? . . . There is a certain interior phantom one must paint."

Thirty years later Ferlinghetti would use almost the same idea to explain his own paintings: "This figure will spring up on the canvas, will surge out of the paint, like where did it come from? It's as if they're existing for all time to spring up on your canvas at this instant."

He concluded his review by remarking at the "gone eye of a barbarian" that looked out from Oakland, a phrase which would echo in the title of Ferlinghetti's first collection of poems: *Pictures of the Gone World.*

When he and Kirby moved to an apartment on the second floor of 339 Chestnut Street in early 1953, he began to write the "painter" poems that would eventually constitute the heart of that collection. The hillside house with its fine view of the Bay from Golden Gate south had belonged to another artist, Gordon Onslow-Ford, who had taught at the California School of Fine Arts (now the San Francisco Art Institute), and the Ferlinghettis' second-floor flat had itself belonged to another painter.

The house was distinguished by a "Romeo," an exterior covered stair-case with a small balcony at each level, and the apartment was typical of many in San Francisco, with its five rooms arranged in a line off a long hall. At the front were two living rooms, then a bedroom and a bathroom down the hall, a dining room, and a large square kitchen at the back.

The presence and influence of painters, as well as Kirby and Law-rence's own taste for the offbeat, led to the eclectic decor they gave the place. The kitchen, painted green, looked out on a backyard garden with an avocado tree. The back dining room, offering a view over the housetops to the ocean, was painted yellow, and they painted the long, dark hall "flaming crimson." The bathroom, "a long cryptlike enclosure with a raggedy linoleum floor," according to Janet Richards, was painted red and green. One of the front rooms they painted completely blue, including the floor, except for one wall, which remained covered in the silver paper from cigarette packs that the previous tenant had installed. On the op-posite wall was a fireplace with a gas stove, and on an adjacent wall, Kirby's piano. The furnishings were as various as the color scheme, with bookcases jutting out at angles, pale Persian rugs, and a philodendron growing across the ceiling in front.

It was in the front living room that Ferlinghetti wrote, with no revision, his first "completely San Francisco poem." Like several of the short poems he had written in Paris, it began as a simple description—this time of a woman he had seen from his window who was hanging laundry. The romantic setting highlighted the scene, turning a simple household chore into a portrait of eternal seduction:

> *Away above a harborful*
> *of caulkless houses*
> *among the charley noble chimneypots*
> *of a rooftop rigged with clotheslines*
> *a woman pastes up sails*
> *upon the wind*
> *hanging out her morning sheets*
> *with wooden pins*
> *O lovely mammal*
> *her nearly naked teats*
> *throw taut shadows*
> *when she stretches up*
> *to hang at last the last of her*

> so white washed sins
> but it is wetly amorous
> and winds itself about her
> clinging to her skin
> So caught with arms upraised
> she tosses back her head
> in voiceless laughter
> and in choiceless gesture then
> shakes out gold hair
>
> while in the reachless seascape spaces
>
> between the blown white shrouds
>
> stand out the bright steamers
>
> to kingdom come

Though Michaux was apparently one of the influences on his work, and even more, Prévert, whose own poems were often anecdotal snapshots colored with satirical social comment, the whole process of painting made its way into the poems. Having noted in his journal that "style is a feeling for the weight and arrangement of words on a page," Ferlinghetti wanted to use the page as a canvas. Rather than being restricted to the left margin, these poems were designed to use the whole page, spreading across the surface the way painters spread paint. The idea was that this "open form" would be analogous to the idea of "open form" the abstract expressionists articulated. By utilizing the white space as part of the overall composition, rather than simply having dense, closed, compact blocks of type, the page becomes an accessible field, and the whole poem more available.

While going on to write more San Francisco poems, he continued sending his Prévert translations off to local magazines. One that had published six of them in spring 1953 was a journal that had come out of the Berkeley Renaissance and published just two earlier issues. Pete Martin's *City Lights* caught Ferlinghetti's attention as much because of the name as the content. Charlie Chaplin, the hero of the film of that title, was the perennial outsider—dispossessed, alienated, victimized by the immense mechanism of the modern world. It was a figure with whom Ferlinghetti instinctively sympathized. Though he didn't see himself as a victim like Charlie, he clearly felt himself one of the "common men," threatened by the massed forces of the bureaucratic, materialist, conformist world. The sense of being a perpetual outsider, of never quite belonging, which was a central part of Charlie's character, was something Ferlinghetti also felt strongly.

Martin, son of the assassinated Italian anarchist Carlo Tresca, and a nephew of radical American activist Elizabeth Gurley Flynn, had been a student at Berkeley and was teaching sociology at San Francisco State College. His pop culture magazine only lasted five issues, but it published the first film criticism by fellow Berkeley alum Pauline Kael and eccentric articles like "The Sociological Significance of Moon Mullins." Ferlinghetti's meeting with him, soon after moving to Chestnut Street, though coincidental, was not entirely a surprise.

"I was driving up Columbus Avenue, I'd been painting on Mission Street. It was just when I was discovering North Beach. I'd finally zeroed in on where so-called bohemians were. And I saw this guy putting up a sign where City Lights is, and it said, Pocket Book Shop. So I got out of the car and I went over, and I said, 'What are you doing?' The guy was Pete Martin, and he had an idea that an all-paperback bookshop might support the publication of his magazine. It was just before the paperback revolution that saw major publishers for the first time make 'serious' books available at inexpensive prices. At the time, the only paperbacks except British Penguins were twenty-five-cent Pocket or Avon or Signet popular library editions that were only sold at drugstores or newsstands.

"And Martin said, we're just trying to pay the rent for the magazine office. So he said, who are you? And I said, my name is Larry Ferling. I was still using the abbreviated form of my family name. And he said, 'Oh, you wrote those Prévert translations.' "

The meeting led to a partnership in the bookstore. Each of them put in five hundred dollars, and in June 1953 City Lights Pocket Book Shop opened its doors. By design, the emphasis was decidedly political, with magazines and newspapers all across the political spectrum. During Rexroth's Friday evenings, Ferlinghetti would jot down titles and authors Rexroth mentioned and order them for the store. For his part Ferlinghetti had in mind some of the French bookstores he had known in Paris, and along with Martin, who was led by his own political background, they hoped the store might become the center of an intellectual community, a place where artists and thinkers could meet and gather and find the most current thinking.

From the beginning, they were successful. Open from late morning until midnight, seven days a week, from the first day, the small store was busy, though it took several years before receipts averaged a hundred dollars daily, and in those first years, Ferlinghetti hardly scratched out a living. Right away, Rexroth became a regular visitor, as did many other San Francisco writers and those visiting from out of town.

Soon after opening, Martin, who liked to frequent local bars, met a young, heavy-set Japanese-American named Shigeyoshi Murao, who was tending bar as day manager across the alley at Vesuvio's.

"They gave me a manual how to turn out the lights, scatter the sawdust, and so on," Murao remembers. "I thought it was very silly. I showed it to Pete Martin, who used to come in, and he thought it was funny, too, so we talked, and he decided to hire me at City Lights. They didn't have any money to pay me, so I worked for books for two, three months."

Murao was born in Seattle and spent two years in one of the Idaho internment camps for Japanese-Americans during World War II. Then after volunteering and serving as an interpreter in the Army, after the war he traveled to New York, Chicago, New Orleans, and Reno before winding up at Vesuvio's.

"Meanwhile, the government caught up with me, I owed taxes, so I said I had to have income," Murao remembers. "So City Lights offered to pay the taxes and to pay me."

He stayed on to work and eventually manage City Lights for twenty years. Martin, however, didn't remain nearly as long. A New Yorker, he decided he wanted to return. After a little more than a year, he sold his interest to Ferlinghetti and went back east to open the New Yorker bookstore in Manhattan. His change of heart was not really a loss to Ferlinghetti, though; the partners' business relationship had never become any more than that.

Besides, Ferlinghetti had another idea which had been brewing for a while, though he'd never discussed it with Martin. He wanted to use the bookstore as a base for publishing avant-garde literature. It was something he had seen in Paris, where major publishers like Hachette and Gallimard also operated bookstores, and to Ferlinghetti "it seemed like a logical thing to do. I never understood why bookstores here didn't do it. The bookstore's a natural source of publicity for the press, and a place to sell the books."

His idea was to publish poetry in small, inexpensive editions that people could slip in a pocket and carry with them to work, on errands, anywhere. When he was in France, he'd seen, and read, some of the small, square, paperback *Poètes d'Aujourd'hui* that Seghers published, and as far as he knew, there was nothing like them in America. *Livres de poche*, they were called in French: pocket books. Ferlinghetti decided he would call his "Pocket Poets."

After Martin left, Ferlinghetti began working on the first book. He assembled a collection of twenty-seven short poems he had written in the last six or seven years, about ten of them in Europe before he had come to San Francisco, and the others in the few months after the first Chestnut Street poem. Influenced by Prévert as well as by the French surrealists and other urban poets he had studied, all are rooted in concrete descriptions of the world around, and suffused with the wonder and whimsey that became dominant characteristics of the Ferlinghetti voice. The whimsey becomes in several a strong dose of irony, while the wonder comes in others from transformations that are surreal. In many, as well, there is the sexual content that also became a recurrent theme in later work. And like that first San Francisco poem, none were revised beyond the first draft.

In January 1955 he legally became sole proprietor of City Lights Pocket Book Shop; then on August 10, with the help of David Ruff, who printed the small volume in letterpress, Kirby, and Holly Beye, City Lights Press published "Pocket Poet Number One": *Pictures of the Gone World*. On it, the author used his full name, which he had finally discovered when he got a copy of his birth certificate to establish his identity to apply for a California driver's license. He'd only begun using it for the first time on his *Art Digest* reviews in January—Lawrence Ferlinghetti. Larry Ferling was gone.

5

By late 1954 McCarthy's reputation had been irrevocably damaged when the circus of televised hearings he engineered to expose Communists in the Army publicly exposed his own unsavory tactics. The Senate adopted a resolution of censure, though the presiding officer, Vice President Richard Nixon, exercised his prerogative and had the word "censure" stricken to tone down the criticism. But the public intolerance for anything that could be construed as having the faintest scent of "communism" in its neighborhood was still going strong. It was in this atmosphere that the murals at the San Francisco Rincon Annex Post Office continued to inflame patriotic citizens of the city.

The murals had been commissioned by the Roosevelt administration and painted by Anton Refregier, an artist whose "left wing" political views were known, though there was no protest when the work was unveiled in 1948. However, as San Franciscans, like other Americans, became aware of the "Communist threat," the letters of protest began to come in. From May 1949 to July 1951 the American Legion, the Veterans of Foreign Wars, the Society of Western Artists, and many more all wrote, variously charging that "said murals do not truly depict the romance and glory of early California history," that they were "definitely subversive and designed to spread Communistic propaganda." One mural, entitled "War and Peace," was particularly objectionable: included among the flags of many nations was that of the Soviet Union—clearly a subversive image.

Ferlinghetti had written in his journal in 1952 that "if I could find a

J. M. W. Turner to champion, I might become a great art critic." Though Refregier certainly wasn't a J. M. W. Turner, in April 1953 Ferlinghetti defended the murals in an *Art Digest* article headlined "Muralist Refregier and the Haunted Post Office." In it he reported the latest twist to the controversy—the introduction of a resolution by California Representative Hubert Scudder calling for the removal of all twenty-nine panels, based on a House Un-American Activities report of twenty-three instances of Refregier's association with Communist organizations or organizations of "fellow travelers."

Ferlinghetti wrote that "it was all too evident then that the murals had become the latest battleground of intellectual and artistic censorship." In their defense he described their democratic array of "Indians, conquistadores, padres, nuns, miners, railroad and ship workers, businessmen, vigilantes, soldiers, patriots, judges, earthquake and riot victims, bridge builders, and builders of the United Nations," as well as the recent formation of the Committee for the Defense of the Refregier Murals, which he joined.

The resolution to remove the murals never passed, and as McCarthy's influence waned, the furor subsided. But the issue had occasioned Ferlinghetti's first foray into the political realm. His involvement in First Amendment questions of free speech and expression, however, had hardly begun.

Though the Refregier murals became a local cause célèbre, it was not because of their artistic value; the leading edge of painting fashion at the time was not social realism, or any kind of realism. Rather, the abstract expressionism of New York painters Jackson Pollock, Willem de Kooning, Mark Rothko, and others who burst on the scene in the late 1940s dominated critical attention. Ferlinghetti's own paintings, influenced by Franz Kline, grew from that aesthetic, and his *Art Digest* columns demonstrated the greatest enthusiasm for works of expressionist artists.

Rothko and Clyfford Still were two of these abstract expressionists whose work Ferlinghetti, like many others, thought very important. In 1953–54 Rothko was visiting San Francisco and teaching at the California School of Fine Arts along with Still. In late fall of 1954 six young painters who had been associated with the California School of Fine Arts, some of whom had been students of Still and Rothko, opened their own gallery in a converted auto-repair garage on Union and Fillmore, and called it simply the Six Gallery. Some of the others were attracted to the new figurative painting, which was just beginning to claim attention that had been going almost exclusively to abstract expressionism for the previous seven or eight years; but what all these young artists, including James Weeks, Jay DeFeo, Fred Martin, and Wally Hedrick, had in common was an interest in a new aesthetic and a variety of artistic experiment. Their intent at the Six Gallery was to "combine the showing of painting with music and poetry, and, moreover," according to Ferlinghetti's brief review in the January 1955 *Art Digest*, "make poetry pay." It was a novel idea in San Francisco at the time.

The project was viewed with some skepticism by the local art pundits, but Ferlinghetti seemed to be excited by the idea, if not by what it had accomplished to that point. "So far," he wrote, "the '6' has not fallen on its eager, upturned face, though it cannot be said to have reached any delirious heavens." He went on to describe a Sunday afternoon showing of abstract film; the painting and poetry, shown together, of Fred Martin (Ferlinghetti was much more enthusiastic about the poetry, quoting a ten-line poem written "in the style of a popular song"); and a poetry reading that featured Robert Duncan.

Earlier that year, Duncan's play *Faust Foutu*—or *Faust Fucked*—had been given a reading there; one of the readers was a young student who had come to San Francisco partly in pursuit of the woman who would become his wife, and partly to learn more about the "gestural" painting of Still and Rothko. Michael McClure never painted, but he was interested in the aesthetic of these painters and the ideas behind them—especially the biological basis of the work that might be incorporated into his poetry. When he found that the two painters were not at the California School of Fine Arts that year, he went on to enroll at San Francisco State College and took a poetry class there with Duncan.

Duncan took a liking to McClure and his poetry, and the young poet quickly became involved in the Bay Area literary world. That year of 1954, McClure had gone to a party given by Ruth Witt-Diamant, the director of the San Francisco Poetry Center, for W. H. Auden's reading, and at that party had met both Auden and Allen Ginsberg.

Ginsberg had come to the Bay Area from Mexico, where he'd spent the first four months of 1954 exploring Mayan ruins in Yucatán and seeking out psychedelic drugs which he took in Indian ceremonies and by himself. In May he'd come to San Jose to stay with his close friend and sometimes lover Neal Cassady and Cassady's wife, Carolyn, but by the fall the young poet was living with a woman he had met in San Francisco after being kicked out of Cassady's house by Carolyn when she came home one night to find Ginsberg and her husband in bed together. By winter Ginsberg got a job doing market research for Towne-

Oller, met and fell in love with Peter Orlovsky, and in mid-February got an apartment on Montgomery Street in North Beach.

Ginsberg had brought with him a letter of introduction to Rexroth from William Carlos Williams, who had lived near Ginsberg in Rutherford, New Jersey. Ginsberg had sought Williams out there, and Williams, with the generosity toward younger poets for which he was noted, had encouraged him. That first winter in San Francisco, Ginsberg had called on Rexroth, who suggested he meet several of the other writers in the area. As a part of the neighborhood, and of the literary life there, Ginsberg became another of the regular visitors to City Lights. He introduced himself to Ferlinghetti, and also at Rexroth's suggestion, tried to interest Ferlinghetti in publishing *Empty Mirror*, a collection of his own poems, with an introduction by Williams. Ferlinghetti read them, but he wasn't overwhelmed, and at any rate didn't have the money to do another book just then. He was already planning to do two more Pocket Poets books, by Kenneth Rexroth and Kenneth Patchen.

Ginsberg recalls that "I was a little upset, because I thought it was a good book and it was up his alley." But the younger, aggressive, voluble New Yorker, with his energy and brilliance, became one of the circle surrounding City Lights and North Beach, as he and Ferlinghetti struck up a friendship based on their common interest in literature and politics. Like Ferlinghetti, Ginsberg had studied at Columbia, with some of the same teachers (though they hadn't known each other there), and also like Ferlinghetti, Ginsberg's interests extended far beyond literature, especially in its academic guise. He had a real taste for experience, both physical and mental, and an attraction to the alienated, the dispossessed, the down-and-out, the whole wildness of the bohemian life. Though Ginsberg seemed more interested in pushing his rebellion and curiosity beyond the limits of the acceptable—Ferlinghetti's own style had nothing of Ginsberg's flamboyance—Ferlinghetti was more than sympathetic with that rebelliousness. The two began to see each other regularly, at the bookstore, at nearby Mike's pool hall where they would go for beer and hamburgers along with Ferlinghetti's dog Homer, and occasionally at Rexroth's and other literary gatherings.

By the end of April the restless, energetic Ginsberg wanted to move on from the workaday grind at Towne-Oller. He talked with his bosses there and finally persuaded them that they would be far better off replacing him with a computer, and he would help them do it; in exchange for that arrangement, they agreed to let Ginsberg collect unemployment compensation. Ginsberg happily took off and went to work on his poems.

Ginsberg and Kerouac had both been working to bring the immediacy of experience into their writing. For Kerouac this effort took the form of the "spontaneous" prose of his novels, which was increasingly informed by his studies of Buddhism, an interest Ginsberg had sparked in 1953. Ginsberg's own intensive studies of Chinese and Japanese religion, art, and literature had begun in the spring of 1953. His poetry was increasingly influenced by this, as well as by his interest in the poetry and visionary qualities of both William Blake and Walt Whitman. In late August he finished the first part of a major new poem addressed to his friend and former fellow patient at Columbia Psychiatric Institute, Carl Solomon, and titled it "Howl for Carl Solomon."

Ginsberg had enrolled in graduate school in English at Berkeley for the fall term, and at the beginning of September, moved to a small cottage across the Bay in Berkeley and was working on the poem again—revisions of what he had sent Kerouac, and a whole new section based on a peyote-inspired vision he had had of the Sir Francis Drake Hotel while he was living on Montgomery Street. The cottage was spare—at first he couldn't even afford to get the phone connected, as he reported in his later poem "Sunflower Sutra," but he had a phonograph (as the poem also mentions), books, and time to write.

He continued working on the poem and in early September saw McClure. A little earlier Wally Hedrick had run into McClure on the street in North Beach and asked him if he wanted to organize a poetry reading, or some event, at the Six Gallery. McClure said yes, but at the time, he was busy working at the San Francisco Museum of Art, and Joanna, now his wife, was pregnant; the project languished in the back of his mind. When McClure saw Ginsberg in September, they talked about what they were doing, and McClure told him that among other things, he wanted to put together a reading at the gallery, but didn't really have time. Ginsberg was interested and said he'd do it. He wanted to have Kerouac and Cassady read, but neither was interested; at the same time, he set about contacting some of the other poets he'd met.

One of the first he contacted was twenty-five-year-old Gary Snyder, whom Rexroth had sent Ginsberg to meet. Raised in rural Oregon and intimate with the outdoors, Snyder gave the impression of ruggedness, though he wasn't really a big man. He had worked as a fire lookout in the High Cascades and had come to the Bay Area to do graduate work at Berkeley in 1951. After living in North Beach for two years, he was back in Berkeley working on his thesis (the later published *Myths and Texts*, based on American Indian lore) and learning Japanese in preparation for going there to live and study Buddhism. Like Ginsberg, he was living in a small cottage, and very nearby; diligently cultivating his garden in traditional Japanese-style robe, he was also writing plain, unornamented poems, rich with simple images, about the natural world.

Philip Whalen, also a serious student of Buddhism, had been a roommate of Snyder's at Reed College in Portland, and had also worked as a fire lookout, having left and come to San Francisco in September. Ginsberg met him through Snyder. The other poet he invited to join the reading was Philip Lamantia, whose poems Ginsberg had first read and liked in 1945 in *View*, a New York surrealist magazine. He'd met him in 1948 at the San Remo Bar, a New York hangout for artists and writers and musicians.

Ginsberg asked Rexroth if he would be willing to emcee, and the older poet agreed. Ginsberg finalized arrangements with the gallery, made up postcards announcing the reading for October 13, and stopped at City Lights to drop off a bunch and let Ferlinghetti know about the reading.

"Six poets at the Six Gallery," the card read. "Kenneth Rexroth, M.C. Remarkable collection of angels all gathered at once in the same spot. Wine, music, dancing girls, serious poetry, free satori. Small collection for wine and postcards. Charming event."

The afternoon of the reading, Ginsberg and Kerouac, who had been staying with Ginsberg in Berkeley, took the train across the Bay, arriving at the Key Terminal at the same time Whalen arrived with Snyder. The three poets spent the rest of the afternoon together and met Philip Lamantia for dinner at the New Pisa Restaurant near City Lights on Grant Street, then all went over to the gallery. Ferlinghetti and Kirby drove over separately with other friends, the Richardses came with Weldon Kees, and dozens of other artists, writers, friends, and aficionados all found their way as well.

The gallery itself was two adjoining rooms, and it was filled—over a hundred people packed the room, using all the chairs, standing up in back, sitting on the low platform stage. Behind the podium someone had constructed, sculpture by Fred Martin was exhibited—"pieces of orange crates that had been swathed in muslin and dipped in plaster of paris to make splintered, sweeping shapes like pieces of surrealist furniture," McClure described them. The six poets sat in a semicircle on the stage behind the podium, and the reading itself was delayed while Kerouac went out and got a gallon jug of red wine. Finally Rexroth, in a pin-striped cutaway coat he'd bought at a thrift shop for the occasion, got up to begin the event.

He made a joke about the sculpture, suggesting it might be furniture for a Japanese dwarf, then went on in a more serious note. Characteristically political in his reference, he likened San Francisco at the time to the Barcelona of the Spanish Anarchists—a kind of island where the best of the culture survived, even flourished; though even here in San Francisco, there was no escape from the world of the cold war. Then he introduced Lamantia, who chose not to read any of his poems, but several by John Hoffman, a young prose poet who had recently died. McClure read poems focused on the natural world, and our own animal nature, and Whalen read a humorous poem about confronting metamorphic change.

Ginsberg read second to last. Clean-cut, with thick, curly black hair and black horn-rimmed glasses, he began to read his new poem, the title now shortened to simply "Howl." He had tried it out a few evenings earlier on Whalen and Snyder, both of whom had liked it. As it picked up momentum with its repetition of "who" clauses that went on to describe in vivid, arresting, continual invention the lives of those with the "best minds of my generation destroyed by madness," Kerouac began shouting, "Go! Go! Go! Go!" as if it were a jazz set, and beating rhythm on his wine jug. By the end of the poem, many of the audience had joined the demonstration, stamping feet, snapping fingers, and shouting and chanting with Kerouac and Ginsberg.

When it was over, and the last echoes of the "saxophone cry that shivered the cities down to the last radio / with the absolute heart of the poem of life butchered out of their / own bodies good to eat a thousand years" had died out, the room exploded. The poets themselves were amazed. Kerouac told him the poem would make him famous in San Francisco, but Rexroth insisted his fame would spread further, saying, "This poem will make you famous from bridge to bridge."

McClure said, "I felt there was a line that had been drawn, and either we had to stand at that line or else we had to step back from it. I was an apolitical young man until 'Howl.'"

Snyder finished the reading with his long poem, "A Berry Feast," about a traditional Indian celebration in a modern context, which celebrates the ongoing vitality and power and mystery of the traditional ways allied with nature. Afterward the poets and some of their friends all went to a celebratory dinner in Chinatown, then to The Place, a popular North Beach bar.

Ferlinghetti and Kirby weren't, however, "part of the scene," as he termed it, and didn't go. The power of Ginsberg's poem still rang, though, and when Ferlinghetti got home, he went upstairs to his study and typed out a two-sentence telegram to Ginsberg. Copying the sentence Emerson had sent to Whitman as part of a letter when Emerson first read a copy of *Leaves of Grass*, Ferlinghetti added one more: "I greet you at the beginning of a great career. When do I get the manuscript?"

Another small-press publisher, Berne Porter, had also been at the reading and approached Ginsberg afterward about publishing the manuscript, but Porter wanted to put it out as a limited edition of a hundred copies in rare-book style, with no reprints, and priced at thirty dollars. Ginsberg much preferred the idea of Ferlinghetti's Pocket Poets books. Unlike the often expensive, arty fine-press editions of much avant-garde poetry, these books were designed to be, like Ferlinghetti's own poetry, accessible; they were small (4″ by 5″) and inexpensive (seventy-five cents to a dollar). And Ginsberg liked the poems of *Pictures of the Gone World* for their warmth, their humor, and their clarity. City Lights seemed exactly the right publisher for "Howl."

When he brought the poem to Ferlinghetti, it was in four parts, including the section later called "A Footnote to Howl," with its chanted list of everything holy. Ginsberg had begun the third section at the same time he wrote the first, and finished that and the rest of the poem, including "Footnote," later in the fall. When he read the "Footnote" to Rexroth, however, the older poet had reacted against it, saying, "No, no, that's enough." Still, Ginsberg felt it belonged to the poem. The solution was to separate it from the body of the poem and give the separate but related title. Ginsberg made several other attempts to continue the poem, but these, too, were never successful and were published variously as separate poems—"Fragment 1956," "Many Loves," and in 1958, "The Names."

For the rest of the book, Ginsberg and Ferlinghetti settled on five of the other recent poems Ginsberg had written that fall and through May 1956, during the period they were assembling the manuscript: "A Supermarket in California," about a dream encounter with Walt Whitman at a supermarket; "Transcription of Organ Music," a more lyric, Buddhist vision of solitude in his Berkeley cottage; "Sunflower Sutra," another Buddhist-influenced meditation on a sunflower growing amid urban wastes; "America," another aspect of Ginsberg's grim re-visioning of Whitman's euphoric national portrait; and "In the Baggage Room at Greyhound," the newest poem about insight achieved at his latest temporary job.

About the "Greyhound" poem, Ginsberg wrote in a letter to Ferlinghetti from Alaska when the book was being assembled that he thought it "stinks on ice." "I thought it was scatterbrained," he explained years later, "just mechanical notation, and it didn't seem to have any élan or much of a visionary quality."

Ferlinghetti liked it, however, and Ginsberg agreed to include it in the collection. He also included "America" at Ferlinghetti's suggestion.

"I thought it was just silly, shallow," Ginsberg remembers about that poem. "It was more his style; kind of joking. But he really liked it, so I thought, jeez, it must be good."

Ginsberg also wanted to publish "The Green Automobile" in the collection, but Ferlinghetti discouraged it, thinking it would displace other, more important and effective poems.

They then went through some of his earlier work—more lyrical poems which used shorter, alternately indented lines reminiscent of William Carlos Williams—and chose four to fill out the collection. At Ginsberg's suggestion Ferlinghetti wrote the seventy-two-year-old Williams and asked if he would contribute an introduction. Having read the almost final manuscript Ginsberg sent him in the spring, Williams agreed to write the introduction, and his response was as much as—more than—Ferlinghetti and Ginsberg could have hoped. In part, he said:

> It is a howl of defeat. Not defeat at all for he has gone through defeat as if it were an ordinary experience, a trivial experience. Everyone in this life is defeated but a man, if he be a man, is not defeated.
>
> It is the poet, Allen Ginsberg, who has gone, in his own body, through the horrifying experiences described from life in these pages. . . . He proves to us, in spite of the most debasing experiences that life can offer a man, the spirit of love survives to ennoble our lives if we have the wit and the courage and the faith—and the art! to persist. . . . Poets are damned but they are not blind, they see with the eyes of the angels. This poet sees through and all around the horrors he partakes of in the very intimate details of his poem. He avoids nothing, but experiences it to the hilt. . . .
>
> Hold back the edges of your gowns, Ladies, we are going through hell.

Ginsberg's collection would be number 4 in the Pocket Poets series; numbers 2 and 3, already in process, would come out during 1956: Kenneth Rexroth's *Thirty Spanish Poems of Love and Exile* and Kenneth

Patchen's *Poems of Humor and Protest. Howl and Other Poems* was planned for fall 1956.

In that spring following the Six Gallery reading, the poets repeated the event at Berkeley to another wildly enthusiastic audience, and thanks to Rexroth, Ginsberg himself, and others, news about the burgeoning poetry scene in San Francisco was beginning to spread. Photographers came all the way from Vancouver to take pictures of the Berkeley reading, which was also professionally recorded for Fantasy, the Berkeley record company, and later in the spring New York poet and critic Richard Eberhart came to meet Ginsberg and others, and to write an article for the *New York Times* about the San Francisco poetry renaissance.

In summer Ginsberg shipped on board a freighter to Alaska; he got back to San Francisco just in time for the appearance of Eberhart's article on September 2, titled "West Coast Rhythms." Eberhart wrote, "The West Coast is the liveliest spot in the country in poetry today," going on to note the contribution of City Lights Pocket Book Shop and the press. He mentioned the Patchen and Rexroth books, the reissue of Williams's thirty-year-old *Kora in Hell: Improvisations*, and coming first books by Denise Levertov and Marie Ponsot as well as *Howl*.

Mademoiselle magazine had also got wind of the excitement and sent a photographer to get pictures of the poets and the new San Francisco scene. With all this publicity the San Francisco Renaissance was launched. All through the summer and fall, a number of the poets had been hanging out together, and with other poets and artists, around the apartments and cafés of North Beach. But despite Ginsberg's vision of a unified Beat front, several of the more significant talents remained outside. Robert Duncan, who had long been in San Francisco, neither had nor wanted any part of the Beats; Rexroth, as a sort of elder statesman, also stood apart, as did McClure, who apparently didn't want to lose his individual identity to any hyped-up movement. And Ferlinghetti also remained apart. As proprietor of the main literary bookstore, and publisher of Ginsberg and others to come, he was sought out, and City Lights was a central pole of the neighborhood; but the main Beats—Ginsberg, Kerouac, Corso—were really New Yorkers who were all friends before they came west, and who happened to gravitate to San Francisco for what turned out to be a fairly brief time.

In September the first fifteen hundred copies of *Howl and Other Poems*, in a saddle-stitched (that is, stapled) letterpress edition, arrived at City Lights from the printer, Villiers, of Great Britain. Ferlinghetti had chosen the overseas printer because of their substantial experience with typesetting and printing for small presses and their reasonable prices. At Ginsberg's suggestion Ferlinghetti had sent copies of *Howl* galleys to some of Ginsberg's former teachers at Columbia, among them important eastern critics Lionel Trilling, Mark Van Doren, and Joseph Wood Krutch, as well as to Malcolm Cowley, whom Ginsberg had met before. Though none had anything good to say about the new work, they all became aware of it. Now Ginsberg sent copies of the book to all his friends as well as to writers, critics, and others of national fame who he thought should pay attention: Charlie Chaplin, Henry Miller, Robinson Jeffers, W. H. Auden, T. S. Eliot, Ezra Pound, Marianne Moore, e. e. cummings, and nearly a hundred more.

Though the book sold well in San Francisco, elsewhere it was hard to get. In October Ginsberg did a wild reading in Los Angeles in which he took off his clothes, inspiring more renown, then went down to Mexico for a brief stay. In November he went back to New York, where he met Eberhart and dozens of other literary lights and tried to drum up publicity for the book. When he heard that Ferlinghetti had ordered a second edition of fifteen hundred copies, he wrote in December saying that no one he knew in the Village had seen it and asked, "Can you sell them?" He brought a copy with him to the *New York Times*, where he was interviewed, and by the end of the month the Eighth Street Bookshop had sold out its copies; the book was beginning to move.

When the second printing arrived the following March, Ginsberg was on his way to Europe, and the edition ran into trouble. A magazine called *Miscellaneous Man*, published in Berkeley and also printed by Villiers, had been recently seized for alleged obscenity, according to Section 305 of the Tariff Act of 1930. Thus, the authorities were alerted to Villiers as a printer of "obscene" literature for U.S. publishers. On March 25, 1957, Chester MacPhee, collector of customs, saying "The words and the sense of the writing is obscene" and "you wouldn't want your children to come across it," ordered 520 copies of *Howl and Other Poems* seized.

Ferlinghetti wasn't taken by surprise. Before the manuscript had even gone to the printer, suspecting trouble, he had contacted the American Civil Liberties Union and asked if they would defend it in court, if need be. On April 3 they told MacPhee and customs that they did not consider the book obscene and would contest the seizure. Meanwhile, Ferlinghetti made arrangements to have an entire new photo-offset edition of *Howl* printed within the United States, thus circumventing customs. On May 19 William Hogan gave his Sunday *Chronicle* column to Ferlinghetti to write a defense of Ginsberg's work. Ferlinghetti wrote:

It is not the poet, but what he observes, which is revealed as obscene. The great obscene wastes of "Howl" are the sad wastes of the mechanized world, lost among atom bombs and insane nationalisms. . . . Ginsberg chooses to walk on the wild side of this world, along with Nelson Algren, Henry Miller, Kenneth Rexroth, Kenneth Patchen, not to mention some great American dead, mostly in the tradition of philosophical anarchism. . . . Ginsberg wrote his own best defense of "Howl" in the poem itself. Here he asks:

> *What sphinx of cement and aluminum bashed open their*
> *skulls and ate up their brains and imagination?*
> *Moloch! Solitude! Filth! Ugliness! Ashcans and unobtainable*
> *dollars! Children screaming under stairways! Boys sobbing in*
> *armies! Old men weeping in the parks!*

A world, in short, you wouldn't want your children to come across. . . . Thus was Goya obscene in depicting the Disasters of War, thus Whitman an exhibitionist, exhibiting man in his own strange skin.

The U.S. attorney in San Francisco finally decided against initiating condemnation proceedings, and on May 29 customs released the books it had been holding. The real battle was just beginning, however.

Captain William Hanrahan of the Juvenile Department of the SFPD had taken MacPhee's warning about children to heart. The first week in June, he sent two of his officers to City Lights. Ferlinghetti wasn't in the store at the time, but Kirby was, and remembers them looking like well-groomed college students.

"They were terribly nice, really," she said. "I would have sworn they were just out of Yale. They said it was all in the line of duty, ma'am, and I guess I got a little emotional about the whole thing and told them there were a lot more obscene things in books you can buy every day at any bookshop. I think they might have been just a little embarrassed about the whole thing."

One of them purchased a copy of *Howl* from Shigeyoshi Murao, who was tending the cash register, then left. A little later, Murao got a phone call telling him he was under arrest, and he would have to come down to the city's Hall of Justice to be booked and fingerprinted. Ferlinghetti contacted the ACLU, which put up bail to free him. The complaint charged Ferlinghetti with willfully printing and selling lewd and indecent material, and Shig with selling it.

The ACLU saw this as a fundamental free-speech issue and got two top lawyers to defend Ferlinghetti and Murao. A third lawyer, J. W. K. ("Jake") Ehrlich, had been practicing in San Francisco since 1922, and though he had not handled many First Amendment or civil rights cases, he had gained a major national reputation for defending condemned murderer Caryl Chessman, whose endless appeals from death row had forestalled his execution; and Ehrlich's fame and his courtroom style did much to focus attention on the case. The ACLU's lead trial counsel, Lawrence Speiser, who himself had much experience working on civil rights cases, had brought in Ehrlich as a volunteer. The other lawyer, Albert Bendich, was a staff counsel for the ACLU and was about to succeed Speiser. Ehrlich had the "pizazz and visibility," as Bendich remembers. While Speiser and Ehrlich were responsible for preparing witnesses, Bendich did the legal analysis and the preparation of briefs. Their combined grasp of the fundamental issues at stake and their command of courtroom strategy soon proved them well suited.

Opposing them was prosecutor Ralph McIntosh, an assistant district attorney who had worked his way through law school as a linotype operator on a paper. Thus, he had experience with the world of typesetting and publishing. But more important, he had a long history of involvement in legal actions against nudist publications and pornographic movies. The judge assigned to the case, Clayton Horn, was one of the four city police magistrates. He had recently received some national attention for unique sentencing: he had ordered five women convicted of shoplifting to see the movie *The Ten Commandments* and to write essays on its "moral lesson." It was a sentence the ACLU had protested and that the *San Francisco Chronicle* and others had also criticized, all of which combined to focus attention on the *Howl* case.

The trial itself received national attention as it began in mid-August and proceeded through the rest of the summer. The municipal courtroom was jammed to its capacity of 150 or so every day, including a full complement of press, and observers with beards and sandals, jeans and work shirts, attire which was scandalous at the time.

The prosecution's case began with the arresting officer, Russell Woods, testifying about going into City Lights and purchasing a copy of *Howl* from Shig. McIntosh then read the list of the offending book's contents into the record, and the dedication to Kerouac, Burroughs, and Neal Cassady, which also mentions their books. When he got to the last

72 • *Barry Silesky*

sentence—"All these books are published in Heaven"—he paused and said, "And I don't understand that, but let the record show anyway, Your Honor, it's published by the City Lights Pocket Book Shop."

Following Russell's testimony, Ehrlich picked up the copy of the book that had been introduced as Exhibit One and asked the rhetorical question: "Is there anything about this book that indicates that there is something in it which would lead to a moral breakdown of the people of this city, to say nothing of Police Officer Woods?"

After a pause for effect, he went on, "We are confronted with the manner in which this book is to be evaluated by the court. As I understand the law, the court must construe the book as a whole. I presume that I could take the classic *Leaves of Grass* and by cutting it to pieces find a word here or there or an idea that some people might not like. But in *Leaves of Grass* there is the intent of the poet to convey a certain idea, not lewd and lascivious or licentious or common, but a story, laying out a certain format concerning life itself."

Ehrlich may not have been a literary critic, but he had done some homework. Ginsberg's poems, and "Howl" in particular, were directly in the tradition of Whitman and the vision of America he had spent his career articulating a hundred years earlier. Ginsberg had used Whitman's device of repetitious chant and his long free-verse lines, which Whitman had crafted to fit the nature of the expanding nation he saw, with its myriad faces and limitless possibilities. Like Whitman, who was the first American poet to write of the city and urban life as a central subject, Ginsberg wrote of the modern metropolis. But instead of the religious paeans Whitman constructed, Ginsberg was portraying another America—the nation that Whitman's dream had in fact become.

Even the homosexuality that is explicit in some of Ginsberg's poems is also present, if more subtly, in Whitman; though Whitman's homosexuality wasn't revealed until fifty years after his death, a careful reading of his poem shows it clearly in some lines. And in its time, and later as well, *Leaves of Grass* was also controversial, having been banned in certain places. Whitman had lost a job with the federal government on account of it.

A week after the trial began, charges against Murao were dropped because it could not be ascertained that he had actually read the book or was aware of its "obscene" content, and under California law, "lewd or obscene intent" had to be demonstrated. But the poets, critics, and readers who were familiar with "Howl" and with Whitman realized the connection; and the array of voices who contributed statements on behalf of the defense reads like a "Who's Who" in American literature of the time. They included James Laughlin, publisher of New Directions; poets Kenneth Patchen and Robert Duncan; poet and professor Thomas Parkinson of the University of California; Henry Rago, editor of *Poetry Magazine*; Barney Rossett, editor of Grove Press; and Donald Allen, his coeditor of *Evergreen Review*, the leading avant-garde literary magazine, which published "Howl" in a 1957 issue.

Wrote Duncan, in a statement coauthored with Ruth Witt-Diamant: "Howl is a significant work in American poetry, deriving both a spirit and form from Walt Whitman's *Leaves of Grass*, from Jewish religious writing. . . . It is rhapsodic, highly idealistic and inspired in cause and purpose. Like other inspired poets, Ginsberg strives to include all of life, especially the elements of suffering and dismay from which the voice of desire rises. Only by misunderstanding might these tortured outcryings for sexual and spiritual understanding be taken as salacious. The poet gives us the most painful details; he moves us toward a statement of experience that is challenging and finally noble."

Parkinson said: "*Howl* is one of the most important books of poetry published in the last ten years. Its power and eloquence are obvious, and the talent of Mr. Ginsberg is of the highest order. Even people who do not like the book are compelled to testify to its force and brilliance."

Judge Horn considered the array of expert witnesses and statements the defense assembled, concerning their admissibility as evidence. Finally he said, ". . . it is obvious that you are never going to get unanimous consent on anything that is involved in this case. That's the reason why the freedom of the press should be so stringently protected, so that no one segment of the country can censor to the injury of the rest, what they can read, see and hear and so forth. That is why this case is such an important one, why I am giving it such a lot of time and consideration."

McIntosh, however, rose in protest. "You can see how far this thing can get out of hand," he said, "both sides bringing down all kinds of expert witnesses and telling Your Honor how you should decide when Your Honor has your own set of rules there. I think Your Honor can fairly and conscientiously interpret the rules as set down, trying to take an objective view of it through the whole community and decide it yourself."

But the expert witnesses were called to testify. The first was Mark Schorer, also a professor at the University of California, who, in response to the first question about the kind of writing he had done, listed his credentials: "I have published three novels, about seventy-five short stories, thirty-two of them collected in one volume, more pieces of literary criticism than I know the number of, in practically every periodical one might name." He also testified that he was an adviser to Harvard University Press and Princeton University, a paid consultant to the Army regarding textbooks for educational programs, and was at work on a biography of Sinclair Lewis. It was a formidable résumé.

After establishing Schorer's credentials, Ehrlich asked, "Do you have any opinion as to the literary value of Exhibit One, to which we refer as *Howl and Other Poems*, by Allen Ginsberg?" Schorer's response was well prepared: "I think that 'Howl,' like any work of literature, attempts and intends to make a significant comment on or interpretation of human experience as the author knows it. And to that end he has devised what we would call an aesthetic structure to sort of organize his material to demonstrate his theme. . . . The theme of the poem is announced very clearly in the opening line, 'I saw the best minds of my generation destroyed by madness, starving hysterical naked.' Then the following lines that make up the first part attempt to create the impression of a kind of nightmare world in which people representing 'the best minds of my generation,' in the author's view, are wandering like damned souls in hell. That is done through a kind of series of what one might call surrealistic images, a kind of state of hallucination. Then in the second section the mood of the poem changes and it becomes an indictment of those elements in modern society that, in the author's view, are destructive of the best qualities in human nature and of the best minds. Those elements are, I would say, predominantly materialism, conformity and mechanization leading toward war."

Schorer continued to characterize the third section of "Howl," in which the poet proclaims his empathy with Carl Solomon ("Carl Solomon! I'm with you in Rockland where you're madder than I am . . ."): "And then the last part is a personal address to a friend, real or fictional, of the poet or the person who is speaking in the poet's voice—those are not always the same thing—who is mad and in a madhouse, and is the specific representative of what the author regards as the general condition, and with that final statement the poem ends."

Then Schorer went on to speak directly to the offense the authorities, and many other readers of traditional poetry, took at the poem for its "dirty" language. "To write in the language of the streets," he said, "really meant not to write in the language of poetry; this is the language narrowly determined by critics to be the proper language for poetry. One must always be in rebellion. Each person had to determine his or her own language—from the level of their own body."

In case Schorer had used any critical abstractions that might have confused Horn, the defense asked a final, clarifying question to nail the point about Ginsberg's language unmistakably: "So that the use of a particular word, which some think offensive, is necessary to paint the picture which the author tries to portray?"

The answer: "Definitely."

Schorer's articulate explanation of Ginsberg's revolutionary poem could not have been more effective. It expressed eloquently the ideas animating the poem and the tradition from which they came. And to have this explanation come from an eminent university professor of unimpeachable credentials, and not some bearded "beatnik"—and there were plenty of them in and around the courtroom—gave Ginsberg's poem and the whole aesthetic behind Beat literature a currency that established it permanently as deserving of serious consideration.

McIntosh's cross-examination began by trying to suggest the poem's incomprehensibility. He asked Schorer about the meaning of such an obscure term as "angel headed hipsters." Schorer answered, "You don't understand the individual words taken out of their context. You understand the whole impression that is being created. . . . You can no more translate this back into logical prose English than you can say what a surrealist painting means in words. . . . Poetry is a heightened form of language through the use of figurative language. . . ."

McIntosh went on to list the specifically "obscene" terms in the poem—"cock," "balls," "pubic beards"—then went on to point out a place in the poem where "there are just little dots down there." Finally he read the passage, "Who blew and were blown by those human seraphim, the sailors, caresses of Atlantic and Caribbean love," and asked Schorer if he really thought those lines were necessary.

Schorer answered that "the essence of this poem is the impression of a world in which all sexuality is confused and corrupted. These words indicate a corrupt sexual act. Therefore, they are part of the essence of this picture which the author is trying to give us of modern life as a state of hell."

Schorer apparently misread, at least in part, Ginsberg's intent here, which doesn't so much seem to have been the depiction of "confused and corrupted" sexuality as an affirmation of homosexual love, proclaiming it to be as beautiful, as "angelic," as heterosexual love. And this affirmation is part of the Whitmanic universality of his message. But by this time, Schorer had clearly made the point that the poem was serious literature and that its method and language were essential to its work. The prosecution was certainly not interested in taking up fine points of critical interpretation.

McIntosh then asked Schorer about the "essence" of the poem "America."

"I think that what the poem says," Schorer responded, "is that the 'I,' the speaker, feels that he has given a piece of himself to America and has been given nothing in return, and the poem laments certain people who have suffered at the hands of—well, specifically, the United States Government, men like Tom Mooney, the Spanish Loyalists, Sacco and Vanzetti, the Scottsboro boys and so on."

"Is that in there?" McIntosh asked.

"That's on page 33," Schorer answered. "In other words, that is the speaker associating himself with those figures in American history whom he regards as having been martyred. He feels that way about himself."

Kenneth Rexroth also testified eloquently for the defense. When asked to describe Ginsberg's work, he said, "The simplest term for such writing is prophetic. It is easier to call it that than anything else because we have a large body of prophetic writing to refer to. There are the prophets of the Bible, which it greatly resembles in purpose and in language and in subject matter. . . . The theme is the denunciation of evil and a pointing out of the way out, so to speak. That is prophetic literature."

Several other witnesses testified for the defense in the same vein: William Hogan, the *San Francisco Chronicle* book review editor; San Francisco State College professors Herbert Blau, Walter Van Tilburg Clark, Arthur Foff, and Mark Linenthal; poet and novelist Vincent McHugh; and *San Francisco Examiner* book editor Luther Nichols.

Nichols's testimony was also particularly effective. In the beginning he described his view of the poem: "Mr. Ginsberg is expressing his personal view of a segment of life that he has experienced. It is a vagabond one; it's colored by exposure to jazz, to Columbia, a university, to a liberal and bohemian education, to a great deal of traveling on the road, to a certain amount of what we call bumming around. He has seen in that experience things that do not agree with him, that have perhaps embittered him. He has also seen things at a social level concerned with the atom bomb, and the materialism of our time. In sum, I think it's a howl of pain. . . ."

The prosecution followed with only two "expert" witnesses of its own.

The first was a private elocution teacher who testified that "you feel like you are going through the gutter when you have to read that stuff. I didn't linger on it too long, I assure you."

Gail Potter, the other, was an instructor from the Catholic University of San Francisco. When asked her qualifications, she drew a laugh from the courtroom by answering that she had rewritten *Faust*. "Took three years to do that," she said, "but I did it." Also, she said, "I rewrote *Everyman*."

In response to McIntosh's question about the nature and value of "Howl," she answered, "To have literary style you must have form, diction, fluidity, clarity. Now, I am speaking only of style, and in content, every great piece of literature, anything that can really be classified as literature, is of some moral greatness, and I think this fails to the nth degree."

The defense chose not to bother to cross-examine.

In the defense summation, Counsel Bendich cited the Supreme Court standard for judging obscenity: "The First Amendment to the Constitution of the United States," Bendich said, "protecting the fundamental freedoms of speech and press, prohibits the suppression of literature by the application of obscenity formulae unless the trial court first determines that the literature in question is utterly without social importance. . . .

"The record is clear that all of the experts for the defense identified the main theme of 'Howl' as social criticism. And the prosecution concedes that it does not understand the work, much less what its dominant theme is."

On October 3 Judge Horn found Ferlinghetti not guilty of publishing or selling obscene writings. In a thirty-nine-page opinion, he said, "I do not believe that *Howl* is without even 'the slightest redeeming social importance.' The first part of 'Howl' presents a picture of a nightmare world; the second part is an indictment of those elements in modern society destructive of the best qualities of human nature; such elements are predominantly identified as materialism, conformity, and mechanization leading toward war. The third part presents a picture of an individual who is a specific representation of what the author conceives as a general condition. . . . 'Footnote to Howl' seems to be a declamation that everything in the world is holy, including parts of the body by name. It ends in a plea for holy living. . . ."

He had been completely convinced by the defense. His description of the structure and intent of the poem echoed Schorer almost exactly.

He went on to set forth twelve rules for determining obscenity, among them, first: "If the material has the slightest redeeming social importance it is not obscene because it is protected by the First and Fourteenth Amendments of the United States Constitution, and the California Constitution." Third, "The test of obscenity in California is that the material must have a tendency to deprave or corrupt readers by exciting lascivious thoughts or arousing lustful desire to the point that it presents a clear and present danger of inciting to anti-social or immoral action." Fifth, "If the material is objectionable only because of coarse and vulgar language which is not erotic or aphrodisiac in character it is not obscene." Horn's eleventh rule quoted Justice William O. Douglas of the Supreme Court, who wrote: "I have the same confidence in the ability of our people to reject noxious literature as I have in their capacity to sort out the true from the false in theology, economics, politics, or any other field." And his last rule: "In considering material claimed to be obscene it is well to remember the motto: *Honi soit qui mal y pense* [Evil to him who thinks evil]."

The victory for Ferlinghetti, Ginsberg, and *Howl and Other Poems* was complete. Besides establishing the "nonobscene" character of the book, the trial ensured its financial success, and as a result, the future success of City Lights Books as a publisher. In September *Life* magazine had run a photo story on the trial and the San Francisco poetry scene under the headline "Big Day for Bards at Bay." Headlines and stories throughout the trial had made both Ferlinghetti and Ginsberg famous. The *Chronicle* called the decision a "landmark of law" and reported that it "was hailed with applause and cheers from a packed audience that offered the most fantastic collection of beards, turtle-necked shirts and Italian hair-dos ever to grace the grimy precincts of the Hall of Justice."

Ferlinghetti had nothing to say to reporters, however. After accepting congratulations from the assembled well-wishers, he went straight back to the store. Throughout the trial, copies of the banned book had been displayed in the window; now they could be freely sold for their list price of seventy-five cents each, and the trial publicity had ensured unprecedented demand.

As for Ginsberg, he was still out of the country. He had been in Tangier during the trial, taking in the faces, the sensations of its exotic, gritty streets, while staying with William Burroughs, who was at work on his own "sensationalistic" novel. Its working title was "Word Horde," but he would publish it under another title, one that Kerouac had suggested: *Naked Lunch*. Ginsberg didn't know yet that ten thousand copies of *Howl* had been printed by the trial's end, on its way to becoming one of the best-selling poetry books in American history. In fact, one of the only poetry books whose sales surpassed it would be one published two years later, written by his own publisher: *A Coney Island of the Mind*, by Lawrence Ferlinghetti.

6

In the fall of 1952 Scribner's published John Clellan Holmes's first novel, *Go*. Based on his own life and that of some of his friends, including Jack Kerouac, Neal Cassady, and Allen Ginsberg, it tried to capture the combination of skeptical wariness and furious urgency along with the voracious appetite for experience that drove them. Part of his method was to transcribe directly some of their conversation; in fact, he had taken sections verbatim from Kerouac's journals. And in the book he referred to his characters by a term Kerouac had first used in a conversation the two had had in 1948 when they were trying to characterize themselves and others like them—the "beat generation."

Gilbert Millstein, editor of the *New York Times*, read the book and was interested. He asked Holmes to write an article defining the term. On November 16 Holmes's "This Is the Beat Generation" appeared. It credited Kerouac with inventing the term, then went on to describe the young people to whom it referred.

"The problem of modern life," Holmes said, "is essentially a spiritual problem." These young people "drink to 'come down' or to 'get high,' not to illustrate anything. Their excursions into drugs or promiscuity come out of curiosity, not disillusionment."

Despite Holmes's explanation, and explanations later in essays by Kerouac that "beat" came from "beatific," the term took on a life of its own. America's eternal fascination with the outlaw led the press to seize on the new "Beat hipster" as the latest incarnation. Articles by Norman Mailer in *The Village Voice*, by Anatole Broyard, and a 1957 essay by Holmes in *Esquire* stressed the alienation of Beats and the violent crimes of "hipsters."

Then in May 1958 the *San Francisco Chronicle* ran a three-day series emphasizing the wildness of the North Beach Beats: "Far out in the faceless jungle of nothingness . . . their capital [North Beach] . . . is dangerous to outsiders who roam its cobbled streets at night . . . ," ran part of the lead. Such publicity helped to precipitate a campaign of police harassment against the Co-Existence Bagel Shop, The Place, and other popular hangouts; anyone out in the neighborhood at night became a target. By late June, when *San Francisco Chronicle* columnist Herb Caen coined the disparaging term "beatnik"—because the Beats were as "far out" as the Russian satellite *Sputnik*—the term had become synonymous with a young, rebellious, offensive, often criminal element, though even some of the extreme manifestations of the "Beat life-style" would pale in comparison with what would come from the younger generation a decade later.

For the increasing numbers of Americans actually living in the suburbs, working at their careers, raising their children, firm in their faith in America and its moral rightness, these scruffy, ragged, oddly dressed young people with their hip slang, affecting "cool" indifference to all that "normal" people believed in and worked for, could only be a threat—a black spot, like the color of their jeans and turtlenecks, on the shine of the American Dream.

If Ferlinghetti also wore jeans, he didn't think of himself—then or ever—as a Beat. Still as slender, clean-cut, and fit as ever, with his dark hair thinning now above his receding hairline as he approached forty, he even looked the part of the respectable San Francisco small businessman, except that he rarely wore a sport coat or tie. Further, in 1958, with the financial help of his mother-in-law, he and Kirby had moved into their own home on Potrero Hill, a quiet old Russian neighborhood well removed from the North Beach hustle. The two-story frame house nearly at the top of the hill on Wisconsin Street cost less than ten thousand dollars, as it had been abandoned for nine years and fallen into complete disrepair. It had plenty of space, however, and offered a spectacular view of the city and the Bay. Looking north from the unfinished attic, they could see all of downtown, and past it to Mount Tamalpais and the Golden Gate Bridge. To the east, the view extended across the Bay to Oakland and Berkeley and the hills beyond.

They set about restoring it before they could move in, Ferlinghetti himself working alongside a carpenter he hired. In addition to necessary repairs, he turned the attic into a study where he could write and paint, installing a large picture window there, and built a porch outside it to take advantage of the panoramic view. Kirby, especially, had been hoping for some time to become pregnant, and their new home must have seemed a perfect place for the family they hoped to have. For his part, Ferlinghetti seemed to eagerly take on the role of householder, spending long hours on home repair when he wasn't working at the store or on his own writing.

But these exterior elements of respectability were neither the only thing nor the main thing that separated him from other Beats. For one thing, he was a few years older than Kerouac, Ginsberg, and the other central Beat writers. Further, his shyness kept him from affiliating with any group, as did the sense of alienation he had grown up with, which supposedly marked the Beats. More important, there was a distinctly anti-intellectual component to the Beat identity, particularly as various media characterized it, that was never part of Ferlinghetti. Though he had rigorously dissociated himself from academia since his one summer teaching at the University of San Francisco, he had, after all, got a Ph.D., and his own work and interests from his earliest days were as much of the mind, of the discourse of ideas, as they were of everyday life.

Perhaps even more to the point, Ginsberg and Kerouac were primarily concerned with capturing the immediacy of consciousness and direct experience in their writing; in Kerouac's case—and his novels provided the main models of "Beatness"—of a kind of feverish, manic experience involved in the search for meaning amid the lifeless straight world. Though Ferlinghetti's poems were certainly grounded in the ordinary sights and sounds of daily life, and several satirized the straight world, they had nothing of the manic pace and intensity of either Ginsberg's poems or Kerouac's novels. And while his novel *Her*, which he was to publish in 1960, did have a similar intensity, it had none of the immediate accessibility that made his and Ginsberg's poems, and Kerouac's novels, so popular.

But most significant, the "disengagement" of the Beats, the term by which Rexroth had characterized them in a 1957 essay, and which had become so much a part of their public image, was an image directly opposed to Ferlinghetti's thinking (and Ginsberg's as well, for that matter). By 1956 City Lights was a going concern, a business on the way to success, even if it hadn't shown much profit. Shig Murao had become the everyday manager, but Ferlinghetti was still spending long hours at the bookstore, getting his publishing business started, then coming home to write or paint in his studio in the Audiffred Building. His affiliation with the Committee for the Defense of the Refregier Murals and his work as publisher of *Howl* were neither peripheral nor accidental; they were an integral part of his social and political commitment.

In a statement he published (more than once) in 1958, he made his position clear:

> William Seward Burroughs said, "Only the dead and the junkie don't care—they are inscrutable." I'm neither. Man. And this is where all the tall droopy corn about the Beat Generation and its being "Existentialist" is as phoney as a four-dollar piece of lettuce. Because Jean-Paul Sartre cares and has always hollered that the writer especially should be committed. *Engagement* is one of his favorite dirty words. He would give the horse laugh to the idea of Disengagement and the Art of the Beat Generation [the title of Rexroth's essay]. Me too. And that Abominable Snowman of modern poetry, Allen Ginsberg, would probably say the same. Only the dead are disengaged.

But if his sense of alienation was not as keen by now, as he had begun to make the place for himself in San Francisco that he had never quite had anywhere else, he still felt sympathy with those aspects of the Beat sensibility described by Kerouac and by Holmes's *New York Times* article. The curiosity, the dissatisfaction with prevailing social mores, the sense of being an outsider, were strong.

Yet, despite his increasing involvements and the busyness they brought, he still found time to spend a few hours regularly in the small Trieste Cafe, across the street and around the corner from City Lights on Grant and Vallejo, or one of the other old cafés or coffeehouses in North Beach. Writers, artists, and other neighborhood types would drop in to talk or just hang around, and no one seemed in a hurry to make sure the customers were consuming at a brisk enough pace. At these places Ferlinghetti found a little of the Parisian ambience he had sought from San Francisco in the first place, and took in the faces and scenes that went into poems.

In the previous years he had continued working on his novel, going through three more drafts, but had put it aside after *The Stone Angel* was rejected by Lippincott in June 1954, though again with encouragement. In the letter to Ferlinghetti's agent, Margaret Christie, Lippincott editor Pascal Covichi wrote, "Your Mr. Lawrence Ferling has considerable ability and should by all means be encouraged. His novel *The Stone Angel* however I'm afraid is much too thin in material and overwritten even though at times beautifully expressed."

Since then, between hours at the bookstore, he had focused on occasional Prévert translations and his own poems. In 1955 he'd sent a few of the translations to New Directions, for which Rexroth acted as a West Coast consultant-reader. Like Grove Press, the only other really avant-garde publisher of the time, New Directions was interested in writing which was more literary and outside the mainstream, and though they hadn't wanted to publish the Prévert translations immediately, the response he got in March had been encouraging:

"Thank you for sending us some of your translations from Prévert. We would like to hold them for consideration later when our Prévert project gets under way and hope you will have patience with us until that time."

Almost immediately he sent off some more, and in May got a similar answer—the "project" was still in the "vague planning stage." At the time, Laughlin himself was in India, where he had been for a prolonged period, and day-to-day matters at New Directions were being handled by others. Thus, though Laughlin was in touch with his assistants, not much new was being undertaken.

Then in August *Pictures of the Gone World* came out and got reviewed in *The Times Literary Supplement* of London as well as in the *San Francisco Chronicle*. One of the very first original paperback poetry books to be published in America, to get that much attention for such a paperback was an unusual stroke of fortune. The paragraph-long review in the *Times* was more negative than positive, but it was nonetheless encouraging not only in some of its content but in the very fact of its attention. "The ebullient Mr. Lawrence Ferlinghetti has zest but almost no discipline at all," was the judgment. "*Pictures of the Gone World* is a headlong canter through a private gallery of memory in which the selection of detail is too haphazard to allow any coherent impression to emerge. But a few individual images stand out: 'and the coach / creaking through the corn-fields / so slowly that / butterflies / blew in and out.' "

Rexroth, however, in reviewing the book for the *Chronicle* in October, was unconditional in his enthusiasm. Pairing it with a collection by Holly Beye which she and her husband published, he called them "two of the best books to come out" of the "San Francisco school." He went on to describe *Pictures* as a "remarkable first book, because it speaks with an achieved personal idiom—something it usually takes years to develop. [Ferlinghetti] is completely independent of any other poet writing in English. His dry humor and acid bite resemble most the French poems of Raymond Queneau and Jacques Prévert. And he shares with them a genuinely popular diction."

With that kind of encouragement, in these days of 1956, Ferlinghetti was most excited about the new poems he was writing. In *Pictures* he had come to a way of writing that felt right, bringing together his interest in painting, the lyricism of some of Eliot and of Thomas Wolfe, the flavor of the urban metropolis which pervaded Apollinaire and others he had studied for his dissertation, and the detached, critical, faintly whimsical view of so much that went on around him that he had come to share with Prévert. It was impossible now not to look around and see the eccentricity, the irony, in events out there that begged to be written.

The new poems were a natural extension of the ones in *Pictures*, but his political and social concerns, fed by Rexroth, Patchen, and his own drive, seeped into them with increasing force. And they came faster. In a few months, working in the front room of the Chestnut Street flat, at the Mission Street studio where he still went to paint, and occasionally at a café, he composed a whole new group of twenty-nine poems, all without revision. Like those in *Pictures*, these were essentially short poems, using the open form and the lyricism he had been perfecting. He thought of them as a single collection, and borrowing a line from Henry Miller's *Into the Night Life*, he titled it *A Coney Island of the Mind*.

When Ferlinghetti finished the new group of poems, he sent the whole collection to New Directions. On December 2, 1956, Laughlin, now returned from India, wrote back:

> . . . I am only just now getting down to selecting material for ND 16, and I want to tell you that one of the most interesting things I found in the manuscript box was your "A Coney Island of the Mind" collection. You are certainly getting to be a very good writer of poems. I'm impressed.
>
> Might I pick out a couple of these poems for use in ND 16? Please let me know right back by air because the printer is breathing down my neck. . . .
>
> May I keep the rest of the collection a bit longer? I'd like to think more about it for a possible little book, something along the line, perhaps, of your wonderful little Pocket Poets series, which I greatly admire.

Rexroth had been telling Laughlin much about City Lights and the San Francisco writers that he thought New Directions should begin publishing. Now Laughlin also wanted to know where he could find Kerouac and Ginsberg, whose work he wanted to include in the annual, and mentioned two new books by Rexroth—*In Defense of the Earth* and *100 Chinese Poems*—that he hoped Ferlinghetti would display prominently at City Lights.

Ferlinghetti was, of course, delighted at Laughlin's response and wrote back immediately, giving Laughlin permission to choose some poems. Laughlin wrote again, praising Ferlinghetti further and making the seriousness of his interest clear:

> For your own poems it is terribly difficult to choose because I find them all quite irresistible (or able, I could never spell that word). I don't know when I have felt so drawn to a new poet, not that you are just beginning to write, but, what with other pre-occupations, I haven't before really registered. We really must try to think up some larger project for you. I think you could have here the kind of success that Prévert has had in France if one could just think up the formula for getting it across. But more of that later.

Laughlin was drawn, he remembers, by "the free, open and humorous" quality of the work, which also had "a lot of wit, a charming, sort of kidding attitude."

And while they were corresponding, Laughlin had come out to San Francisco, as he did almost every year after he supervised the spring closing of the ski resort he owned at Alta, Utah. Rexroth brought him to City Lights, where he saw Ferlinghetti's *Pictures of the Gone World* and met Ferlinghetti. From the first, he liked Ferlinghetti, as he did his poems.

"He was a slow talker," Laughlin recalls, "hesitant and thoughtful." And unlike so many writers, "he never gossiped."

Laughlin settled on three for the *New Directions Annual*, titled from their first lines: "In Goya's greatest scenes," the first poem in the collection; "Sometime during eternity"; and "See, it was like this." When the issue came out in July 1957, he was in good company: a section from Kerouac's *On the Road* was included along with other work by Rexroth, Ginsberg, Henry Miller, and some of the first published poems of Denise Levertov, whom Rexroth was also championing.

Laughlin was indeed serious about a "larger project" as well. As the "Howl" uproar drew national attention to Ginsberg and Ferlinghetti, as *On the Road* began getting prepublication publicity, and as other articles in national media covered the San Francisco scene, it seemed the time for New Directions to take advantage of the interest. On September 16, 1957, Laughlin again wrote to Ferlinghetti:

> . . . I have been meaning to write you from day to day, as I am really enthusiastic about your poetry and, of course, with all this publicity breaking (the good piece in *Life* on your poets group there in San Francisco, and the preview of Kerouac's book) the time is ripe to do something.
>
> I must say, however, that I am very lukewarm on the idea of doing just another poetry book in the usual format, with all the limitations of the customary poetry market. I understand that Grove Press has had pretty good success doing new poetry in paperback form and I think we ought to experiment with this, and that you are just the man to begin with, because you are so lucid, not to mention your wonderful wit and verbal color.

Though Grove editor Fred Jordan says their three original paperback poetry publications at that time, which had all come out only that year, could hardly be termed "good successes" in terms of sales, Laughlin was of course aware of the experiment and of the possibilities of the growing paperback market.

> Now such a book ought to be at least ninety-six pages [Laughlin went on], and that means that there isn't enough material in the "Coney Island," so what have you got that we could add to it to bulk it out? What would you think of picking up again the poems which you had in your "Pocket Poets" selection, which both I and my wife liked so much? What has the sale on that volume been? To what extent has it been around in the same channels that our paperbacks would reach? I see no reason why such a volume should not also contain some bits of prose. So why don't you turn it over in your mind and shoot on to me whatever you have ready that you think might fit in well. To capitalize on the present publicity, we ought to get going right away. And there might, of course, be a few hundred copies bound up in hard covers, which you might sign, or something, to justify the considerably higher price that would be necessary to float the binding.
>
> I am very much interested in what you told me about the

other books that you are working on, and I hope that if we can get off the ground successfully on this first venture, a long and mutually interesting publishing relationship will develop. Not, of course, that you haven't already made a fine start for yourself with the first book, but I suppose any poet likes best to be published by somebody else. . . .

Laughlin went on in the letter to take note of another experiment Ferlinghetti had been trying to which Rexroth had initially recruited him. It had led to several new poems of a whole other sort which Ferlinghetti had written since finishing the *Coney Island* group, and had already generated quite a public response:

Kenneth brought me a copy of your Fantasy record to Wyoming, and I enjoyed it very much. Extremely powerful stuff, and this kind of mounting will obviously create an enlarged poetry public. The only thing I didn't like was the monotony of the verbal tone. Both you and Kenneth seemed to have your voice at the same pitch all the way through. Good old Dylan, as I recall, used to put a lot of variation into his readings, almost as if he were an actor acting the lines, and I think that helped to put it across. Not that I like very soupy readings of poetry, but I think some variation in pitch and force would help. . . .

The recording had been made at a club on Green Street called The Cellar earlier in the year. There, a series of jazz-poetry evenings had been started at the beginning of the year which featured the house jazz quintet, consisting of the two club owners and three other musicians— Bill Wisjahn on piano, Max Hartstein on acoustic bass, Sonny Wayne on drums, and various drop-in horn players—playing behind various poets. To many of the writers at the time, this combination of poetry and jazz seemed a logical extension of both forms. Poetry had been, after all, an oral medium in the beginning, and all good poets still composed with close attention to the sound of their words, to the rhythm of the line; to the "beat." And the irregular, improvisational rhythms of jazz seemed naturally suited to poetry. The solo techniques and unpredictable movements as the piece unwound corresponded to the movement of modern free-verse poems.

In a 1959 interview Ferlinghetti explained, "The printing press has made poetry so silent that we've forgotten the power of the oral message.

What about the Salvation Army street singer? And the whole oral tradition? This has been forgotten about in poetry. Up to the Beat poets, or up to poets of the late 1950s, poetry was a great big mumble. Poets were contemplating their navels or talking to themselves in a low mumble and no one was listening because they weren't saying anything relevant to the average person in the streets. Allen Ginsberg comes along with 'Howl' and he's saying something very important to everybody."

Though the Six Gallery reading that premiered "Howl" certainly helped ignite the performance side of poetry, the crowd that had filled the gallery that night was not the first to see poetry go public. Long before Dylan Thomas's fabled appearances in 1951 and 1952, Kenneth Rexroth had read poetry to jazz accompaniment in Chicago with Langston Hughes and in New York's Greenwich Village with Maxwell Bodenheim. Rexroth had always been an emphatic advocate for a public poetry which reached more people than the intellectual, academic verse whose audience would always be strictly limited. In San Francisco the new wave of public poetry that Thomas's readings may have seeded was furthered in February 1955, when poet Weldon Kees, who also played piano, joined with clarinetist and fine printer Adrian Wilson, a guitar player, and a washboard player-vocalist to put on the first of two "Poets' Follies." The vaudevillian performances included such featured acts as stripper Lily Ayres reading "Sarah Stripteasedale," and provided the occasion of Ferlinghetti's first public performance. In the clear, faintly droll tone that highlighted the dry humor of the lines, he read some of his translations of Prévert to the enthusiastic audience.

But the jazz-poetry sessions at The Cellar became by far the most popular of all these performances. Rexroth had invited Ferlinghetti to join him in the 1957 performances, and they filled the club from the beginning. Only about a hundred could fit into the room, but on the very first night, some five hundred more lined up outside to get in and a fire marshal had to be called to clear the hallway. It seemed to everyone an idea whose time had come, and the idea spread quickly. Soon Kenneth Patchen tried a more elaborate technique at the nearby Black Hawk using formally scored music. The experiment moved to New York when Philip Lamantia, who was living then in Greenwich Village, teamed with poet Howard Hart, who was also a jazz drummer, French horn player David Amram, and Jack Kerouac to perform New York's first jazz-poetry reading at the Brata Gallery. Very soon thereafter, Patchen did a series of performances in New York, including appearances at the famous jazz club the 5 Spot. Rexroth appeared there as well, and TV star Steve Allen picked up on the idea, thinking it would be interesting to have spontaneously scored jazz accompany a Kerouac reading of his "spontaneous prose." He recruited Gilbert Millstein to arrange an event, and Millstein convinced Allen himself to play behind Kerouac. In 1957 *Time* magazine wrote about some of these performances; and in the space of the next two or three years, recordings of Kerouac, Phillip Whalen, Patchen, and Rexroth were made in addition to the one Laughlin had mentioned. And by 1959 Patchen had carried his synthesis to West Coast college campuses, to Vancouver, Canada, and to Los Angeles' Jazz Concert Hall, where he performed for two months.

The music at The Cellar was loose, improvisational, "semi-spontaneous"; but the musicians were generally more interested in their own self-expression than in creating an ensemble that supported or harmonized with the poetry. Neither Ferlinghetti nor Rexroth had any musical training, and most music aficionados felt the performances weren't particularly successful, despite their popularity at the time.

David Meltzer, who also performed at The Cellar, was perhaps the only poet who had begun as a musician, having studied music theory, performed as a child in New York, and played guitar with his wife at Berkeley folk clubs. He felt that of all those who tried combining their readings with music, Kerouac was the most effective.

He "had the truest ear and spirit for it," Meltzer wrote, "his language responding to the music easily. His work on record with Al Cohn and Zoot Sims displayed some lovely possibilities."

Michael McClure, who was interested, but didn't try performing with music himself until much later, felt that Meltzer himself was by far the most successful.

"David was a musician, so he had an advantage over Lawrence and the Kenneths in that sense. Musicians and poets did not quite know what they were doing with each other, except it was something new at the time. Meltzer could compose his poems for poetry and jazz with the idea that he was another instrument in a combo."

On the whole, however, Meltzer didn't think any of the experiments particularly effective. "Jazz and poetry was an interesting attempt that failed to advance beyond its hybrid and awkward propositions," he wrote. And on reflection, Ferlinghetti agreed, concluding that "it was an interesting experiment, but generally it wasn't very successful. The musicians generally . . . well, their attitude was usually, 'Like, go ahead and read your poetry, but we got to blow.' And you ended up sounding like you were hawking fish on the street corner trying to be heard above the din."

The collaboration did, however, spur Ferlinghetti to write the poems which would complete the *Coney Island* collection. Designed to be read with jazz accompaniment, these were longer, befitting a jazz composition, and stuck to the left margin of the page; their visual appearance was intended not to distract from their aural characteristics. He called them "oral messages" and sent them to Laughlin, with a note to be published with them, explaining their origin:

"These seven poems were conceived specifically for jazz accompaniment and as such should be considered as spontaneously spoken 'oral messages' rather than as poems written for the printed page. As a result of continued experimental reading with jazz, they are still in a state of change."

Despite the note, it would be misleading to think of them as entirely "spontaneous." Though they were composed in a short time, Ferlinghetti had done some revision, making substantial deletions of lines. Further, their composition was obviously informed by his wide reading and education as well as by his personal experience. Throughout the "messages," as well as the other *Coney Island* poems, he draws on literary tradition, quoting phrases from Yeats, Eliot, Whitman, Keats, and many others, much as a jazz musician might quote licks from well-known compositions. This poetic technique is intended to enlarge the meaning and experience of the new work by bringing into it the context of the old work. The juxtaposition of the two creates resonances which make the new poem richer and multifaceted. And though Ferlinghetti asserted the continuously changing nature of these poems, he stuck pretty exactly to the written text in his readings over the next few years—further evidence of the care and intentionality that went into the original composition.

By the time *A Coney Island of the Mind* came out in mid-1958, Ferlinghetti's work, like that of several other poets associated with San Francisco and the Beats, had drawn wide notice. The publicity surrounding the *Howl* trial was certainly a major factor that focused attention on literary San Francisco. And by 1957, besides other articles in national magazines which had taken up the Beat phenomenon, several of the most important literary magazines of the time had also devoted all or large parts of issues to these writers. Even before *New Directions Annual 16* came out, Barney Rossett had published the first two issues of his new *Evergreen Review*, designed to showcase the newest avant-garde writing. The second issue featured the "San Francisco Scene" and contained Ginsberg's "Howl," work by Rexroth, Duncan, Brother Antoninus (the name William Everson took as a member of the Dominican Order; he didn't actually live in San

Francisco, but down the coast), Henry Miller (who also lived not in San Francisco, but at Big Sur), Kerouac, McClure, and Ferlinghetti's poems numbered 3, 6, and 7 and "Dog" (one of the "oral messages") from *Coney Island*. Besides the poems, *Evergreen* also published Ferlinghetti's "Horn on Howl," which detailed the *Howl* trial and its significance, and an essay by Rexroth, in which he first applied the term "San Francisco Renaissance" to the literary ferment there.

In the essay Rexroth attacked capitalism, doctrinaire leftists, and the literary establishment, claiming San Francisco's uniqueness and importance. "I always feel like I ought to get a passport every time I cross to Oakland or Berkeley," he wrote, then went on to describe the "new San Francisco writers."

Ferlinghetti, he said, "is a lazy-looking, good-natured man with the canny cocky eye of an old-time vaudeville tenor. . . . His verse, so easy and relaxed, is constructed of most complex rhythms, all organized to produce just the right tone. Now tone is the hardest and last of the literary virtues to control and it requires assiduous and inconspicuous craftsmanship. Ferlinghetti is definitely a member of the San Francisco School—he says exactly what Everson, Duncan, Ginsberg say."

The equivalence Rexroth asserted among the four poets is grossly unfair to the varying complexities in all of their work, but his essay helped to underline their importance and the uniqueness of the Bay Area as a literary center.

At the same time, Michael McClure and James Harmon had taken over editing *Ark* magazine in Berkeley, changed its name to *Ark II-Moby I*, and brought together the new Beat writers (publishing one of Ferlinghetti's *Coney Island* poems, among others) with East Coast "Black Mountain" poets Charles Olson, Robert Creeley, Louis Zukofsky, and Cid Corman, some of whom had studied with Olson at Black Mountain College. Though *Ark II-Moby I* didn't have the kind of national circulation these others did, it was another of the forces that helped to spread further the influence of the San Francisco scene and connect it with a vital branch of avant-garde literature centered in the East.

In a February 1957 issue, the national newsmagazine *The Nation* also published a Ferlinghetti poem, and in Chicago, Irving Rosenthal and Paul Carroll, the young editors of the *Chicago Review*, had taken note of the new writing and conceived a San Francisco issue. The spring 1958 issue contained Kerouac's introductory essay, "The Origin of Joy in Poetry," work by Duncan, Ginsberg, Lamantia, McClure, Whalen, and others, and a poem by Ferlinghetti and his "Note on Poetry in San Francisco."

In the "Note," Ferlinghetti denied the existence of the "school" Rexroth had asserted, saying,

> There are all kinds of poets here, writing very dissimilar types of poetry (as this issue ought to show). But I should say that the kind of poetry which has been making the most noise here is quite different from the "poetry about poetry," the poetry of technique, the poetry for poets and professors which has dominated the quarterlies and anthologies in this country for some time and which of course is also written in San Francisco. The poetry which has been making itself heard here of late is what should be called street poetry. For it amounts to getting the poet out of the inner esthetic sanctum where he has too long been contemplating his complicated navel. It amounts to getting poetry back into the street where it once was, out of the classroom, out of the speech department, and—in fact—off the printed page. The printed word has made poetry so silent. But the poetry I am talking about here is spoken poetry, poetry conceived as oral messages. It "makes it" aloud. Some of it has been read with jazz, much of it has not. A new "ashcan" school? Rock and roll? Who cares what names it's called. What is important is that this poetry is using its eyes and ears as they have not been used for a number of years. "Poetry about poetry," like much non-objective painting, has caused an atrophy of the artist's senses. (I walked thru Chinatown recently with a famous academic poet, and he never saw the whole schools of fish gasping on counters, nor heard what they breathed.)

Ferlinghetti's qualification of the "San Francisco school" is one he has made over and over through the years. "They're all just New York carpetbaggers, including me," he has said, still fighting the media distortion which lumped all of them together. The San Francisco poetry scene had of course been going for many years before Ginsberg, Kerouac, and Corso arrived from the East Coast for a brief stay, and it has continued to be as vital since they left. It is a distortion which also contributed to a good deal of resentment on the part of more native San Francisco writers like Rexroth (though he, too, had only come for the first time in his twenties).

When *A Coney Island of the Mind* did come out, as with Kerouac's work, and the work of other "Beats," critical reaction was mixed. Critical taste, as at most times, was largely ruled by formal, academic standards, and the apparent verbal and sensual excesses of Kerouac and Ginsberg on the one hand, and the populist accessibility of Ferlinghetti on the other, were not the sorts of writing that appealed to that taste. Still, some of the critics gave significant positive assessments. Critic and literary editor of *The Nation* M. L. Rosenthal noted that Ferlinghetti had "learned some useful things, and gladly," from various "European and American experimenters." He called him a "deft, rapid-paced, whirling performer [with] a wonderful eye for meaning in the commonplace."

Other reviewers were less generous. Writing in the *New York Times*, Harvey Shapiro called Ferlinghetti "highly readable and often very funny," but termed the book "a grab bag of undergraduate musings about love and art, much hackneyed satire of American life and some real and wry perceptions of it." Hayden Carruth, writing for *Poetry*, was unconditional in his dislike, finding "no trace of understanding for language's capacity and no sensitivity to sound."

In the case of *Coney Island*, however, sales and popularity seemed to have little to do with reviews. The romantic side of the American temper had been captured by the outlaw Beats, and though Ferlinghetti was much different from Ginsberg, Kerouac, and others the media associated with that term, the poems of *Coney Island* attracted readers with their combination of openhearted lyricism and satirical wit. They set Ferlinghetti squarely in the tradition of the outsider, that timeless American hero, and invited everyone to join. The invitation was irresistible. New Directions sent the book into a second printing even before the official publication date. By the fall of 1958 it was in a third printing, with two more to come in 1959, which would put a total of 15,000 copies in print. That was only a fraction of the 40,000 copies of *Howl* that were in print by that time; but by 1989 *Coney Island*, in its twenty-eighth printing, had nearly doubled *Howl*'s record, having sold almost 700,000 copies in America and over a million worldwide in various translations—all together, more than any single book by any living American poet.

Lawrence came to read for *Big Table* in October 1959. I found an old theatrical hall in the Loop on Randolph Street [the Oriental Theater] and rented it. It was the first time I ever saw native beatniks in their own habitat with the black turtleneck sweaters, the black dungarees, the sandals, even though it was October, clutching icons of Zen paperbacks, and they all had come to hear the prophet reading. And it was an enormous crowd—oh, several hundred, which at the time was a tremendous crowd for a poetry reading. And I couldn't resist teasing them just a little bit. I was inspired by the intensity and the evangelical quality of the beatniks. I said, Lawrence has a most interesting background. He was raised by the family that founded Sarah Lawrence College, and he was a football and basketball player. In World War II he was a lieutenant commander in the United States Navy. He holds a doctorate from the University of Paris, a Ph.D.

"At that point several beatniks fainted, and I could not resist, I proceeded on. I said he was an employee of *Time* magazine for a while. And he subsequently became a very successful and honest businessman in San Francisco, and he tells me with good cheer that he has made enough money so that he can buy a house for himself and his family on Potrero Hill. More beatniks fainted. And I said he married the young woman who is here with him tonight, Kirby Smith, who is a descendant of the last Confederate general to surrender in the Civil War. And in addition to being a successful businessman with his bookstore, City Lights, and his publishing firm, City Lights Books, he is also a very nice guy.

"You see, none of those things were supposed to be. Then I turned the microphone over to Lawrence and he said, 'Everything Paul said is unfortunately true.' He gave a terrific reading."

Paul Carroll's new magazine, *Big Table*, had begun when he was editing the *Chicago Review* with Irving Rosenthal, both of them young graduate students at the University of Chicago. After the spring 1958 San Francisco issue, they had pursued their interest in these new writers and got excerpts from William Burroughs's new novel, *Naked Lunch*, about the surrealistic world of heroin addiction, as well as contributions from Kerouac, Corso, Ginsberg, and others. Officials of the University of Chicago, however, offended by the "obscenity" of some of the work, and of the Burroughs manuscript especially, had refused to allow the magazine to be published. Rosenthal then sent the Burroughs manuscript to Ferlinghetti, thinking he might want to publish it, but Ferlinghetti didn't see it as a unified piece.

Further, he commented recently, "I was very straight at the time, and the junkie mentality really turned me off. The whole death mystique is so strong with hard-core druggies. It was just a matter of taste. I figured, if you like to eat shit, then okay, but I didn't like to eat shit and that's the way *Naked Lunch* affected me.

"Later when you have a chance to read all of Burroughs's work, then you see *Junkie* and *Naked Lunch* as part of a great worldview. Burroughs's whole sensibility comes into focus. But having only the very early version of scattered pages of *Naked Lunch* which had been sent to me . . . it was a lot less than finally came out when he published *Naked Lunch*. It was scattered pages that Ginsberg had gathered up from under the bed and elsewhere; if it hadn't been for Allen the book probably never would have been published.

"There was enough for a book, but I didn't see it as a book. It's like, for instance, if you were Shakespeare's editor and you came upon manuscripts of his early history plays, what's called the 'bloody plays,' and you think, well, this is about on the level with Marlowe, it's really not the greatest in the world. Maybe Marlowe even wrote these. But then a little later on when Shakespeare writes his other plays, you begin to see that he's a real genius."

Carroll, however, was certain the work was too important to be ignored, or suppressed by University of Chicago officials concerned with propriety. He decided to begin a new magazine which would publish the material (the title was another suggestion of Jack Kerouac's), and set about raising the money to underwrite it. Toward that end, Ginsberg, his lover Peter

Orlovsky, and Corso came to town to do a benefit reading to help, followed a little later by Ferlinghetti.

When Ferlinghetti said that Carroll's introduction at the *Big Table* reading was "unfortunately true," it wasn't that he necessarily felt the biographical facts Carroll listed in his introduction were unfortunate, but by this time Ferlinghetti was a celebrity, and the portrait Carroll sketched was not quite consistent with the public image that had been built around him. Ferlinghetti's comment was an acknowledgment of that inconsistency, delivered, no doubt, with the dry irony that suffused his poems, though the audience may have been too worshipful to detect it.

The irony was to remain a signature element of all the poetry as well, but the inviting warmth of lyricism that surrounded it in *Pictures of a Gone World* and *A Coney Island of the Mind* was to give way to a sometimes more strident tone in the coming years, in response to his own widening engagements.

In May 1958 he had written his first really full-fledged political tract-poem: "Tentative Description of a Dinner to Promote the Impeachment of President Eisenhower," which he read at the last "Poets' Follies" performance. It was based on a much longer poem by Prévert in the French edition of *Paroles*, titled "Tentative Description of a Dinner of Heads in Paris, France," that Ferlinghetti tried to translate, but gave up because the numbers of word plays and specific French references made it too difficult for an American audience. Like Prévert's, Ferlinghetti's poem was political satire, and the irony which moved it was not at all subtle. In the tradition of Swift's "A Modest Proposal," which coolly outlines the advantages of cannibalism as a solution to seventeenth-century Ireland's economic woes, Ferlinghetti's poem fantasizes Eisenhower's bewilderment in the face of atomic horrors, and suggests his resignation as the appropriate consequence. It made a terrific reading piece for audiences disaffected from the "silent generation." They shared fully the poem's view of Eisenhower as an all-encompassing symbol of cold war whose inept confusion in the face of the atomic bomb amounted to madness:

> And after it became obvious that the word Truth had only a
> comic significance to the Atomic Energy Commission while
> the President danced madly to mad Admiral Straus waltzes
> wearing special atomic earplugs which prevented him from
> hearing Albert Schweitzer and nine thousand two hundred
> and thirty-five other scientists telling him about spastic

generations and blind boneless babies in the strange rain
from which there was no escape—except Peace
And after it became obvious that the President was doing everything in his power to get thru the next four years without
eating any of the crates of irradiated vegetables wellwishers
had sent him from all over and which were filling the
corridors and antechambers and bedchambers and cham-
berpots in the not-so-White House. . . .

The poem was the first of several about the presidents of the next thirty
years, the first of many which directly took up contemporary political
issues, and it was published in many different places, including his next
book. Like other public poems he went on to write—many of which were
never included in collections—it was tremendously popular with audiences, and though Ferlinghetti acknowledges that the interest of most of
them is circumscribed by the specific events that were their occasion, he
has always believed in the importance of writing them and reading them,
in trying to reach as many people as possible.

Poet Robert Bly, for instance, remembers that he and James Wright
were just starting their magazine, *The Fifties*, when the poem was being
widely published.

"It was the first time I realized that political poetry was possible, that
it could be powerful," Bly says. "Up until then, everything was square
stanzas about the latest trip to Italy to see the statues."

Though "Howl" certainly didn't fit the "square stanzas about the latest
trip to Italy" description, Bly goes on to say he felt that poem "was more
about Ginsberg than it was about the world. And real political poetry
must be about the world."

In January of 1959 Ferlinghetti's political interests were sharply focused
by the first extended trip he took away from San Francisco since he
arrived in 1950. He and Allen Ginsberg, along with twenty-five other
writers from fifteen American nations, were invited to attend a writers'
conference at the University of Concepción in Chile sponsored by the
Communist Party. Though he had lived in France, had been politically
alert and active ever since he first came to San Francisco, he hadn't
traveled abroad in nine years and never to Latin America. Nothing had
prepared him for what he was to see and hear.

The invitation had been extended partly due to a Chilean poet who
was teaching at the University of California–Berkeley, and neither Ferlinghetti nor Ginsberg was aware that most of the participants in the

conference would be Communists. For these foreign intellectuals, "revolution" was not an abstract term bandied about by academics and rebellious beatniks; it was an urgent goal essential to transform the dirt-poor, overwhelmingly illiterate countries which were their homes. As poets, they saw their work as vital in this process. Poetry was a special language which could reach people, touch them as nothing else could, and spur them to action in the interests of their country and themselves. They pointed out the difference between this active concern and the more unfocused, passive rebelliousness of American Beats; and Ferlinghetti was drawn to these poets who saw themselves and their work not as eccentric, but as vital, fully integrated with and inseparable from the day-to-day world.

Their most intense interest at the time was directed at Cuba, where with America's blessing, Fidel Castro's guerrilla army had driven out the corrupt dictator Fulgencio Batista on New Year's Day and taken power in Havana a week later, just as the conference opened in Concepción. Saying, "Power does not interest me and I will not take it. From now on, the people are entirely free," Castro flew to Washington and assured eighteen congressmen in the Foreign Relations room that his movement was "not a Communist movement." He went on to tell them that "we have no intention of expropriating United States property, and any property we take, we'll pay for." Though by summer he had suspended habeas corpus, ended rights of appeal for convicted defendants, established military tribunals, and assumed dictatorial powers, in these first days of the revolution he was an international populist hero. And Ferlinghetti, like all the Latin American writers at the conference, supported him (though not uncritically).

Conversations with the other participants also helped give Ferlinghetti a different perspective on the U.S. role in Latin America from that which the media suggested. Conference presentations and tours focused on the poor, and on U.S. support for the wealthy and privileged at their expense. Ferlinghetti wrote in his journal that "the impression I have is that a great, fat, omnivorous crab named United States of America is sitting on top of the Pan American Hemisphere, sucking the marrow from its soft underside."

One of the most affecting experiences for him was a tour of the coal mines near the resort town of Lota. In contrast to the beautiful botanical gardens and the flavor of wealthy tourism were the coal miners whose "working conditions were like those in the United States seventy or eighty years ago," Ferlinghetti wrote. At the end of the conference he was asked to complete a twenty-five-item survey with such questions as "What strikes you as the most important thing you've seen in Chile? What is the most important poetry that you've seen in Chile? Who were the most important literary personages in Chile?" For every answer, Ferlinghetti wrote the same single sentence: "The faces of the miners in their cages at Lota."

After the conference, Ginsberg stayed on with Nicanor Parra, the Chilean poet he and Ferlinghetti had met, spent three weeks in La Paz, then traveled on to Peru and continued his experiments with native psychedelic drugs. Ferlinghetti and Kirby made their way back north slowly, traveling through Bolivia, Peru, Central America, then up to Mexico City before coming back to San Francisco. Throughout, Ferlinghetti was struck by the vivid contrast between the physical beauty of parts of the cities and countryside along with the wealth of some of the people on the one hand, and the stark poverty of the majority of the population on the other. At the conference itself he had heard again and again about the all-pervasive influence of the United States in contributing to these conditions, and his journal comments on this as well as on the force of what he saw.

In one passage he compared Lima, Peru, to the European capitals of Vienna, Paris, and Madrid; but La Paz he found a "miserable, mud covered, dung hole of humanity at the top of the world, with one fine tree-lined Prado cut through and above the sink hole city of decaying Indian beggars, con men and German fascists. . . ." He went on to note, "There's no middle class in most South American countries. In the outskirts of Lima, there's a small neighborhood of the first middle class."

In Mexico, on the other hand, he seemed to feel much more comfortable, enjoying the look and feel of the people and surroundings. It had both the exoticism and interest of a wholly other culture, yet was close enough to be relatively accessible, and in the coming years, Ferlinghetti would return many times to spend days or weeks in different parts of that country.

When they got back, Ferlinghetti's interest in Latin America, its politics, and the United States' hand there had been stirred, and one of his first acts was to publish a selection of Parra's poems. Like Ferlinghetti himself, Parra was a poet who was rebellious and whose work was concerned with social injustice and the hypocrisy of established institutions. But also like Ferlinghetti's, his work was satiric, humorous, and a break from conventional forms. Underlining this break, and the nontraditional subject matter, he titled the collection *Anti-Poems*.

As spring turned to summer, Ferlinghetti noted in his journal, "Ginsberg says that 'the major beat figures have already published their major sounds and what's left is an exfoliation of the original insights and methods.' . . . I did not agree . . . [and] said it would run another ten years." ("But," Ferlinghetti notes thirty years later, "they became Long Distance Runners.")

As if to assert that continuing vitality of the Beat spirit, Ferlinghetti got involved in another cooperative editorial project, this one focused in his own North Beach neighborhood. There, poet Bob Kaufman, John Kelley, William Margolis, and Ginsberg, who had spent the summer of 1959 in San Francisco participating in some of the early experiments with LSD that Gregory Bateson was conducting at Stanford, conceived the idea for a new magazine that would convey the sense of radical openness and free exchange they felt was at the heart of literary San Francisco. It would be called *Beatitude*—the term given to the blessings pronounced by Christ at the Sermon on the Mount—and the term Kerouac had said was at the root of the term "beat." The magazine was to be done by mimeograph—no fancy, expensive production, but something that, like the blessings themselves, would be easily accessible to all. The editors announced that it would be a "weekly miscellany of poetry and other jazz designed to extol beauty and promote the beatific life among the various mendicants, neo-existentialists, christs, poets, painters, musicians, and other inhabitants and observers of North Beach, San Francisco, California, United States of America," and that it would be "edited on a kick or miss basis by a few hardy types who sneak out of alleys near Grant Avenue." Ferlinghetti also became involved, and the editors gave notice that beginning with number 17, the magazine would issue "spasmodically from the underground caves of City Lights bookstore through whose subterranean passages some of the original editors may be reached. But manuscripts will not be returned, even if accompanied by the usual return postage. (The stamps will be unlicked and used for evil purposes.)"

In the table of contents of *Beatitude #17*, the only issue Ferlinghetti edited, his playful side took over in the distortion of some well-known contributors' names—Ginsberg became "Ellen Ginsboig"; Ferlinghetti, "L. Foolingheppi"; Gregory Corso, "Gregoire de Corse." These distortions mocked the pretentious formality of the traditional literary review and emphasized that this was "street poetry"—writing of and for common and ordinary people, and people with a sense of humor about themselves and the world.

Other well-known contributors included McClure, Whalen, Kerouac,

Lamantia, and Bob Kaufman. Ferlinghetti included his poem "Over-population" in the magazine as well as an excerpt from the Paris novel he had begun working at again, now titled *Her.*

Besides his interests in politics and his engagement in the larger world, a part of him was turning inward as well, to his family and his own past, a direction which the renewed attention to *Her* also reflects. The mystery of that past had never been resolved, and though he hadn't actively pursued answers to it—he hadn't had the time, for one thing—like all writers, he was fundamentally introspective, and that absent piece of his life, crucial to anyone's sense of identity, loomed large. The trip to Latin America had stirred those interests again. During it, he had turned forty; for most people the crossing of a decade marks a time for reassessment, for measuring what has been and what is to come. Though Ferlinghetti probably didn't think of it in those terms, such forces were at work.

In the summer of 1958, with *Coney Island* published and selling well, he had begun working on the novel again—rewriting the draft he had completed during his last year in Paris and set aside. Its events were taken directly from his hours at the Montparnasse cafés and surrounding streets, and images of his "two-room cave" on the rue de Vaugirard. During his wanderings that year he had kept a "black book" in which he wrote what became the novel. Heavily influenced by Djuna Barnes's *Nightwood*, it follows that novel's tripartite structure and uses a similar "Spielmann"—in this case the headwaiter in the Lubin café—who is a direct copy, Ferlinghetti acknowledges, of Barnes's Matthew O'Connor. The novel is a 150-page mostly interior monologue about the search for a meta-physical center, for some ultimate identity—the quest to find and know the self, to integrate the rational and irrational, the male and female, to achieve a whole. Its central metaphor, "Her," includes his mother, Aunt Emily, various lovers, and other women—in short, the essential archetype of the female, the ubiquitous presence which is part of him but which eludes him.

When he finished it at last, in the early summer of 1959, he sent it to his publisher. James Laughlin wasn't especially enthusiastic about it, find-ing it dense and difficult, albeit fascinating. "I suspect that it is an im-portant book," he wrote, though "it is much harder to get into [than *Coney Island*], being so tightly packed." Despite any reservations, however, he felt the book was "logical" in terms of Ferlinghetti's European con-nections and experience; but he did suggest that Ferlinghetti divide the single sentence which comprised the book into three sections, to give some sense of progression to the narrative. Ferlinghetti took the suggestion, and New Directions brought out the novel in 1960 with a reproduction of a Ferlinghetti painting as the cover.

Ferlinghetti's major reputation as a poet by this time ensured some attention from reviewers, but their reactions to such a dense and complex novel were predictably mixed.

Commonweal wrote that "sentimentality lies at the core of Ferlinghetti, both when he succeeds and when he fails. . . . Such devotion to a theme often leads to excess, and excess, as Blake has said, helps a man to stumble into the path of wisdom. The difficulty is that the stumbling, aside from its lack of grace, is often repetitious and dull."

In *The Village Voice* Paris Leary wrote, "Mr. Ferlinghetti, while dispensing with Plot, still remains on the outside of experience, as it were, quite failing to achieve the internal action or drama we have come to expect from modern writers. Too much preoccupation with the momentary effects of excited language and sexual imagery keeps the book from being really successful on any level."

But in the *San Francisco Chronicle* Vincent McHugh praised it as "a great triumph of narrative" and "the most important American prose work I've seen in the last twenty years, decidedly the pleasantest."

Regardless of critical reception, as with his poems, Ferlinghetti had developed a large, interested audience, and the book sold—by 1988, in its thirteenth printing, nearly 100,000 copies had been published.

In his continual exploration of the personal and political and the relation between them, it represents the extreme of the personal in his work. He had long been working to integrate the two, and he didn't see them as conflicting; now with a successful book of poetry, the novel finally finished, and an established and successful business, he planned another trip which would answer questions in both areas.

Ever since his aunt Emily disappeared from the Bislands, Ferlinghetti's family background had been largely lost to him. His brief visits with his mother and brothers had left them virtual strangers, and in the decade that he had been in San Francisco, he had entirely lost touch with them. But while he was corresponding with William Carlos Williams about the publications of *Kora in Hell* and *Howl*, Williams had mentioned that his own parents had been married at the residence of someone named Monsanto in Brooklyn; and that his mother's family, who had come from Puerto Rico, knew of other Monsantos there.

At the same time, Ferlinghetti had learned through another poet in San Francisco, Tram Coombs, that he might have relatives living on St. Thomas in the Virgin Islands. Coombs had moved to Charlotte Amalie, on St. Thomas, and Ferlinghetti had stayed in touch with him. Coombs told him that Gladys Woods, the local telephone operator, was the daughter of Jean-Baptiste Mendes-Monsanto and the half sister of Ferlinghetti's maternal grandfather, Herman Monsanto. Ferlinghetti called Woods, and they had a long conversation; he decided that he would indeed come to visit.

In November 1960 Ferlinghetti and Kirby went first to Chicago, where Ferlinghetti gave another reading for *Big Table*, this time at the Gate of Horn nightclub, then on to his alma mater at Chapel Hill, where he read and met with the current students of his former English professor, Phillips Russell. He also met the granddaughter of Presley and Anna Bisland, Anne Oakes Scarborough, who was living there with her husband and with whom he had corresponded on and off through the years. The Ferlinghettis then traveled to Florida to visit Kirby's family, and down to Puerto Rico and the Virgin Islands. There Gladys Woods showed them around the island, which had not yet become a commercialized tourist center, and told him what she knew of his family. He also learned that he had another aunt, Jean McGrath, who was Gladys's sister, living in Bolinas, just north of San Francisco.

The experience was profound for Ferlinghetti, the orphan. He met eighty-one-year-old William Smith, one of his "ancestors," who stood "in straw hat, glasses, one eye totally blind." He lived "in a Gauguin shack with tin roof, inside walls plastered with newspapers, posters, cardboard, two beds—made up neat—a seaman's pad at wind's end."

"When I shook his hand," Ferlinghetti wrote, "I was meeting my Father for the first time . . . Ulysses on the beach beside the fishnets where the boats knocked."

At his uncle Desir Monsanto's house, Ferlinghetti was shown old daguerreotypes of his grandfather Herman as a vigorous thirty-year-old man, and Herman's brother, both of whom looked "like Spanish Lotharios." He learned that Herman had "left his French wife (my grandmother), returned from New York to the islands, and philandered into various other women, then got involved in Guatemalan revolution, contracted yellow fever or something and returned to St. Thomas to die at age thirty-eight."

After the visit to St. Thomas, the Ferlinghettis went to Haiti. There they witnessed scenes of poverty more extreme than anything they had seen before in Latin America. Those extremes, coupled with the guidebook comments written by "a noted American poet," reinforced impressions he had gained in his Latin American adventure of the previous year, of the terrible living conditions so many of the people there suffer, and the insensitivity of the United States government, and most of its people, to them. In his journal Ferlinghetti wrote:

> Some desolation photographer ought to . . . take pictures of the *real* "picturesque" island life—for the tourists—shit, hunger, and pissing death—rags and broken shoes—kids with pieces of men's shoes tied to the feet, open sewers seething with revolution. Haiti still 85%–95% illiterate. . . .
>
> The coins all read LIBERTE, EGALITE, FRATERNITE. These noble savages are all absolutely equal, except for the six percent who own everything not owned by foreigners. If money's the blood of the poor, in the Port of the Prince, the blood has black corpuscles. The Prince has long washed his hands of it. . . . Ah, but our guidebook tells us, "Tourists beset by beggars, fresh children, arrogant young men and petty thieves will do well to remember that the first and last belong to the declassed riffraff found in any large city, and the others are insecure members of a rising and still unaccepted middle-class. . . ." It goes on to say that the average cash income of the Haitian is under $75 a year.

They only stayed one day, then went on to Jamaica, which Ferlinghetti found similarly depressing: "All together a very mournful episode in my life, this British Crown Colony."

On December 3 they flew to their other major destination—the new revolutionary state of Cuba. Always sympathetic with the oppressed and disenfranchised, Ferlinghetti, like many intellectuals, completely supported the stated goals of Castro's revolution to improve the lot of the majority. The U.S. Government's opposition was a tragedy, as far as he could see, based on unjustified distrust and the economic greed of the privileged who had benefited under Batista. In his journal Ferlinghetti noted parallels between the Cuban Revolution and the Spanish Civil War of the thirties, in the U.S. failure to see and support the armed opposition to fascism in Spain.

When he arrived in Havana, the first thing Ferlinghetti noticed was the huge red lettering on the terminal building spelling out "Cuba Territorio Libre de América—Patria o Muerte" (Free Cuban Territory of America—Our Country or Death): an announcement that this was indeed a new country. And on the drive from the airport, he noted the beauty of the country and the sense of freedom and calm:

". . . not a single question asked us at the airport. . . . Sixteen-mile drive from Airport to Havana—Dramatic waterfront in Havana—Sea beating great long seawall Northside of city—Morro Castle at one end —Didn't see an armed soldier all the way to the city. . . . Beautiful city! Beautiful trees on the Paseo del Prado. . . . First we met a Greek in the lobby who says he's been here a month and 'everybody's happy and like brothers.' "

The first night they went to a "Cow Fair" in the center of Havana on the capitol grounds. There were soldiers there, some of them armed, but apparently just milling about, like the other visitors. There were others with guns also—a man setting up microphones on a stage for a concert by soldiers, two young soldiers, "one looking a little like Jean Louis Barrault in his teens," but "lots of kids and mothers. . . . Everyone sitting on wooden chairs looking very peaceful." He also noticed that at the fair "there aren't *any* people who look like the usual well-dressed upper middle class. Everyone in the park looks like the working class." But most important, he learned that "at 11 P.M. tomorrow night the money from the Fair will be used to present a cow to every farmer."

He did encounter some hostility toward Americans from a hotel clerk and a young Venezuelan who were angry at the U.S. attitude and mounting government pressure against Castro. But he sympathized. The tourist trade which supported St. Thomas, Jamaica, and previously Cuba had completely stopped—due, Ferlinghetti felt, to the biased media reporting which mouthed the government line and drew an exaggerated picture of danger. And the pressure was designed to defeat a regime which was sincerely trying to better the lot of its people. As far as Ferlinghetti could tell, the new regime was already succeeding:

"All I've seen so far indicates Havana, and Cuba in general, are much, much better off economically than all other Caribbean countries, including even British Jamaica, U.S. Puerto Rico (which is considered a U.S. imperialist colony here), and U.S. St. Thomas. . . . Went out to offices of newspaper *Revolución* at ten P.M. on Plaza Cívica—a huge empty space with modernist buildings spaced far apart—walked across it and down a smaller plaza in the dark to get to the newspaper building—No one fired at me in the night—as I was led to expect by U.P.I. and A.P. dispatches—I saw only one soldier—sitting down guarding a garage— And one at entrance desk of *Revolución* escorted me upstairs. . . . Back on the great square by the Paseo del Prado at midnight, I came upon a group of about 35 to 45 campesinos from the cow fair—of various colors—in the midst of a big political argument."

Throughout the visit, Ferlinghetti notes, there was no sense of a "guided tour"; he went wherever he wanted to, whenever he wanted to. In fact, for the first two days, he couldn't get in touch with anyone official, though he tried. When he did finally get in touch with the editors of the literary supplement, *Lunes de Revolución*, with them one evening he actually met Castro:

"He came out of the kitchen of the restaurant where we were eating," Ferlinghetti wrote. "He must have been having supper back there. He was smoking a big stub of a cigar. One guard had a submachine gun. Both in the usual fatigues. . . . He walked out the door, glancing at us as he went past, nodding slightly. . . . By the time I got up to speak with him, he was already outside on the sidewalk. I rushed out past the yard and shook his hand saying, soy poeta Americano. He looked at me smiling slightly . . . and shook my hand . . . I said, gracias . . . I mumbled a few more insane phrases like, soy amigo de Allen Ginsberg y Leroi Jones (who he talked to at length once last summer and in New York recently), but someone else rushed up and embraced him and he went on, having said not a word. He was gentle, very shy. His handshake was soft, at least not hard."

If the idyllic view of Castro and Cuba that Ferlinghetti recorded in his journal seems a bit naive, or even the anticipated self-fulfilling prophecy, it is important to remember that it was a view shared by numbers of Americans who were skeptical of official public attitudes which insisted anything having to do with communism must be bad. A year after the revolution, though Castro's rule had been consolidated, he had also set in motion programs and institutions that would reduce illiteracy, improve medical practice, and generally raise the standard of living. The Soviet Union provided much of the assistance that made these advances possible, but from the point of view of many international observers, among which Ferlinghetti included himself, the revolution made everyday life significantly better for the masses of Cuban people.

Ferlinghetti was dismayed, however, by the lack of interest, even opposition, of other American writers to what was going on in Cuba. That writers whom he respected, even published, could be misled, or uninterested, was disturbing, and further underlined his own distance from the public idea of the "Beat Generation":

"U.S. Beats not angry with anyone—too cool for that—And Jack Kerouac told me before I left for Cuba, 'I got my own Revolution out here in Northport—the American Revolution.' His is a typically selfish view. Other writers in U.S. today—older ones especially—mostly not interested in coming down here to see for themselves—I tried to get

Rexroth interested—He wouldn't go—put down the whole idea of reporting it."

But while he was there, he did meet another Latin American writer
who was even more directly involved in politics. The former Chilean
ambassador to China and to France was in Havana and scheduled to give
a reading of his poetry. Ferlinghetti had seen the poster announcing the
reading by Pablo Neruda, and Pablo Armando Fernández, the young poet
and editor of *Lunes*, the literary supplement of *Revolución*, which had
published some of Ferlinghetti's poems, told him that Neruda was staying
at the former Havana Hilton, now called the Cuba Libre.

When Ferlinghetti called him, he invited Ferlinghetti to visit him at
the hotel; Kirby, unable to tolerate the fleas in their hotel bedroom, had
gone home alone. Ferlinghetti spent several hours visiting in French
with Neruda and his wife, Mathilde, at the hotel, as that was the one
language in which they had common fluency. Ferlinghetti hoped to interest Neruda in publishing a Pocket Poets book with City Lights, and
though that never came about, they got along well. When a driver from
the House of the Americas, which sponsored the reading, came to take
him there, Neruda insisted that Ferlinghetti accompany him in the official car. Ferlinghetti understood some of the Spanish, but mainly was
impressed with the enthusiasm of the audience, most of whom were
soldiers. Neruda knew well how to communicate with his audience, and
they responded readily to his poems in praise of revolution and against
U.S. imperialism.

On December 8 he left Cuba, and upon returning to San Francisco,
focused a part of his experience there by writing "One Thousand Fearful Words for Fidel Castro." The poem was read before it was published, in mid-January at a rally in San Francisco's Civic Center
sponsored by the Fair Play for Cuba Committee. Loaded with irony,
and written in the easy, conversational style of the *Coney Island* poems,
the poem's first lines immediately dispelled the tension that hung over
the hall at the rally:

> *I am sitting in Mike's Place trying to figure out*
> *what's going to happen*
> *without Fidel Castro*
> *Among the salami sandwiches and spittoons*

Its free-swinging irony went on to satirize mainstream America's opposition to Castro and to portray him as a tragic hero:

It's going to be
a big evil tragedy
They're going to fix you, Fidel
with your big Cuban cigar
which you stole from us
and your army surplus hat
which you probably also stole
and your Beat beard
History may absolve you, Fidel
but we'll dissolve you first, Fidel

Finally the poem compares Castro with Abraham Lincoln:

Well, you've got your little death, Fidel
like old Honest Abe
one of your boyhood heroes
who also had his little Civil War
and was a different kind of Liberator

Such sentiments in this kind of political poem guaranteed Ferlinghetti the disapproval of established literary critics, and not entirely incidentally, also earned him attention from the FBI. Still, Ferlinghetti's hope for Cuba was shared by all at the rally and by thousands, if not millions, of Americans. At City Lights he published the poem as a broadside along with a note on the back saying in part:

"There are not one thousand words here. The author has left room for a happier ending, in case the relentless hostility of government and press in the U.S. should somehow not triumph in the end. . . ."

The poem's concern turned out to be prophetic. Four days before the Ferlinghettis had arrived in Havana, Allen Dulles, the head of the CIA, told President-elect John F. Kennedy of a plan the CIA had devised. Though Kennedy was initially skeptical, Dulles convinced him the plan couldn't fail. Three months later, on Monday night, April 17, 1961, a few hundred defected Cuban assault troops, called La Brigada, trained and encouraged by the CIA and led by American frogmen, landed at Cuba's Bahía de Cochinos—the Bay of Pigs. They had been promised that American military might was right behind, about to help them and guarantee the overthrow of Castro.

The American support never arrived, however, and it took less than three days for the poorly planned, poorly executed invasion to be thoroughly smashed by Castro's loyal and well-trained militia in a humiliating foreign policy debacle for the new President. The cold war had suddenly grown hotter. And at almost the same time, Kennedy's advisers were also orchestrating American military involvement much farther away—across the Pacific in the jungles of Vietnam. It was getting harder for anyone to be really "disengaged." Soon it would be just about impossible.

In the fall of 1960 Allen Ginsberg flew up to Boston with Peter Orlovsky and his brother, Lafcadio, to meet Dr. Timothy Leary of Harvard and participate in some of Leary's first experiments with the consciousness-altering drug psilocybin, derived from the *Psilocybe mexicana* mushroom. Both Ginsberg and Kerouac had long been interested in exploring the mind, and Ginsberg, particularly, had been pursuing these explorations widely. He had already traveled through Mexico and tried various Indian drugs in the mid-fifties, and as early as 1959, had written the poem "Lysergic Acid" about his insights under the influence of that drug.

High on psilocybin that fall night, according to Ginsberg's biographer Barry Miles, Ginsberg called Kerouac and told him to take a plane to Boston immediately because "the revolution is beginning," and "it's time to seize power over the universe and become the next consciousness."

Kerouac, characteristically, said he couldn't leave his mother, but in January 1961 Leary flew down to New York himself to visit Ginsberg and Kerouac and continue his experimental testing of psilocybin's effects on artists. Alcoholic, depressed, and increasingly isolated from his friends and the rest of the world, Kerouac was taking a brief vacation from Northport, where he had been browsing the *Encyclopaedia Britannica*, which he had bought with the intention of perusing the accumulated knowledge of scholars from the beginning to 1909. Staying with Ginsberg at Ginsberg's 70 East Second Street apartment, under the influence of Leary's psilocybin Kerouac continued to drink wine, smoke cigarettes, and stomp around yelling and telling stories. When Leary tried to discuss the implications of altered mind states, Kerouac answered that "walking on water wasn't built in a day." His final conclusion, however, was more prosaic: "Everybody is full of shit."

For Ginsberg his psychedelic experiences were interior parallels to his worldwide traveling. Having already journeyed through Mexico, Europe, and down to Tangier, in March 1961 he would again leave for Paris, the Middle East, and then India and Japan, where he would rendezvous with Gary Snyder. Ginsberg's two-year sojourn ultimately served to solidify his immersion in the Buddhist viewpoint that would inform all his future poems.

The psychedelic experience did nothing, however, to change the course of Kerouac's increasingly precipitous slide toward alcoholic oblivion. Later that January, Kerouac got a dozen of the psilocybin mushrooms from Leary and ate them all in one afternoon. Euphoric, playing with Leary in the snow, he came to the realization that there was no "new life" for him. In his memoir *Flashbacks*, Leary remembers Kerouac as "an old-style Bohemian without a hippie bone in his body," who "opened the neural doors to the future, looked ahead, and didn't see his place in it. Not for him the utopian pluralist optimism of the sixties." Like its most famous figure, the whole Beat phenomenon, thoroughly plumbed and picked over by the media, was nearing the same exhaustion. Or more accurately, it was beginning to become something else.

In 1959 University of California President Clark Kerr had said that the current generation of college students was "going to be easy to handle. There aren't going to be any riots." But a year later, students flooded the San Francisco City Hall to quietly support several public school teachers and a Berkeley sophomore, rumored to be "leftists," who had been subpoenaed to appear before the House Un-American Activities Committee in San Francisco. Seats filled, and as police blocked the entrance of other supporters to the hearing room, one cop slipped and fell; others drew nightsticks, then fire hoses appeared.

One undergraduate who was beaten said, "I was a political virgin, but I was raped on the steps of City Hall."

And Jessica Mitford wrote in *The Nation*, "The current crop of students has gone far to shake the label of apathy and conformity that had stuck through the fifties." She went on to predict that some would dedicate themselves to "shaping the future of the world."

A few weeks earlier, on February 1, 1960, four black students at North Carolina Agricultural and Technical College bought a few small items at the F. W. Woolworth drugstore in Greensboro, then sat down at the whites-only lunch counter and ordered coffee. When they were refused service, as they expected, they refused to leave, stayed until closing, then returned the next morning with five friends. The following day more black students joined them, and in the next two weeks their action was repeated at Woolworth stores in a half dozen other southern cities. The demonstrators called the actions "sit-ins."

The sit-ins continued, and on May 10 the demonstrators won their first victory when six lunch counters in Nashville were desegregated. But the demonstrations continued and spread, directed against other segregation laws, and on October 19 police in Atlanta arrested fifty-one demonstrators. Among them was the Reverend Martin Luther King, Jr.

And equally important, on May 9, 1960, the day after the San Francisco City Hall disruption, the Food and Drug Administration approved for sale Enovid, a pill developed by G. D. Searle & Co. It was the first oral contraceptive, making it possible for women to have sexual intercourse without fearing the consequences of pregnancy. The sexual restraints thus loosened opened the way to what became a sexual and social revolution.

Then two years later, in June 1962, forty-five young people in Port Huron, Michigan, gathered at an old UAW-CIO summer camp and discussed a sixty-two-page manifesto drafted by twenty-two-year-old Tom Hayden. The organization they founded was to be called SDS— Students for a Democratic Society. Though it came to be associated with some of the worst of the radical violence of the late sixties, Hayden's manifesto renounced violence, and cited racism and the cold war as the two greatest threats to society. The solution, he wrote, was to "replace power rooted in possession, privilege, or circumstances by power and uniqueness rooted in love, reflectiveness, reason and creativity."

In those first years of the 1960s, Ferlinghetti wasn't directly involved in the civil rights movement or in much other political activity, however. As he continued to work daily at the store, on the publishing, and to give readings around the country and write his own poems, his attention also focused much on his family. In the last week of February 1961, Kirby and Ferlinghetti adopted a baby girl they named Julie, who had been born on the fifteenth. Then a few months later, Kirby finally became pregnant after years of hoping and, on July 5, 1962, delivered a boy, Lorenzo, at Kaiser-Permanente Hospital in San Francisco while Ferlinghetti waited in the hospital's maternity waiting area for fathers, called, he remembers with a laugh, the "Heir Port."

At the same time, he was interested in the exploration of consciousness that Ginsberg and other friends were pursuing, an interest no doubt encouraged in part by his friendship with Ginsberg, and by the steady stream of letters Ginsberg continued to send from his outposts. Much of Ferlinghetti's practice in meditation and consciousness exploration was centered at Bixby Canyon in Big Sur, where he had first bought a parcel of land in 1957 for five hundred dollars, "just a thicket," he described it, from "an old bohemian who owned a gallery on Upper Grant Avenue and never got down there." The land had a stream running through it, and with the help of a carpenter from Carmel, Ferlinghetti built a small cabin there. The place was in a narrow part of the canyon, however, and only got a few hours of light in the winter, so in 1960 he bought a parcel of meadowland, sold the cabin, and built another one. Some two hundred miles south of San Francisco, Bixby was relatively undiscovered, and the simple cabin itself was truly isolated. A narrow dirt road connected it to California State Highway 1, and the cabin sat beside a creek near the point where the road itself leads into a footpath down to the beach.

In September of 1961 he spent an afternoon there sitting naked in the lotus position, reading the Kamasutra, while his wife and mother-in-law were in San Francisco. Then in October he took a short trip by himself to Mexico. It was the first of many such Mexican odysseys in the next two decades. He spent two days with friends in Tijuana, and three alone in Ensenada. Though he had liked Mexico more than any of the other Latin American countries he had visited in his 1959 and 1960 trips, his experience in Ensenada this fall was quite otherwise. Far from achieving enlightenment, he noted with reference to Malcolm Lowry's protagonist in his novel of alcoholic self-destruction, *Under the Volcano*, "This is the most depressing journey I have ever been on . . . I can see why Consuls drink themselves to death in towns like this, out of pure desperation. Help! . . ."

As always, he was both aware of and involved with the political currents stirring beyond his doors; and all these interests are reflected in the fourteen poems of *Starting from San Francisco*, his second collection from New Directions, published in 1961. Less lyrical but more diverse than either *Pictures of the Gone World* or *A Coney Island of the Mind*, the poems are a continuation of his efforts to bring together the personal and the political; to encompass and address the greater issues in the culture. Politics in particular are at the center of several of these poems, and present in some way in all of them. Sex is here even more directly than in *Coney Island*. And always, there is the ironic voice inviting the reader into the joke, pointing out absurdity, foolishness, contradictions.

Taken together, the poems constitute a certain kind of travelogue of the previous years; journeys to Chile and Latin America, to Cuba, across America to the East, and from New York City to Albany, are all occasions for poems. In that expansiveness, the collection might be termed "Whitmanic," though the poems generally lack Whitman's celebratory voice.

"The Great Chinese Dragon," the one poem where that voice does sound clearly in its wild description of the transcendent title figure at the head of the annual Chinese New Year's parade in San Francisco, also demonstrates the other characteristic elements Ferlinghetti gathers. The flavor of Whitman here, as in other poems, is heavily mixed with surrealism, underscoring the magic, the larger than lifeness of the whole affair, as well as its absurdity. In one long sentence, and line, the dragon is portrayed as "a monster with the head of a dog and the body of a serpent risen yearly out of the sea to devour a virgin thrown from a cliff to appease him and . . . a big red table the world will never tilt and . . . the cat with future feet wearing Keds . . ." and so on.

But the surrealism here, as in other Ferlinghetti poems, also underscores an irony used to criticize some aspect of contemporary affairs. In this case the target is "the great concrete walls of America" which the dragon might "melt down" by "belching forth some strange disintegrating medium." To restrain it, the ubiquitous "they" of the mainstream institutional world "have secretly and securely tied down the very end of his tail in its hole." That is, the dragon is a mystical, sexual, potentially unifying force which "they" must keep in control. The poem ends with the dragon's "one wild orgasm"—the attraction of sex, which helped make *Coney Island* so popular, and energizes many of these poems.

That sexual explicitness, like Ferlinghetti's politics—a literal aspect of his politics, actually, in its challenge to convention—also foresaw social changes in the American fabric. Three years later California designer Rudy Gernreich introduced the topless bathing suit, which was soon followed by bare-breasted waitresses at chic, then not so chic bars; transparent dresses; and by the mid-sixties, mini-, then micro-skirts cut up the thigh almost to the crotch.

Still, though the dominant metaphor is unmistakably sexual in the poem, it is not primarily sex that the poem celebrates. The dragon is a fundamentally spiritual force, and the urge toward transcendence that the poem embodies was a central aspect of the consciousness exploration in which Ginsberg, Ferlinghetti, and others were increasingly engaged. As the 1960s went on, such explorations would become, along with anti-Vietnam politics, a central part of what came to be the counterculture.

In "Big Fat Hairy Vision of Evil," the poet sees "pot visions"; and other poems—"New York-Albany," which is essentially a religious vision, "Hidden Door," about the search for some transcendent knowlege, and "He," which portrays a kind of super-Ginsberg as a mystical, surrealistic shaman—all manifest this fundamentally spiritual interest. "Euphoria" and "Flying out of It" are even more directly about the urge for transcendence: "As I approach the state of pure Euphoria / my eyes are gringo spies and I / may anytime be changed to birds . . . ," he says in "Euphoria." That poem concludes with the poet's transportation to some other state by a girl who has "turned me on. . . . Her breasts bloom / figs burst / sun is white / I'll never come back. . . ." Here, it isn't religion or drugs, but again sex—the powerful, worldly, human impulse—which is most immediately associated with the transformation. Though not exactly the cause, it's the essential, final element. Ultimately, always, Ferlinghetti's concern resides with things of this world.

Two poems written in the mid-sixties were added to a new edition published in 1967—"Berlin" and "The Situation in the West Followed by a Holy Proposal"—and both are also very secular; the "Holy Proposal" is, in fact, universal sex. It was a way perhaps of putting "love" ahead of politics, reflecting the youth culture's movement at the time. The 1961 book, however, ended with three overtly political poems—"Tentative Description . . . ," "Special Clearance Sale of Famous Masterpieces," and "One Thousand Fearful Words for Fidel Castro." It is as if Ferlinghetti wants to be sure we understand that despite any appearance of frivolity, poems, poet, and audience must be grounded in the ominous, everyday world where we actually live.

Reviews of the book were mixed, as usual, but generally favorable. All commented on the record of Ferlinghetti reading, which was included in a back cover pocket of the first, oversized edition, but dropped in later, standard-sized editions. Writing in the prestigious Chicago literary magazine *Poetry*, poet-professor Alan Dugan said, "Oral poetry has to fit the speaker's voice. . . . Mr. Ferlinghetti's verse is perfectly suited to his style, and his style of delivery is effective and engaging. . . . He treats political problems with wit, insight, and frankness, and reads . . . well on the record."

San Francisco poet James Schevill also praised the book: "Ferlinghetti is perfectly aware of the risk he is running in using political-topical themes . . . yet one cannot deny the excitement he stirs up in an audience. Entertainment in the true sense of that corrupted word."

In the *New York Times Book Review*, however, another poet-professor,

X. J. Kennedy, was harsh in his assessment: "Ferlinghetti has won a large audience, apparently made up of people who wish poetry, like TV, to be bright, laden with gags, and undemanding. . . . Listening, I wonder: shouldn't an oral poetry oftener have interesting sounds in it? Ferlinghetti reads flatly; there are few audible patterns. Lacking such patterns, his product seems mostly an amusing talk."

The academic Kennedy was obviously out of touch with the larger poetry audience which from the first flocked in huge numbers to Ferlinghetti's readings, and with most critics as well, who even when they didn't like the poems on the page, generally agreed that Ferlinghetti's "flat" oral delivery was always powerful and effective. Regardless, as with *Coney Island*, negative reviews seemed to have little effect on the book's sales. Ferlinghetti was a popular figure, and though the book didn't sell nearly as well as *Coney Island*, it did far better than almost any book of poetry. The 15,000 copies of the first edition sold out within five years, leading to a 1966 second printing with the two new poems, but without the record of him reading. The printing then was over 100,000; the swelling youth culture had discovered that these poems spoke to the heart of their most urgent interests.

After the publication of *Starting from San Francisco*, Ferlinghetti wrote no poetry for almost three years. In part, he was more involved at home fixing up the Wisconsin Street house; and both the bookstore and the press were busier than ever. His popularity led to numerous invitations to read all over the country, and he had become much less involved in the bookstore, leaving it almost entirely in the hands of Murao. Further, in 1961 City Lights Books published six books, no small undertaking for a small press whose day-to-day operations from manuscript preparation to final book, and all related business affairs, were still managed almost completely by Ferlinghetti alone.

One of the major publication projects was one that Allen Ginsberg had been urging almost since Ferlinghetti first met him; Ginsberg thought City Lights would be exactly the right publisher for Kerouac's poetry. Ferlinghetti, for his part, had not liked it much at first. Though he would later say that not publishing Kerouac earlier had been a mistake, in late 1957 he had turned down Kerouac's *Book of Blues*. Kerouac then offered him several more manuscripts—a long one-line poem called "Lucien Midnight," which Ferlinghetti wasn't taken with, then "Book of Sketches" and "Some of the Dharma," the second a long dissertation on Buddhism and religion. Ferlinghetti read both of these in 1959, but neither of them appealed, either. In 1960 he did publish a broadside of a Kerouac poem about Arthur Rimbaud, but he still was more interested in Kerouac's fiction. The trouble was, almost all of it was sold by his New York agent to commercial publishers. Ferlinghetti and Kerouac continued to correspond, and in 1959 Kerouac sent him his "Book of Dreams" manuscript, an enormous prose collection from his dream diary. It was far longer than anything City Lights had published, and more than Ferlinghetti thought would make sense for the City Lights book list, but he didn't want to dismiss it, either.

Meantime, in April 1960, Ferlinghetti had gone east for readings in New York, Vermont, and New Hampshire, and spent a night with Kerouac in New York City. Though they had met before, they had never spent any time together; now they got to know each other. Like Ferlinghetti, Kerouac had a French background, was a high school athlete and a Navy veteran, and admired Thomas Wolfe and Baudelaire. With all this in common, they got along well, and the evening ended after 3 A.M. at the apartment of a woman Kerouac knew, with Kerouac offering him "her services."

For Ferlinghetti, engagement meant not just political actions—writing manifestos, signing petitions, speaking—but supporting and advancing other writers who were doing important work, not just by publishing them, but in whatever ways seemed necessary. Not only did he always pay royalties on time—itself an unusual practice for such struggling small publishers, and many large publishers as well—he had even sent advances to Gregory Corso in Europe and to Ginsberg when they needed money, and encouraged them and other writers to use City Lights as a San Francisco mail-message-meeting place. By the late fifties he and City Lights had come to serve as just that literary-political-cultural center he'd always intended for the community of writers centered around it. For him the store and the press weren't bounded by the door of 261 Columbus or the study in his Wisconsin Street house on Potrero Hill.

Now in June, when Kerouac wrote to Ferlinghetti describing his suffering in Northport—phlebitis, stomach cramps, insomnia, nightmares, and general attacks of depression and craziness—Ferlinghetti invited him to come out to his Big Sur cabin to get away. Kerouac jumped at the chance, half of him craving isolation, half just wanting escape, and eager also to work with Ferlinghetti on his manuscript. In mid-July he came out to San Francisco, having arranged with Ferlinghetti to call him from the airport, where Ferlinghetti would pick him up and get him on the road to Bixby without telling anyone he was coming. That way, Kerouac figured he would avoid the temptation of his San Francisco drinking buddies and get right to work. It seemed a great idea back in Northport, but when Kerouac got to San Francisco, Ferlinghetti waited in vain for the call to pick him up. Instead, Ferlinghetti ran into him hours later at Vesuvio's bar, across the alley from City Lights.

After a two-day drunk in the city, Kerouac finally took a bus to Monterey late Sunday night, then a cab to Bixby, where he wandered about the meadow with his railroad lantern looking for the cabin until he gave up and fell asleep. Ferlinghetti had come down for the weekend and discovered him a short distance from the cabin the next morning. That afternoon he took Kerouac into Monterey to buy enough groceries to last three weeks, at which point the plan was for Ferlinghetti to come down for another weekend, when Kerouac would take a break, and they would stock up for another three-week stretch. Leaving Kerouac installed with the "Book of Dreams" galleys to correct, Ferlinghetti went back to the city.

Though Kerouac may have done some writing, he was too nervous and high-strung to take the isolation for the full three weeks, and after a little more than two weeks, made his way back to San Francisco for another siege of drinking and partying. On the third weekend, when Ferlinghetti had planned to go back to Bixby, he drove his Jeep down with Shig Murao, following Kerouac, Lew Welch, and Whalen to Neal Cassady's house in Los Gatos. They had planned to meet Henry Miller in Carmel—Miller had written a favorable introduction for Kerouac's novel *The Subterraneans*—but they went out for pizza with Cassady, and Kerouac got so drunk he missed the meeting.

Ferlinghetti had admired Miller's work since the forties, and he lived in a cabin at Parlington Ridge, only fifteen miles from Ferlinghetti's, but he was a notorious recluse. When Ginsberg had written from San Francisco asking if he could drop in, Miller's response had been short and curt: "Dear Friend. Please do not drop in." He did later agree to meet Ferlinghetti, however, perhaps because they were neighbors, and Ferlinghetti arrived with a bottle of French wine, knowing "that was the only way an outsider would be welcome." Ferlinghetti had some hope that he might publish something of Miller's, but Miller seemed completely uninterested in City Lights or in any of the literary activity going on in San Francisco. He did, however, urge Ferlinghetti to find out about publishing work by French fiction writer Albert Cossery. Ferlinghetti followed up and found that Cossery's *Men God Forgot*, a collection of Egyptian stories for which he was best known, was out of print and available, and he added it to City Lights' 1961 list.

At the cabin they were all joined as well by actor Victor Wong and by Michael McClure and his wife and daughter. They had a log-chopping contest—which Ferlinghetti won—and a cookout on the beach; altogether a fine evening. The next day they went to a nearby hot-springs bathhouse owned by one of Kerouac's friends.

Kerouac went back and forth to San Francisco again over the next weeks that August, with stops at Cassady's in Los Gatos, drinking and keeping company with a woman Cassady had set him up with. Then, after a drink-inspired night of nightmares at Bixby, he wound up back in San Francisco. At that point Ferlinghetti counseled him to drink burgundy instead of the sweet wine that was making him sick and to eat plenty of fruit and cheese. He shaved Kerouac; Wong cleaned him up, then took him to his own father. Wong's father advised him to go to the mountains and become a Zen monk, writing and drinking as much as he wanted. Not surprisingly Kerouac was incapable of heeding the advice. Ferlinghetti then suggested it might be best for Kerouac to return to Massachusetts and his mother there. At the beginning of September he stayed for two or three days in the attic at Wisconsin Street (Kirby remembers him perpetually drunk), before Ferlinghetti took him to the airport and a plane back east.

In an intense, Benzedrine-fueled ten-night streak a year later, Kerouac would write his novel *Big Sur* about his six weeks there that summer. In it he would characterize "Lorenzo Monsanto," a fictionalized Ferlinghetti, as a "genial businessman," in Ferlinghetti's phrase. Though it is ostensibly fiction, Kerouac's characters were known for being as close to authentic transcriptions as he could create, and it is a characterization Ferlinghetti continues to resent. In fact, both the characterization and Ferlinghetti's attitude underline again his own distance from those Beats with whom he is so automatically associated by media.

Though Kerouac and Ferlinghetti were hardly in touch again after that summer, "Kerouac felt ambivalence toward everyone," Ginsberg says, insisting that "Kerouac formed an enduring respect" for Ferlinghetti, and "still relied on Larry as sort of elder or father figure and publisher and refuge provider."

And Ferlinghetti relates that the month before Kerouac died in 1969, Kerouac offered him the chance to publish *The Legend of Duluoz*. But it was a novel Kerouac had never been able to complete, and "he called me up at three in the morning from Florida, and wanted me to say on the phone that I would publish the whole thing uncut—without even seeing the manuscript. He said he wouldn't even send it unless I told him on the phone we'd publish it." Of course, Ferlinghetti could not make such a commitment.

As for *Book of Dreams*, the final version that City Lights published in 1961 was less than half the original manuscript Kerouac had sent, and Ferlinghetti says, "I see it now as pretty stupid. I should have published the whole thing." Still, he was clearly pleased to add what he was sure was a unique and important work by another major writer to the City Lights list.

Besides the Kerouac and Cossery books, he also published Edward Dahlberg's *Bottom Dogs* in 1961, an out-of-print novel by a writer with a large underground following, and *Kaddish and Other Poems*, containing Ginsberg's long title poem on the death of his mother, which many critics think his best. At the same time, two other editorial projects engaged him, one involving McClure and young poet David Meltzer, who had approached Ferlinghetti with an idea for another magazine. Ferlinghetti joined them as coeditor, producing the first issue of the *Journal for the Protection of All Beings* at City Lights. Subtitled "Love-Shot Issue," it was to be a "Visionary Revolutionary Review." The thrust here was directly political, and though more "professional"-looking than *Beatitude*, it like-wise envisioned a kind of populist dialogue which the editors hoped would appeal to a broader audience. The editor's statement said, "We hope we have here an open place where normally apolitical men may speak un-censored upon any subject they feel most hotly & cooly about in a world which politics has made.

"We are not interested in protecting beings from themselves, we cannot help the deaths people give themselves, we are more concerned with the lives they do not allow themselves to live and the deaths other people would give us, both of the body & spirit."

In keeping with the sense of threat the magazine was conceived to address, the copyright page carried the notice: "Due to the transitory nature of life on earth this Journal is not sold on a subscription basis."

The eclectic collection of readings all spoke to this theme, and it took some time for the editors to assemble contributions they liked. Meltzer wrote a piece called "Journal of the Birth," for which the printer refused to print "various anatomical explicatives," as Meltzer described them. Ferlinghetti then said he would take the entire job away from the printer in protest, but when they discovered how much such a move would cost at such a late stage of production, they decided, grudgingly, to compro-mise. The settlement caused them, in Meltzer's words, "to insert Victorian dashes between the first and last letters of the offending words."

Finally, however, the magazine was released with a star-studded cast of contributors. Norman Mailer offered "An Open Letter to JFK & Castro," attacking U.S. policy toward Cuba and accusing the media of distorting the truth about the situation there. Other contributors included Thomas Merton, Bertrand Russell, Gary Snyder, Gregory Corso, Robert Duncan, and a three-way conversation among Ginsberg, Burroughs, and Orlovsky, who were in Tangier. The issue also included a group of documents, including Nez Percé Chief Joseph's surrender speech (". . . Hear me, my chiefs. I am tired; my heart is sick and sad. From where the sun now stands, I will fight no more forever") and a "Declaration of Rights" by Percy Bysshe Shelley (beginning, "Government has no rights; it is a delegation from several individuals for the purpose of securing their own").

These and similar sentiments located the magazine within the anarchist-pacifist tradition articulated by Rexroth and other literary-political activists whom Ferlinghetti had known and associated with since his early days in San Francisco.

The other editorial project was equally a reflection of his activist side. Titled simply *City Lights Journal*, it was conceived to be an annual. The first issue contained work by Kerouac and Burroughs, but the majority of the magazine was given to writers who were new or little known at the time. Ed Dorn and Daniel Moore were among them, along with poet Harold Norse, whose early collections were among the first paperback poetry originals Grove Press had published in 1957. Also included was fiction writer Richard Brautigan, who had been writing and reading his poetry around North Beach since the fifties, even selling copies of his poems for small change on street corners. Three sections of Brautigan's strange, inviting, deceptively simple *Trout Fishing in America* appeared; it was an important early exposure for him that helped open the way to a wider audience, and to publication of that novel in 1967, as well as his previously written comic *Confederate General in Big Sur* in 1964. Both of them became best-sellers, and by the late sixties, Brautigan's following had grown from a tiny cult to a huge section of the swelling counterculture, rivaling that of Ginsberg and Ferlinghetti himself.

The centerpiece of the issue, however, came as the result of Ginsberg's and Snyder's Indian adventures. The cover was a picture of Ginsberg, beardless, wrapped in a blanket, somewhere in India. Inside, he introduced poets of the "Hungry Generation" he had met in his travels there, and Snyder contributed a prose travelogue, "A Journey to Rishikesh and Hardwar."

For Ferlinghetti these projects were a natural extension of his political awareness; and now, with the new wave of civil rights activism and the heating of the cold war, this kind of awareness was beginning to spread. Still, despite all the work involved in these enterprises, Ferlinghetti's creative impulse wasn't channeled entirely into publishing and editing. In 1962 his own writing took another new turn.

"What turned me on to doing it was a couple things," he said in a 1963 interview. "I read Kenneth Tynan's book of criticism called *Curtains* and realized what wasn't being done in the modern theater. There's a hiatus there too. Nothing is happening. Where are the great playwrights in this country—after the generation of Miller and Tennessee Williams? . . . They've got all these theater groups but they keep having to import British and French plays. There don't seem to be any great young playwrights. And the European theater, even Beckett, hasn't really been brought over into this country by playwrights. Play groups bring them over and produce the original works, but there doesn't seem to be any continuation in what is being done over here by playwrights."

Ferlinghetti was excited by possibilities Tynan's book suggested of doing something larger than the representational American theater, which was a dead end as far as he could see. At the Caffe Trieste he began to write the one-act plays, continuing the work at his Wisconsin Street study. Less than a year later he had finished nine of them, which he sent to New Directions with the title *Unfair Arguments with Existence*.

As with the novel, what interested him was the European avant-garde—Breton's *Nadja*, the theater of Eugene Ionesco, of Jean Genet, of Samuel Beckett, and especially of Antonin Artaud. Though Artaud had repeatedly spent time in insane asylums through his life, and his plays weren't very successful, many found his ideas powerful. His "Theater of Cruelty" was particularly influential to Genet, Ionesco, Beckett, and other writers.

"Everything that acts is a cruelty," Artaud had written in *The Theater and Its Double*. "It is upon this idea of extreme action, pushed beyond all limits, that theatre must be rebuilt." His idea was to utilize the whole arena—stage, auditorium, audience—instead of relying so heavily on language, and by so doing to break down the barrier between actor and audience. He wanted to make the events on stage dramatic equivalents of emotional states. In the same work he said, "The theatre restores to us all our dormant conflicts and all their powers, and gives these powers names we hail as symbols—and behold! Before our eyes is fought a battle of symbols . . . for there can be theatre only from the moment when the impossible really begins and when the poetry that occurs on the stage sustains and superheats the realized symbols."

It was a theater of confrontation, of sensation, where what happened on stage challenged, even offended, the audience. The end was to be an epiphany of some kind: an emotional and spiritual realization which would transcend any ordinary, passive theatrical experience, and heighten both the actors' and the audience's sense of life.

In 1962 Ferlinghetti made plans with Jack Hirschman to publish a large collection of Artaud's works. Hirschman was teaching at Dartmouth when Ferlinghetti had come there for a reading in 1960, and they had met then. In the next four years, influenced partly by his friend Anaïs Nin, "and most of all by the visionary avant-garde and narcotic texture of those Kennedy–pre-Vietnam days," Hirschman remembers, he assembled the texts by Artaud that became *The Artaud Anthology* that City Lights published in 1965. Ferlinghetti's support of experimental theater also led to his publication of work by Julian Beck and the European Living Theatre Company and by other playwrights.

Though he saw the plays in *Unfair Arguments* as "moving progressively from the representational toward a purely non-objective theatre," even "The Soldiers of No Country" (the first play, whose idea came from his adventure to Ensenada) is hardly the "exercise in conventional realism" he termed it in his introduction to the collection. The "womb-like cave" where the four misfits of the play find a sort of shelter is located nowhere (or anywhere); and the characters themselves play out a desperate, damaged parody of human roles. He had absorbed the ideas of Artaud and the other avant-garde playwrights completely, and all the plays demonstrate this "new theater" he was working to create.

With the encouragement of Laughlin and others, Ferlinghetti continued working in his newly discovered form. Just six months later, in July 1964, he finished another collection of a dozen even shorter plays he called *Routines*, written entirely at a back table at the Trieste. Even less dramatic in the conventional theatrical sense, he saw these theater works as part of a "Third Stream Theater," as he termed it in the introduction to that collection. This third stream lay "between Well Made Plays (with their coherent pictures of coherent worlds which now turn out to be the falsest) and those free form Happenings made of primitive perceptual chaos. . . ." The theater, he went on, was a theater of transition "from all this so-necessary dramatic anarchism to pure Poetic Action not necessarily logical or rational but with, at best, that kind of inexpressible inchoate meaning that springs from wild surmises of the imagination."

Despite Ferlinghetti's prominence as a poet, however, and the plays' grounding on the frontiers of serious writing, they didn't receive the kind of major attention he hoped for them. One problem was no doubt their very experimental nature. Most were too brief for conventional productions, and in genuine avant-garde tradition, they just didn't have the kind of immediate accessibility that helped make his poetry so popular.

In June 1962 "The Alligation," probably the most producible of any, was performed at the San Francisco Poetry Festival, and again in November and December at the Hamlet in Houston, Texas. In the next decade that and other plays were given numerous performances by small theater groups across the country, and in 1970 three of them were finally given eight performances in New York City and reviewed by established theater critics.

Clive Barnes in the *New York Times* had some praise for the themes, saying they were "vast and gutsy, and they talk . . . about the decay and dissolution of our civilization." But his criticism was also severe: "They are windy allegories set on some far horizon of poetic sensibility." And John Simon, writing in *New York* magazine, seemed not quite to know what to make of them. He found a "mildly poetic, markedly absurdist, satirical but arcane atmosphere in all of them" that made them variously "diffuse," "smilingly impenetrable," "fairly obvious," and "flirting with opacity."

None of these productions, nor those since, ran more than a few days. A main reason Ferlinghetti's third-stream theater never succeeded much beyond this limited exposure, however, probably had less to do with its avant-garde nature than that Ferlinghetti himself remained outside the theater world and had no association with any company or acting group to hone the plays through performance as playwrights invariably do. Nonetheless, his enthusiasm continued into the sixties and was reflected in some of the contributors to future issues of *City Lights Journal*—Artaud, Julian Beck, Barbara Garson, Kenneth Brown, Alexandro Jodorowski, and others all have plays or theoretical essays in the issues published in 1964 and 1966.

His immersion in avant-garde theater at the time may also have been one of the sources of his enthusiasm for the journey he took between the writing of the two collections. After completing *Unfair Arguments*, he returned to the cradle of that avant-garde which had so captured him initially and in which he was now completely immersed again. In the last eight years Ginsberg, Corso, Burroughs, Kerouac—writers he knew well and associated with—had all been to Europe and beyond. Ferlinghetti, however, hadn't been overseas since leaving France in 1950. Now, with the store in Murao's competent hands, and his own books of poetry enormously successful, he had the means and the time to taste some of the adventures of traveling himself.

With two children under two years old, it would have been difficult for the whole family to travel, and not surprisingly Kirby "wasn't too enthusiastic," as Ferlinghetti put it, about his leaving. But she was a full-time mother, and her experiences in Latin America hadn't exactly whetted her taste for overseas adventure, either. On the other hand, Ferlinghetti's career must have seemed to him to justify (if not require) this trip as much as any "business" trip was required of someone in the commercial world. For the point was discovery, as much as it was pleasure—and the pleasure was equally important and necessary for his writing. As a successful poet, his time was much in demand in San Francisco. In order to continue to "make it new," as Ezra Pound had commanded, he had to break away periodically from the demands of home and its routine to get a fresh view. Though he didn't necessarily see it in these terms, the trip would be a return to what was both a geographical and a spiritual center, a reconnection as important as his journey to the West Indies had been. Thus, in late May, like his isolated, alienated characters, Ferlinghetti went alone, back to his youth, to what was in so many ways a source of his creative energy.

On the way to Paris he stopped first in London, visiting the Tate Gallery, and seeing Pablo Armando Fernández, now in London as a diplomatic officer. He spent one entire day with Fernández, walking from the upper-class beginning of Portobello Road with its expensive furniture and antique stores, to the end in a West Indian neighborhood with its market full of plantains, guavas, and tropical fruit.

But the most interesting aspect of his London stay was probably his visit to William Burroughs, some of whose work he wanted to publish. Burroughs was living in a basement apartment on Lancaster Terrace, and in his journal Ferlinghetti recorded the visit in some detail:

> I go to see Wm. Burroughs underground. He too under glass. Two floors down, in a subbasement with no windows but a French door leading nowhere but onto a concrete triangular area like an airshaft. He says it's convenient for his cat who craps there. In the little room there is only a couch, a small table, a portable typewriter, no books in sight. The cat is there. There is an alcove. He serves me some tea out of it. Burroughs

receives me like T. S. Eliot. He is alive. He came up the winding basement steps and let me in, saying he didn't hear much "down here." (I'd had to knock many times.) He's perfectly dressed, a British accent, etc. . . . I look around & ask him what he does down here "all the time." He looks at me straight & says "Just work." It's cheap, he says, and explains to me his money difficulties & adds that he's soon going to Tangier, via Paris, where he has to pick up some money. He doesn't say "Bread" for money, or any of that jazz. Talking about people in Tangier, he says so-and-so are always Bad News wherever you run into them—always getting "arrested." He doesn't say "busted," etc. . . . He gets up and closes door to concrete outside & lights a joss stick of some kind of cheap incense & sticks the end of it in the tapestry or wallpaper, saying, "the cat-crap gets to smelling out there." We agree to publish a book. I tell him I never really dug his writing until the "Soft Machine." . . . He agrees to come to a party . . . I leave. It's dusk outside in Lancaster Terrace. There are lilacs in bloom in the great park. Burroughs is underground.

Then on May 30, 1963, at eleven at night, he arrived at the Gare du Nord in Paris. He had no particular agenda; his business seems to have been only to touch again a significant part of his past, to measure how far he had come. His journal records that he thought about other women and past lovers, and his writing was suffused with sexual energy, but his interest was not in an affair. As an orphan, who for most of his formative years had been disconnected and isolated, connection with the past which had been mostly lost was not so much a frivolous luxury, but an effort to bridge the chasm of that wound, though he would not have thought of it that way. It is a healing that is always imperfect and incomplete at best, but it was an effort toward the kind of continuity and wholeness most take for granted.

Of course Paris had changed: "Already I'm getting used to this new brighter Paris and already hardly remember the image of the old Paris," he wrote on his third day there. But there was the same dreamy quality to it, or at least to his days there. He walked down the old streets, visited the old places, even went up to the two-room basement apartment he lived in while at the Sorbonne, and rang the bell. No one answered, however; what he learned was what most who take such journeys learn, what his onetime hero Thomas Wolfe learned when he wrote, "You can't

go home again": the streets, the buildings, the people were all there—
but the place was gone.

For the first week the overwhelming sensation all the time that he
recorded was of loneliness.

"The city itself doesn't exist," he wrote in his journal. "It's a dream I
once had. It's a dark place, lost in memory. . . . And such a city of wild
loneliness. . . . Impossible that everyone in Paris could be as lonely as I
always am when I am here! All of a sudden, each time, I become aware
of a great lump of loneliness which seems to have been growing inside
of my body for years and years and only now I discover its real presence
and enormous size. Impossible to cut it out! It's too immense, it's too
boney, too supple, too aqueous, being the body itself. . . ."

But after several days of wandering the streets of Paris and finding
"not a face I've ever seen before," he concluded that "one needs other
people, perhaps especially women, to construct one's own special illusion
of life. . . . The Taxis of the Marne are gone for good. . . ."

After a week, he spent an evening with two acquaintances, then an all-
night session "turned on" with twenty-four-year-old Jean-Jacques Lebel,
who had begun translating some of the Beat writing for an anthology he
would publish two years later. Lebel's father had written a major biography
of artist Marcel Duchamp, and Lebel was a painter and writer himself,
so Ferlinghetti and he had much in common. Further, Lebel had been
born in France but spoke fluent, Brooklyn-accented English, as well as
Italian (he had gone to school in Italy). He and his family had spent the
war years in New York when he was very young, along with other French
surrealists who went to New York after Hitler arrived in France.

On June 7 Ferlinghetti left Paris by train for Limoges and Périgueux
in the Dordogne. He went on to Les Eyzies in the Dordogne and looked
up a sculptor who invited him to stay with his wife and four-year-old son.
Ferlinghetti stayed for two days, sleeping amid his statues ("Head of Jean
Genet looking down when I awoke"), and met a paleontologist who was
digging in old caves in Dordogne, but found him "a car salesman of some
kind in disguise." He might have stayed longer, but was bothered by the
strained relationship between the sculptor and his wife, caused in part,
he thought, by their isolation there.

After his short stay he traveled south for a brief visit to Madrid and
the Prado. He spent a night trying to sleep "out in the coche" in Algeciras,
filled with images from Bosch, Dali, Goya, and Burroughs's *Naked Lunch*,
then after a couple days went down to Tangier, where Burroughs had
lived while writing *Naked Lunch* and which Ginsberg had visited during

the *Howl* trial and again a few years later. He was immediately taken with its exoticism: "fantastic world, strange city . . . overheard conversational mummeries in six languages, kif-pipe everywhere, veiled women making eyes & cruising the Medina & Casbah, the skin of sun, the vaccine of dreaming, came to the edge clear and bright, several scenes I passed through (the celluloid streaming). . . ."

He stayed a week, and went south to Asilah, on the Atlantic Coast, where he visited fiction writer Paul Bowles, one of the inspirations for Ginsberg's and others' explorations, and his wife, Jane, also a fiction writer and playwright. Bowles had lived in Tangier and North Africa off and on since the 1930s, had published three critically praised novels, including the best-selling *The Sheltering Sky*, numerous short stories, travel articles and translations, and had written music for Broadway, for playwright Tennessee Williams, and for others.

When Ginsberg had been in Tangier with Corso and Burroughs in 1961, he had urged Bowles to send some stories to Ferlinghetti to publish, and in 1962, City Lights had published *One Hundred Camels in the Courtyard*, a collection of four stories, all related to the power of the cannabis drug kif to alter consciousness and open the way to enlightenment.

"I was sitting around with Bowles, and he wasn't saying a thing," Ferlinghetti recalls. "Jane finally said, well, why don't you at least offer him some dope. So he said, I don't have any. I think he thought I was a narc. Not really, but . . . I think I was just a straight from the outer world as far as he could see." The encounter, like that with Burroughs, is another indication of how far removed Ferlinghetti felt himself, and felt others saw him, from the Beat center and its immersion in such exotic regions.

After leaving Tangier and Asilah, he headed on to Rabat, Casablanca, and Marrakech, where he stayed two more days, then went to Tunis, immersed in the poverty, the sounds, sights, smells of the Arab world. He wanted to go on to see Sicily, but couldn't make connections, so flew to Rome. When he left North Africa, he noted, "There's always one further place, one stage further away from everything, one further port still untouched or underpopulated. . . . In Tangiers, it's Asilah (a fishing port twenty miles out); in Marrakech, there's the Sahara further south; in Majorca there's still Minorca (or is there); in France there's still—?, etc. etc."

After a night and day in Rome he flew back to France and went to St.-Tropez, where he looked up Albert Cossery, and spent a day on the beach with him and some friends of his. Then, with five days left on his month Eurail pass, he went on to Marseilles, Toulouse, and Rodez before returning again to Paris to read with Harold Norse at the American Centre in Montparnasse. The July 2 event was organized by Lebel, one of a long series of multi-arts festivals and happenings Lebel would present under varying names in the next twenty-five years. The crowd there was large and enthusiastic, and Ferlinghetti recorded having a "fantastic two days" in Paris.

During his month-long odyssey, he had experienced extremes of loneliness, had revisited a part of his past, had celebrated with friends, had explored the exotic capitals of North Africa. Though he kept regular journals, he wrote no new poems, and what he learned seemed to be no concentrated revelation, but a texture, an accumulation of experience that remained now, steeping, to inform the work and the life he resumed when he returned. That work included, not least, the new group of plays—*Routines*—that he set to work at almost immediately.

On July 4 he made the flight back, and in San Francisco began work as well on the second *City Lights Journal*, which would come out in 1964. This one featured on the cover a picture of seventy-eight-year-old Ezra Pound. Italian journalist Grazia Livi's interview with Pound was inside as well as "A Few Bengali Poets," another section selected and introduced by Ginsberg.

Ferlinghetti's own contribution to the second issue demonstrated again his passion for the underdog and for the necessity of free expression. It was an open letter soliciting help for Maurice Girodias, the French publisher of Olympia Press who had been arrested in Paris. Girodias was known for printing pornography, but also for publishing the first English-language editions of works by Genet, Beckett, Durrell, Nabokov, Burroughs, Henry Miller, Corso, "and others now famous or infamous." The engagement in the affairs of the world which had drawn Ferlinghetti to Rexroth, to the Committee for the Defense of the Refregier Murals, to the Fair Play for Cuba Committee, to the very idea of City Lights Books and the Pocket Poets series, and which separated him so sharply from the cool indifference the media associated with the Beats, continued to be right at the surface of everything he did. But the radical, iconoclastic position it was often thought to be was gaining new adherents throughout the growing postwar, baby-boom generation. By the end of 1964 the disengagement of the Beat Generation had reduced to pop-culture memorabilia.

The final seal to its end occurred that fall of 1963 just across the Bay. In late summer the University of California at Berkeley had taken steps banning the solicitation of students for off-campus political or civil rights demonstrations. In response, students spanning the full gamut of political ideology—from far left Maoists to ultraconservative Goldwaterites—banded together to form the Free Speech Movement, or FSM. Mario Savio, a twenty-two-year-old philosophy major from Manhattan, led the group in accusing the university Board of Regents of a conspiracy to turn out white-collar drones who would mindlessly serve "the establishment"—banks, corporations, the great American institutions of business.

"The time has come to put our bodies on the machine and stop it!" he shouted.

In September police dragged eight hundred howling followers out of Sproul Hall, the Berkeley administration building, in an attempt to quash once and for all such upstart behavior. Sproul Hall was turned back to the university administration this time, but the movement itself, and others like it, which it helped inspire, only spread. "The Sixties" had begun in earnest.

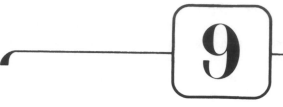

9

"The artists are the antennae of the race," Ezra Pound said in "The Teacher's Mission," a 1934 essay. The analogy calls up the antenna's function of receiver of electronic signals, impulses neither perceptible nor comprehensible to average humans, but which the antenna transmits to other mechanisms—radio, television—which in turn decodes them and makes them comprehensible. Thus the artist, and Pound had in mind particularly the poet, receives and transmits to his fellow humans these signals, messages from other antennae, from elsewhere in the culture, the world at large, even outer space.

This claim for the special function of poets which assigns them to the cultural vanguard may be presumptive, but there is no doubt that poets have been frequently in the forefront of exploration, both personal and cultural. From William Blake and Samuel Taylor Coleridge, whose drug-induced visions shaped poems which are still taught to schoolchildren as part of the foundation of our literature, to Ginsberg's peyote-inspired vision of the Canaanite fire god, Moloch, in "Howl," this exploration has been thought the sovereign province, even the duty, of artists. Their work is the very license to test the limits, balance on the edge. Living lives outside the scope of the normal everyday (as an antenna rises above the surrounding landscape), they give a kind of news about the state of the culture, its issues and concerns; they warn, cajole, prophesize, condemn, inspire.

Or so the mythos goes, at least in America, at least in the second half of the twentieth century. In the 1963 interview that Ferlinghetti published in the second *City Lights Journal*, Pound said, "I believe that the young poet must have an uninterrupted curiosity. That is not sure to be enough to make a writer out of him, but it can, if nothing else, save him from being dried up. The possibility of doing something important depends on that persistent energy." It is of course that persistent energy and curiosity that pushes artists into the position where they may be antennae.

For nearly a decade Ferlinghetti had been building the bookstore and the press as well as doing his own writing. Since the mid-fifties, Shig Murao had assumed most of the day-to-day responsibility for the store; sometime after the *Howl* trial, Ferlinghetti made him a partner, and under his management the store was running well. Its reputation, like Ferlinghetti's, was national among any with interest in current literature. In the late fifties he had also hired two brothers, Bob and Dick McBride, to help with the publishing end. But since *A Coney Island of the Mind* had established Ferlinghetti's reputation as a poet, and invitations to travel and to read arrived steadily from all over the country, the responsibilities of the bookstore, despite Shig's handling of the daily operations, had become something of a burden. In April of 1961 Ferlinghetti had written to James Laughlin about the possibility of selling the store, even inquiring if New Directions might like to buy it. Though nothing came of the inquiry, and Ferlinghetti never seriously pursued such a move, the restlessness—and the curiosity which fed it—were evident in the gesture.

Ever since he read Thomas Wolfe, the attractions of travel, of diverse experience, had stimulated him; but unlike many who are charged in youth by such appetites, take a few excursions, then settle into some version of respectability, Ferlinghetti's curiosity, like any artist's, was never so simply assuaged. Hitchhiking to Mexico while in college, shipping out in the Navy, studying in Paris, and traveling in Western Europe were all adventures that only planted more potent seeds. And as these travels continued to inspire his writing, Wolfe's sprawling vision of the American landscape, Eliot's internal journey of transcendence in *Four Quartets*, and the diverse energies of Europe, particularly Paris, established the personal and literary poles to which he found himself drawn again and again.

At the same time, the ongoing news from friends like Ginsberg about travels, both internal and external, must have helped further to intensify the call to such adventures. Though Ferlinghetti may not any longer have been a "young poet," the elderly Pound's charge clearly applies to writers of any age. Certainly this kind of consecutive thinking wasn't what led to Ferlinghetti's decisions to travel more and more, to explore the reaches of consciousness that were increasingly at the forefront of the times, but his choices were just as surely a product of such forces. Simply put, he traveled more and more, and immersed himself further and further into the explorations of the times, both because he was keenly attracted to such frontiers and because he could.

In February 1965 he began another extended trip to Europe, this time with his whole family. For the first three weeks he rented a house in Nerja, Spain, some thirty miles east of Málaga. At the time, Nerja itself was a small coastal town of about three thousand, not yet overrun by "turismo," and he found the house, about a block from where the poet Federico García Lorca had kept a summer house, by simply walking around and inquiring after they arrived. The house was in a beautiful setting, on the unpaved Calle Caribeo, a "dirt street full of big rocks and broken cobbles, on cliffs over the beach," as he reported in his journal on February 21, and with its white walls, tile floors, and tiny terrace overlooking the street, it must have seemed quaint and charming. But it was also very small—only twenty feet wide, with three small rooms.

An extended vacation was part of the plan, but as always, so was the business of seeing and recording what could be seen. Despite the apparently idyllic setting, things did not go very well, at least the first week—the house was cold, and the weather was "too cold and windy to do anything but huddle in house over smokey fire of madera wood & charcoal." The situation was made even worse by "terrific racket all day" from street repairs and blasting for a sewage drain.

On March 15 they moved to a much larger, two-story house a little farther down the same street "with six big bedrooms, a big dining room & kitchen, a single bathroom with cold water, a sink in the kitchen made of a piece of marble, a big long empty studio upstairs and a tile veranda downstairs opening onto a vegetable & fruit garden that takes up all the land of the houses on each side." A peach tree was in bloom in the garden, and the whole scene seems altogether closer to the idyllic circumstances of the Mediterranean vacation they might at first have imagined.

While they were there, they made side trips to some nearby caves, to Granada, to Málaga ("in search of books and bookstores"), and to Sevilla (where Ferlinghetti stopped at Las Escobas tavern, frequented by the likes of Cervantes and Lord Byron), all of which certainly must have made the trip feel like a vacation. But his own solitary, estranged side, an inextricable part of him, was still equally present. In the brief "Darkness, in Granada," which he wrote at the time, he lamented, "O if I were not so unhappy / I could write great poetry!" and invoked García Lorca, who was killed in the 1930s in the Spanish Civil War. The lament must be taken partly as tongue-in-cheek, of course—such an "if-then" cause-effect claim is an obviously affected juvenile voice—but there's no reason to assume the unhappiness that initiates the poem wasn't a genuine feeling.

As always, he was interested in the political situation in the country he was visiting, and during the first part of the spring, read George Orwell's *Homage to Catalonia* about the politics of the Spanish Civil War. At the same time, his political sentiments led to one of his first prose poems, "Telegram from Spain," predictably critical of the dictator Franco, whose fascist forces had won the Civil War and who still held power. The poem imagines that "THE GENERALISSIMO ROSE & SANK FROM SIGHT UNDER THE WEIGHT OF HIS OWN MEDALS MADE OF MERDE & IRONY POLITICAL VEGETARIANS FORCED AT LAST TO FEED ON THE GREAT PORKER HIMSELF. . . ."

Ferlinghetti's sympathy with Castro and revolutionary movements in general had little to do with any Marxist politics; rather, his Rexroth-inspired readings during the fifties had led him to embrace the philosophical anarchism of Herbert Read, which was rooted in a deep-seated mistrust of all governments and their incursions on individual freedom. Reading *Homage*, he was "struck with the similarity [of the Communist Party in Spain in the 1930s] to the position of the Cuban Communist Party at the time of the Cuban Revolution, 1959 or earlier, when the Communists were much to the Right of the Revolutionary (25 of July Movement) Party of Fidel Castro whose barbudos were true revolutionaries in the sense that the working class militiamen in Barcelona were in the early days of the Spanish Civil War."

Though his inherent romanticism informed his views, his analytical side was aware of the tendency to see through that romantic filter of revolutionary enthusiasm, and the way his own expectations about the political situation affected his perceptions. In another entry he noted:

> It is true, as has often been said about foreign correspondents, that we make up our own picture of things to suit our own ideas. We see what we want to see (re: most reports in the U.S. press from Cuba), the would-be revolutionary sees the Revolution as a glorious, euphoric fulfillment, the conservative or reactionary sees it as a tyranny & police state (which is robbing the vested interests). Were this Revolutionary Cuba here, I would no doubt have reported that there were fewer Guardia Civil in evidence "than there are police on the streets of San Francisco" (which

is what I wrote from Cuba in 1961) and that they were on the whole clean cut, innocent-looking, friendly fellows, rather like the young & goofy-looking guard in fatigues I saw guarding Fidel in Havana in 1961. He too carried a little machine-gun over his shoulder. . . . The difference is the Revolution here never happened.

When two Málaga poets with some official standing came to visit, Ferlinghetti was characteristically uninterested in literary small talk, but questioned them about the climate for writing under Franco. Alfonso Canales had just been appointed to the Spanish Royal Academy in Madrid; Rafael León, the other, assured Ferlinghetti that they, and all poets, were free to write whatever they wanted. But at the same time, they admitted that the leading literary reviews in Spain had to pass Franco's censors, a contradiction Ferlinghetti noted in his journal.

As in his journey to Mexico, he was also conscious of the growing tourist industry and both sides of its effects on the pristine charm of the region: "government 'paradors' or resort hotels being rapidly built up and down the Mediterranean Coast, one in Nerja looking like a harmonica, is almost finished on the cliffs above the biggest beach, with a colony of Miami-type duplex houses rising up behind it. . . . Down the coast, on the others side of Málaga, is Torremolinos . . . another picturesque fishing port which has already been turned into a junior version of Miami Beach. This is probably the last year for Nerja and its old way of life. . . ."

But in the same entry, he noted that his regret for the passage of the quaint was probably not shared by the majority who faced the harsher economic facts. "The townspeople," he wrote, "may well be happy to get rid of most of the features of their 'old way of life'—poverty, not enough food and clothing, no plumbing, open sewers, charcoal braziers for cooking, little wood to burn, unpaved streets, no more than a hundred really good houses in a town of ten thousand."

Not surprisingly, given his political interests, Ferlinghetti worked on a long political poem attacking the repressiveness of Franco's military dictatorship. Over the weeks, he built it to some twenty pages in his notebook, but he was never able to satisfactorily complete it. Nonetheless, his political consciousness was stirred and widened by what he saw and did. Though the trip was on the one hand an escape, it was equally an immersion in sights and sounds of the wider world.

As the spring wore on, Kirby began suffering from allergies that irritated an asthmatic condition, another cause for the less than idyllic tone in their days. Her condition worsened, and in the first week of May the Ferlinghettis left Nerja and went to Paris, where they bought a cheap used car and drove to Brittany. Their idea was that the rocky coast with its stone houses would be free of the pollen that plagued Kirby. Near Quimper they rented a completely stone house and tried to settle in, but after ten days Kirby's allergies were as bad as ever, and just as the Cuban fleas had driven her home early during their 1961 visit there, so now she felt she couldn't remain in Europe. They went back to Paris, and Lawrence put Kirby and the children on a plane back to Florida.

"I waved good-bye to him from the plane and didn't see him for three months," she remembers. But the parting was also an indication of a distance between them that had grown far beyond the geographical.

Meanwhile, Ferlinghetti had been invited to read at two international poetry festivals while they were staying in Nerja. The first, scheduled to take place in Paris in mid-May, was the International Festival of Free Expression, organized by Jean-Jacques Lebel. As in his previous trip to Paris, he had many hours to himself before the festival, some marked with the loneliness and nostalgia that he had recorded during his 1963 visit. But at the same time, staying close to Lebel, there were parties and social events surrounding the festival, and much of the sometime magic pervading the mounting counterculture atmosphere of the time and place.

Out on a walk one day before the festival began, Ferlinghetti unexpectedly bumped into his old San Francisco acquaintance Philip Lamantia, who had been in Europe for several years, and a young woman Lamantia had first met in Greece a few months earlier, Nancy Peters. After Lamantia introduced Ferlinghetti to Peters, all three went on to visit Lebel at his flat and spend some hours together. The coincidental meeting would, however, become more than simply a pleasant occasion; though it was five years before Ferlinghetti would again meet Peters, again accidentally on the street, the meeting then would lead to a daily literary and business involvement that would continue to the present.

The festival itself was another in a series of "happenings" Lebel had initiated some five years earlier and had been conducting around Europe. Aiming to break stultified conceptions of art, increasingly dominated by commercial interests, these happenings outraged exactly those commentators who tried to manage public taste, as much as they amused, exhilarated, and plainly *moved* the audiences they involved.

In an interview after his 1965 happening, Lebel explained his idea: ". . . in the [happenings] we have been doing since 1959 in Europe there is a strong necessity to use the artistic language in a specific struggle to survive and that struggle seems not to have been perceived in its correct perspective. We are up against tremendous odds. Organized repression, great invisible brain-washing, computerized patterns of culture. Can we fight all that and still express something illuminating in a private picture or poem? . . . I say that an art which not only leads to action but directly involves action is the only way out. . . .

"What we have been doing with happenings is not just giving people something to look at, we have been giving them *something to do*, something to participate in and create with. We are giving them a language for their hallucinations, desires, and myths. . . ."

His International Festival of Free Expression turned out to be nothing less than wild, and drew some two thousand or more, to participate with the sixty or so performers, as well as major international press coverage. Among the events, Alexandro Jodorowski directed *Sacramental Melodrama*, in which a girl, painted black, washed a girl painted pink, after which the two danced on the roof of a car. Then another girl in a black hood and waders whipped Jodorowski, after which his hair was clipped poodle-style and he was dressed in orange overalls. Then with the black-painted girl tied to him crosswise, he stumbled across the stage while a band played Yiddish music.

Another feature had axes and hammers demolishing a car, then the roar of a motorcycle breaking through the crowd. A nude girl jumped on the bike, which began circling through the audience while she clung to the driver. When she leapt off, the cycle shot on stage while the girl was chased into the audience. Meanwhile, another girl, in bikini and mask, knelt on the roof of the car that had been beaten and crushed in a sort of ritual sacrifice while a boy kneaded her body with spaghetti. Then she began to pick off the spaghetti and throw it at the crowd.

At the end of the first day the director of the American Students and Artists Center, where the festival took place, lamented its outrages and wanted to stop it, but, opposed to censorship and committed to "free expression" himself, felt handcuffed. "If I stop now," he said, "there will be about twenty-eight times the scandal there already is."

The festival went on. The next night a graphic childbirth film was projected backward, in a perfect visual analogue to the adolescent energy fueling the happening and many similar occasions which would follow. Toward the end of the evening, audience members nibbled at girls dressed in cabbage leaves while the girls beat the nibblers over the head with badminton rackets. Then Ferlinghetti read his poem while a couple acted out the motions of sex in a burlap bag. The festival concluded with the sacrifice of another car, the exhausted and exhilarated audience members bearing its dismembered parts home.

It was a kind of art no one had ever seen, though it had its roots in French surrealism and experimental theater; but combined with technology, and on a scale that encompassed its audience, it seemed a whole new public art form was being born. Artists André Breton and Marcel Duchamp came to witness and acknowledge the new form, understanding that these happenings grew clearly from legitimate artistic experiments, while another French critic wrote that "these experiences, without doubt, show that the theater has been profoundly changed."

Lebel, according to reports, saw it all through with the combination of vision and furious energy which would continue to propel similar inventions in the future. Exhilarated at the event, it was probably the most successful, in terms of attention, in the two years he had been organizing them.

"Our generation is inventing a new meaning for revolution," he said in *Time* magazine's account, "a new state of mind based on an enlarged understanding of what freedom means."

Certainly the revolutionary nature of the spectacle must have delighted Ferlinghetti, whose work had from the first been addressing issues of personal and public "liberation." And now that vanguard of which he was part was picking up steam.

While in Paris he was invited to a third international poetry festival on very short notice, this one proving to be even bigger than Lebel's. Scheduled for June 11, at London's Royal Albert Hall, it also was to include Jodorowski as well as Russian poet Andrei Voznesensky, several English poets, Ferlinghetti's old cohorts Ginsberg and Corso, Pablo Armando Fernández, who was now the Cuban cultural officer in London, and Pablo Neruda.

Hearing rumors that Ginsberg, who had recently been expelled from Cuba for writing and speaking in defense of homosexual artists, was going to kill a cock on stage and perform naked, the older, more staid Neruda refused to appear. Some felt that as a Marxist-Stalinist and "elder statesman," Neruda did not want to be associated with such a spectacle. And, they speculate, because of political pressures from their own countries, Fernández and Voznesensky likewise did not perform. But over seven thousand packed the hall to hear their poet heroes, and after all the rumor, Ginsberg read fully dressed, wearing a sport coat. That audience, like so much of the European poetry audience in the sixties and in the decades to come, was made up in large measure of Beat enthusiasts. Even in 1988 Ferlinghetti remarked that at international poetry festivals, almost the only American poets invited seem to be the Beats—Ginsberg, Corso, "and looking through the far end of the telescope" (as he has characterized the view which places him amid the Beats), Ferlinghetti. "More jeans, longer hair, black turtlenecks than any readings in America," he says.

In Europe the breath of fresh air that the Beats represented was even more startling than it had been in America, if that was possible. And perhaps even more important, the new direction it led was, if not always embraced, at least not so resisted by the established artistic and critical community. While conservative academic taste dominated American critical media, leaving the Beats far on the outside despite their popular success, the tradition of the avant-garde was central to the European artistic establishment. Thus the American Beats, who were exploring territories opened up by European surrealists, symbolists, and dadaists, were far more quickly and enthusiastically welcomed there as the newest legitimate incarnation of that rebellious tradition.

The four-hour Albert Hall event with some dozen performers was an unprecedented spectacle, and the poets' presence in London drew major coverage in both the English and American press. *The Times Literary Supplement* declared that the gathering "made literary history by a combination of flair, courage, and seized opportunities." During the evening, according to Alexis Lykiard's account in *Wholly Communion*, the small anthology that grew from the reading, "wierd papier-mache creatures strolled about the aisles; Bruce Lacey's machine structures buzzed, shook, and flashed; poets and hecklers interrupted each other; and a girl in a white dress danced under the pall of potsmoke with distant gestures of dream." A tape recorder played Burroughs's dry, ghostly voice reading, and Allen Ginsberg concluded by "singing to his finger-cymbals and shuffling like a wild-haired bear among the flowers hurled at him," while "he was surrounded by, and finally disappeared in, a mass of foliage-waving enthusiasts."

Ferlinghetti, trim in high-collar Nehru jacket, read "To Fuck Is to Live Again Kyrie Eleison Kerista or The Situation in the West, Followed by a Holy Proposal," which he had written the previous winter and published in the deliberately outrageously named *Fuck You: a Magazine of the Arts*. The poem's title alone made an ironic, striking contrast with his dignified dress, but the explicit equivalence of sex with holiness in the poem was an integral part of Ferlinghetti's political stance: a part of the whole new "revolutionary" vision whose articulation was the poet's province. In 1965, in a world increasingly dominated by the rising youth culture and its insistence on sexual (as well as all individual) freedom, such a statement perfectly expressed those radical new forces. Though the title was shortened by dropping the first clause when it was published in the 1966 second edition of *Starting from San Francisco*, its initial inclusion emphasized its radical idea and certainly drew the immediate attention of the audience.

For the next two weeks Ferlinghetti stayed in London, socializing with some of the other poets and visiting the sights. Then he went on to Rome and Spoleto, Italy, where he had been invited while in Nerja to participate in the First International Poetry Week of the Festival of Two Worlds. The featured guest there was to be Ezra Pound himself; and invitations had also been extended to Pablo Neruda, Russian poets Andrei Voznesensky and Yevgeny Yevtushenko, and the elderly Spanish poet Rafael Alberti, among others. At eighty years old, the "midwife" of modern poetry, as Pound had been called, was no longer active in the literary world, but the festival's intent was to pay honor to the man who had been such an unparalleled force in modern literature.

Soon after Ferlinghetti arrived in Spoleto on June 27, he began to hear various gossip that flew through such gatherings, some of it relating to him, as if to underline his growing international reputation. He heard on the one hand that Yevtushenko had refused to come because Pound would be there and the Russian considered Pound still a fascist; then that Pound wouldn't come as he didn't want to see Ferlinghetti, because of Ferlinghetti's publication of the interview in *City Lights Journal*. Yevtushenko did come, however, but arrived in a diplomatic limousine from Rome and left quickly afterward. Though he and Ferlinghetti later became friends, at this initial contact Ferlinghetti was privately critical of Yevtushenko's apparently aloof arrival and departure, noting in his journal that one of the most important effects of such international conferences was "the establishment of personal rapport & communication with other intellectuals normally unreachable behind the obscene boundaries" of national division.

And despite the rumors, Pound came as well, though he was reduced to a symbol of the force he had been. He had written substantial numbers of his Cantos during the 1950s at the mental hospital at St. Elizabeth's to which he'd been sentenced for his pro-Mussolini broadcasts from Rome during World War II, but as the 1963 interview Ferlinghetti had published showed, Pound's suffering at St. Elizabeth's and afterward had drawn him further and further into silence.

"I don't work anymore," he had said in the interview. "I do nothing.

I have become ignorant and unlettered. . . . I don't think. I have nothing but the certainty of the greatest uncertainty. . . . I can't get at the kernel of my thoughts anymore with words. . . ."

When Ferlinghetti actually met him, the two shook hands, but Pound said nothing, showing no real awareness of Ferlinghetti's presence or identity. He may have been deliberately ignoring him because of offense taken at the interview, which showed him in such unflattering light, but it's much more likely the affront was unfounded gossip, and he simply didn't know, or care anymore, who Ferlinghetti, or any of the new generation of poets, was.

When Ginsberg made a pilgrimage in September 1967 to Rapallo, Italy, where Pound lived, the elder poet was equally unresponsive, despite Ginsberg's persistent attempts to draw him out in a variety of ways. At their first lunch together, Ginsberg sang Hare Krishna and "vigorous loud oom OOOms," but aside from looking a bit startled, the only response Pound offered was an answer in "crisp French" to his companion Olga Rudge's question about the name of a book by Paul Morand that Pound had liked—*Ouvert la Nuit*. Though Ginsberg saw Pound several more times over a six-week period, he never became much more responsive. The power that was Pound had passed; it was a melancholy close to a life of great achievement, and the prose poem Ferlinghetti wrote describing Pound's presence at Spoleto is full of the poignance of that passage:

> . . . Pound tried to rise from his armchair. A microphone was partly in the way. He grasped the arms of the chair with his boney hands and tried to rise. He could not and he tried again and could not. His old friend did not try to help him. Finally she put a poem in his hand and after at least a minute his voice came out. First the jaw moved and then the voice came out, inaudible. A young Italian pulled the stand-up mike close to his face and held it there and the voice came over, frail but stubborn, higher than I had expected, a thin, soft monotone. The hall had gone silent at a stroke. The voice knocked me down, so soft, so thin, so frail, so stubborn still. I put my head on my arms on the velvet sill of the box. I was surprised to see a single tear drop on my knee. The thin, indomitable voice went on. Come to this! I went blind from the box, through the back door of it into the empty upper corridor of the theatre where they still sat turned to him, went down and out into the sunlight, weeping. . . .

Up above the town, by the ancient aqueduct, the chestnut trees were still in bloom. Mute birds flew in the valley below, far off, the sun shone on the chestnut trees, and the leaves turned in the sun, and turned and turned and turned, and would continue turning. His voice went on, and on, through the leaves. . . .

As Ferlinghetti wrote, the voice did go on, has gone on, continues to go on, heard now in other voices—Ferlinghetti's own, and the next generation who inherited the tradition. With these appearances, Ferlinghetti had clearly established himself as an international figure, a role which seemed right, given the internationalism of both his literary and personal background. And the international festivals of which he was part would prove to be models for dozens that would take place over the next twenty years, where promoters and participants hoped to generate some of the same vitality and magic that had been present in Paris and especially in Albert Hall.

When he finally got home in July, he settled again into the business of his work in San Francisco. Most mornings he worked upstairs in his study from eight till noon. An old potbellied stove kept the room warm on winter days, and in one corner of the room, two worktables were set in an "L." One facing the picture window held files, correspondence, and other business of City Lights publishing; on the other, adjacent to the window, sat the old Royal manual typewriter Ferlinghetti used (and still uses in 1990) to compose. A swivel chair let him move between the tables, and his old dog Homer, a large black and white ("front end collie, chassis mid-European schnauzer, rear end shepherd," as Ferlinghetti described him), was a constant companion.

The sweeping view from the picture window and the adjacent porch must certainly have been a pleasure, and it had provided the setting for the beginning of "The Situation in the West . . .":

I see San Francisco from my window through some old navy beerbottles

.   .   .   .   .

There's the Fairmont phallus
There's the Mark masturbation
There's the park there's the cement works
There's the steam brewing factory
There's the actor's workshop
There's the Bay there's that Bridge
There's that treasured island the Navy doesn't need. . . .

After lunch, he would either walk to work—fifty-five minutes exactly, he had it figured—or drive his old black Volkswagen. The store itself had expanded in 1958 to include the larger basement, which now held most of the books, and the upstairs as well, reached by a curving stair, where the foreign-language paperbacks were housed. The small street-level room still contained the magazines—both literary and political. At the head of the stairs leading to the basement, open mailboxes available to poets, friends, passers-through, held letters and messages; below that, a bulletin board overflowed with the kinds of messages that modeled thousands of such boards by the late sixties—posters of announcements, cryptic requests for rides and riders to various destinations, sex partners, roommates, tenants, petitions, even a few odd jobs. The idea was an extension of Ferlinghetti and Martin's original plan for the store—to make it more than a place to buy books and magazines; to be a community center, where artists, poets, aspirants, and aficionados would gather and exchange information and ideas—the commerce of their lives.

The downstairs, more than twice the combined area of the upper floors, contained the store's office as well as all the other poetry and literature. The walls displayed more posters, literary, cultural, and artistic decoration. There was a poster of a naked Ginsberg with Tibetan finger cymbals; Michael McClure posed as a fighter about to take on Billy the Kid and Jean Harlow; a naked McClure shrouded with hair above the declamation "Poetry is a Muscular Principle"; watercolors by Kenneth Patchen. On the door of Ferlinghetti's office, more signs: "No Trespassing" and "Beware of Dog."

The whole place was designed to project accessibility, as if the selling of goods was almost incidental, and what was important was people. It was a spirit that spread—to Berkeley, across the country—and became the fabric of the times. It represented as well a culmination of the vision that had led Ferlinghetti to the corner of Broadway and Columbus, to City Lights, more than a decade before.

In 1966, when writer David Kherdian recorded these elements in a profile of Ferlinghetti, the third *City Lights Journal* came out amid a rising tide of anti–Vietnam War protests and the growing youth counterculture. The crowd in the photo taken outside City Lights in December 1965, which makes up the cover of the *Journal*, captures a slice of the atmosphere, with its assemblage of writers, journalists, artists, actors. Ginsberg, Orlovsky, Robert La Vigne, Brautigan, McClure, Meltzer, and others are spread out below Ferlinghetti, who is holding an umbrella—a visual symbol of the cultural and artistic forces gathered under Ferlinghetti's auspices.

Folk-rock hero Bob Dylan was also there for the occasion, but wasn't part of the group photo. McClure, however, did persuade him to have his picture taken in the adjacent Adler's Alley with himself and Ginsberg. Later Dylan went to dinner with Ferlinghetti, Ginsberg, Italian translator Fernanda Pivano, Shig Murao, and Peter and Julius Orlovsky. Dylan had talked a little about City Lights publishing some of his prose work but nothing ever came of it. On the whole, Ferlinghetti found Dylan as taciturn and enigmatic as the singer's public image. At Tosca's Cafe, across the street from City Lights, the whole group was kicked out when Julius Orlovsky, who had been institutionalized for much of his life, wandered into the women's rest room. It was not until the event appeared the next day in Herb Caen's column in the *Chronicle* that the management learned whom they had evicted.

The *Journal* itself continued to reflect the range of Ferlinghetti's current interests. Sections of poetry from San Francisco, from the poets at Spoleto, and more from India were featured along with three experimental plays—Barbara Garson's *MacBird*, Julian Beck's *Frankenstein*, and Bob Burleson's *The Shouting Head of Prophet John*. Most all the work engaged major issues of the time—the beginnings of the women's movement, Eastern spirituality, the victimization of American Indians, among others.

Though none of the poems bore directly on the Vietnam War, Paul Carroll had first read his ten-page "Ode to the American Indian" at a University of Chicago affair protesting U.S. Vietnam policy that spring. The war was also a significant point of reference in Ginsberg's "New York to San Fran.," and a presence in others. Protests, "teach-ins," and other antiwar activities had spread throughout the country by now, among college campuses and beyond, as the United States military role in Vietnam escalated. In February of 1965 President Lyndon B. Johnson had ordered the bombing of North Vietnam; and on March 8, while Ferlinghetti was in Nerja, 3,500 marines had landed three miles from Da Nang, South Vietnam—the first U.S. ground troops in that country. The following month the Students for a Democratic Society had organized a protest against U.S. involvement which drew 25,000 demonstrators to Washington, D.C. And on October 15 the first nationally coordinated wave of anti-Vietnam protests saw 14,000 march down New York's Fifth Avenue, 10,000 gather outside the Oakland Army Base, and 2,000 others at the Berkeley campus of the University of California. Ginsberg had spoken to the crowd at Berkeley, urging peaceful nonviolence—coining the phrase "flower power"—to describe the force needed to overcome the kind of cultural violence which he felt had spawned the war.

In March 1966 Ferlinghetti participated in a reading at Reed College in Portland, Oregon, with poets Robert Bly, David Ray, James Wright, John Logan, Vern Rutsala, William Stafford, Louis Simpson, George Hitchcock, and Robert Petersen, dedicated to protest against the war. Bly, whose poetry had drawn increasing praise, had been waging his own crusade against conventional, academic poetry since the fifties, and with Wright had started his own magazine, *The Fifties*, then called *The Sixties*, to keep up with the decades. As he later said, Ferlinghetti's "Tentative Description of a Dinner to Promote the Impeachment of President Eisenhower" had first opened to him some of the possibilities for effective political poetry, and by 1966 Bly had written several poems directly engaging the political and cultural issues surrounding the war.

At Reed, Ferlinghetti read "Where Is Vietnam?," a prose-poem satire critical of President Johnson and his role in deepening American involvement in the war. Ferlinghetti had written it the summer before, soon after his return from Europe, and had published and read it several times during the year; but the Reed event became the subject of an article in the *New York Times*, as Bly and Ray formed "American Writers Against the Vietnam War," which went on to sponsor a series of "read-ins" around the country at which some of these and other writers participated. Bly went on to publish *A Poetry Reading Against the Vietnam War*, which collected poems from several poets on this theme, including "Where Is Vietnam?" and statements by the likes of Abraham Lincoln, John Kennedy, Adolf Hitler, and others. In April of 1966, when income taxes were due, Ferlinghetti had notified the IRS that he was withholding a "symbolic portion"—one dollar—of his taxes in protest against their use to prosecute the war; and the following year, when Bly's new collection, *The Light Around the Body*, won the prestigious National Book Award, Bly turned down the award and its substantial monetary prize, using the opportunity to criticize the literary establishment for their silence about U.S. Vietnam policy.

Given the temper of the times, it wasn't surprising that City Lights again ran afoul of the law, though the problem had nothing to do with antiwar activity. Once again, it was the same free-speech issue which had first brought Ferlinghetti attention. In many ways it came as a result of the straight world's hostility to the hippies who had been descending on the Haight-Ashbury district of San Francisco. Spreading their gospel of love, openness, and sharing, in contrast to the competitive, materialist, violent society they saw around them, young people were making San Francisco the capital of the counterculture.

It was in this atmosphere of increasing pressure for personal and sexual freedom that in December 1965 the opening San Francisco production of Michael McClure's play *The Beard*, which eventually won a Tony Award in New York for best play, was shut down for explicit sexual content. Then on January 3, 1966, the Psychedelic Shop opened on Haight Street, with an inventory that included underground newspapers, rolling papers, hookahs, and bongs. An all-purpose general store for the new culture, it quickly became a target for police, who regularly raided it, trying in vain to find real contraband for which they might arrest the proprietors and customers and close the store. By the following year the shop had become a stop on Gray-Line bus tours of the city.

Later in the year, on November 17, when police raided the shop yet again, they arrested a clerk for selling *The Love Book*, a collection of poems by Lenore Kandel. The poems were erotic, explicit, and therefore, police asserted, "obscene." Two days later they arrested a clerk at City Lights Book Shop for the same offense. A warrant was issued for Ferlinghetti as well, but he was giving readings on the East Coast at the time. In protest against what many saw as clear-cut cases of censorship, a group of San Francisco State College professors then staged a public reading of *The Love Book* and the offending scene from *The Beard*, hoping for a mass arrest to further test the First Amendment issue. The police, however, disappointed the protestors by failing to show for the event.

Meantime, as in the *Howl* case, the ACLU came to the aid of free expression and *The Love Book*. This time, however, the case was never tried; the clerk who sold the book was, terribly, killed in a motorcycle accident, and charges were dropped. Still, the stain persisted, as some ten years later, when Ferlinghetti went down to the North Beach police station to help a young clerk clear up a traffic ticket, police computers showed an outstanding warrant for Ferlinghetti himself on charges of "obscenity" and "lewd behavior." Called a pervert and a child molester by a disgusted officer, he was forced to spend several hours in jail before he was finally released. It turned out that the warrant that had been issued against him because of the "obscene" *Love Book* had never been canceled, and that was why he'd been held.

The swelling counterculture of the sixties found any constraints on personal freedom a threat and a rallying point. A kind of guerrilla war began to be waged everywhere, with both organized and spontaneous demonstrations springing up wherever conventional norms could be construed as a challenge to individual freedom. The younger generation, and sympathetic elders, believed they were changing the fabric of the culture itself. Much talk of a new consciousness, heavily influenced by the East, that would replace violent, capitalist Western society, animated increasing numbers. It was directed both at internal realizations that would then somehow change external conditions and at direct action in the larger world.

Ferlinghetti, always the artist engaged in ongoing dialogue with the world, was, along with Ginsberg and other artists, at the center of these explorations. Investigating that transcendent, spiritual experience he'd already heard much about, that July of 1966 at Bixby Canyon he followed one of the internal routes of exploration that many were beginning to try by taking LSD for the first time. One result of the experience was a breakthrough on a major poem he had been working on since the spring. In it he had been trying to somehow encompass the vast new wave of contemporary experience that seemed to be changing his and everyone's lives—indeed, the whole American culture—in a prophetic vision. Titled "After the Cries of the Birds," the poem saw

> the "future of the world"
> > in a new visionary society
> > now only dimly recognizable
> > in folk-rock ballrooms
> free-form dancers in ecstatic clothing
> > their hearts their gurus
> > every man his own myth
> > butterflies in amber
> > > caught fucking life

The poem went on to picture this new "probably pastoral" world where "Mark Twain meets Jack London / . . . The Jefferson Airplane [the rock band] takes off / and circles heaven / . . . ," where there are "nude swart maidens swimming / in pools of sunlight" and other utopian scenes. Near the end the poem sees the Chinese arrive on the West Coast, symbolizing the unity the poem is working toward. Then San Francisco itself, the capital of this new world, "floats away / beyond the three-mile limit / of the District of Eternal Revenue," leaving us "agape"—both openmouthed and in a state of divine love, that being the Greek meaning of the word.

Though he never included the poem in a collection, he published it both in *The Village Voice* and in the underground newspaper the *San*

Francisco Oracle, then in a separate chapbook with an accompanying "explanation" of its sources, "Genesis of After the Cries of the Birds." The *Oracle* was particularly appropriate, both because of the poem's San Francisco center and because of the way it so fully captured the romantic, visionary spirit of the times, in which so many youth-oriented underground papers were rooted.

He had written the "Genesis" on New Year's Day, 1967, two weeks before one of the major celebrations of the hippie-counterculture life, the "Human Be-In" at Golden Gate Park on January 14. Subtitled "A Gathering of the Tribes," the celebration drew some twenty thousand to the four-hour affair, which featured music by the Jefferson Airplane, the Grateful Dead, Quicksilver Messenger Service, and Dizzy Gillespie; guided meditations, chanting, and other rituals; and poems and speeches by Allen Ginsberg, Gary Snyder, Jerry Rubin, psychedelic guru Timothy Leary, and others. It was here that Leary exhorted the gathering to "turn onto the scene, tune into what is happening, and drop out—of high school, college, grad school, junior executive, senior executive—and follow me. . . ." Quickly afterward, the phrase "tune in, turn on, drop out" became a generational slogan.

Ferlinghetti remembers that "to the participants it truly seemed a new age had arrived, with a new vision of life and love on earth." But sometime during the festivities Ginsberg turned to Ferlinghetti when both were on stage and whispered, "What if we're all wrong?" Though to some it may sound ironic, it was certainly not intended as a joke and, despite the reverent chorus of euphoria, hinted at a darker side to the time. The Vietnam War was of course the most visible hint of that side, but for Ferlinghetti, and certainly for others, the times were far from unconditionally joyous. Despite the spirit of celebration, despite his own surging popularity, that same January, as he traveled to read in Detroit and Geneva, New York, on the first leg of another long journey that would take him across Europe and then the Soviet Union, he noted in his journal his personal unease and his need to get away.

Problems with his marriage persisted and continued to deepen, and he was beset, as he had been recurrently, with restlessness and uncertainty about what he was doing and why; it was not a continual condition, but something he'd experienced sporadically and regularly for years. And regularly over the years, Ferlinghetti's journal asks directly the reason for his compulsion to travel, but never finds a direct answer. Such an urge is part of all of us, of course; and in Ferlinghetti's case, opportunities to travel, resulting from the steady stream of invitations he'd received for a decade, made traveling natural. Further, in San Francisco his phone rang steadily; the demands on his time from City Lights and from the literary world were continuous. The opportunity for reflection of the kind that had always led to the writing he felt compelled to do was rare. More and more, then, the new poems he wrote came from his travels.

On January 31, 1967, he arrived in Cologne, Germany, on the way to Berlin, where he would read with Voznesensky at the Berlin Literarisches Colloquium. At Cologne he also began an undertaking he had been thinking about off and on for a half dozen years—a new novel that would be a sequel to *Her.*

"This is a surrealist-expressionist novel I'm starting here, cauchemar Berlin parallel to Paris 'Her' twenty years ago. . . . I am lost in the dark landscape. In this strange place, surrealist city—thru the dark cellars full of jerking dancers to old Beatles records, crowded rock clubs . . . something out of *Steppenwolf,* I go off into the desolate night streets at 3 AM among the monster buildings. . . . Life goes on, time passes, nothing changes."

The working title was "Berlin Blue Rider," the Blue Riders having been part of an influential school of German expressionist painters in the early part of the century. During his days in Germany he made several pages of notes toward the project, but the novel never progressed beyond the note stage, and remained—remains—a project still waiting to be shaped.

On February 8, a week after arriving, he went with others at the colloquium to East Berlin to visit a poet who had not been permitted to come to the West. Like many Westerners, Ferlinghetti found in the eastern sector evidence of a "joyless civilization." In his journal he described the Berlin Wall as a "monster serpent running thru the city, like some kind of barbaric medievalism . . . ," and he was horrified by the insult to civilization it represented. "Every once in a while a new ruse to escape to the West is uncovered & put an end to. Swimmers shot down in dark midnight canals, bodies found in meat freezers in trucks, bodies found strapped under country wagons, anything for freedom. . . ."

He also spent some time with Heiner Bastian, a poet he had known in San Francisco, who now lived in Berlin. Bastian had translated "After the Cries of the Birds," the poem which Ferlinghetti read at the colloquium, and now, as a result of seeing Voznesensky again, Ferlinghetti had the chance to travel with Bastian and extend his journey further, into a country that Westerners didn't often visit. When Ferlinghetti asked about going to the Soviet Union, Voznesensky called up his wife in Moscow, and while it

At Big Wolf Lake in the Adirondacks, about 1939: *standing*, Bisland cousin Gordon Duvall and wife, from Natchez, Mississippi, with unknown man on right; *seated*, Duvall's mother-in-law, Presley and Anna Lawrence Bisland. (*Lawrence Ferlinghetti Collection*)

On board patrol ship in
North Atlantic, 1943.
(*Lawrence Ferlinghetti Collection*)

As CO of USS SC 1308
during Normandy Invasion,
June 1944.
(*Lawrence Ferlinghetti Collection*)

As doctoral student at the Sorbonne, Paris, 1948–50. (*Lawrence Ferlinghetti Collection*)

Ferlinghetti's mother, Clemence Monsanto Ferlinghetti, Baltimore, circa 1950. (*Lawrence Ferlinghetti Collection*)

In front of City Lights, 1958.
(*Lawrence Ferlinghetti Collection*)

Reading at *The Cellar* with
the house jazz band, 1958.
(*Lawrence Ferlinghetti Collection*)

With Kirby on Wisconsin Street, 1959.
(*Harry Redl, Lawrence Ferlinghetti Collection*)

With dog, Homer, on the front steps of
Wisconsin Street home, 1961.
(*Lawrence Ferlinghetti Collection*)

With Kenneth Tynan at City Lights, 1962. (*Harry Redl, Lawrence Ferlinghetti Collection*)

Julie and Kirby in their kitchen on Wisconsin Street, 1963.
(*Ettore Sottsass, Jr., Lawrence Ferlinghetti Collection*)

With Jean-Jacques Lebel, Venice, Italy, 1963.
(*Lawrence Ferlinghetti Collection*)

With Andrei Voznesenski at the Berlin Wall, 1967.
(*Heiner Bastian, Lawrence Ferlinghetti Collection*)

Next to the Trans-Siberian train, 1967. (*Heiner Bastian, Lawrence Ferlinghetti Collection*)

With Ginsberg at the "Human Be-In," in Golden Gate Park, January 14, 1967. (*Paul Kagan, Lawrence Ferlinghetti Collection*)

At Ginsberg's farm, Cherry Valley, New York, just after Kerouac died, 1969. With Gordon Ball, Allen de Loach and Ginsberg. (*Joan de Loach, Lawrence Ferlinghetti Collection*)

At Caffe Trieste in 1970, with Minette LeBlanc, Peter LeBlanc, unidentified man, Ginsberg, Harold Norse, Jack Hirschman, Bob Kaufman. (*Lawrence Ferlinghetti Collection*)

At the "Beat reunion," University of North Dakota, Grand Forks, North Dakota, in February 1974, with (*standing*) Gregory Corso, Miriam Patchen, Kenneth Rexroth, Ginsberg, and (*in front*) Joanna McClure, unidentified woman, Shigeyoshi Murao, another unidentified woman, and Gary Snyder. (*Lawrence Ferlinghetti Collection*)

With Ginsberg and Yevgeny Yevtushenko, in San Francisco, 1975. (*Lawrence Ferlinghetti Collection*)

Standing: Jack Hirschman, unidentified man, Ferlinghetti, Slovak poet Max Bavosky, Jr., Michael McClure, Thom Gunn, William Burroughs, unidentified man, and Jim Gustafson; *seated*: unidentified man and Carol Lee Sanchez at the 1978 San Francisco International Poetry Festival, Palace of Fine Arts. (*Bennett Hall, Lawrence Ferlinghetti Collection*)

City Lights publishing staff in fall 1975: Craig Broadley and son, Ferlinghetti and Pooch, Pamela Mosher, Nancy Peters. (*Lawrence Ferlinghetti Collection*)

At Kerouac's grave
in Lowell,
Massachusetts, 1977.
(*Helen MacLeod, Lawrence
Ferlinghetti Collection*)

On a boat at Anasquam Inlet, Gloucester, Massachusetts, at the time
of writing "The Sea and Ourselves at Cape Ann," 1977.
(*Helen MacLeod, Lawrence Ferlinghetti Collection*)

With Gary Snyder in San Francisco, spring 1980.
(*Chris Felver, Lawrence Ferlinghetti Collection*)

Painting at his studio, 1981. (*Joe Wolberg, Lawrence Ferlinghetti Collection*)

With George and Felicity Whitman, in front of Whitman's Shakespeare and Company Bookstore, Paris, 1984. (*Hans Erixon, Lawrence Ferlinghetti Collection*)

At Bixby Canyon, Big Sur, 1984. (*Chris Felver, Lawrence Ferlinghetti Collection*)

With Studs Terkel at the WFMT studios in Chicago, April 1986. (*Sidney Lewis, Lawrence Ferlinghetti Collection*)

Ferlinghetti at the corner of the newly named Kenneth Rexroth Place in North Beach, 1988. (*Barry Silesky*)

With Amy Scholder, Nancy Peters, Alexander Cockburn, Paul Yamazaki,
Sin Sarocco, Richard Berman at City Lights book party
for Cockburn, 1989. (*Lawrence Ferlinghetti Collection*)

Ferlinghetti and Nancy Peters in City Lights office, 1989.
(*Barry Silesky*)

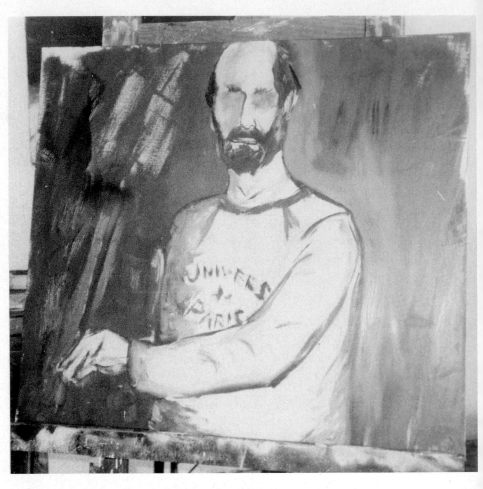

"Self-Portrait," 1987. (*Barry Silesky*)

usually took Westerners months to get a visa to visit there, if they were approved at all, Ferlinghetti received one in two days.

He intended to repeat the journey that French poet Blaise Cendrars had written about in the early part of the century in his prose poem "On the Trans-Siberian." Ferlinghetti planned to ride the Trans-Siberian railway with Bastian for six days and seven nights from Moscow, all the way across Russia, through Kirov, Novosibirsk, Irkutsk, and on to Vladivostok on the Pacific Coast. The trip, however, proved to be not quite the adventure he expected.

He left Moscow with Bastian on February 10, sending a card back to City Lights to let them know he had "made it this far." He had found the "Writer's Union friendly, others not so. . . ." Still, he was apparently looking forward to the trip with some excitement. Then he got on the train.

"It was completely sealed in," he remembers. "There was no ventilation. It was like twenty below outside, but inside was very hot." The landscape seemed some archetypal vision of nineteenth-century Russia. "Everything was completely under the snow. . . ." Still, though the long trip on the train became tedious, he kept his journal, wrote a few poems, and had plenty to eat and "all you could drink. Heavy, red Georgian wine, and I was slugging it down without thinking about it." As the long journey ended, the heat and wine took their toll. "By the time I got to the end of the line," he said, "I was hung over, then I got this fever."

Five years later, reading Yasunari Kawabata's *The Snow Country*, he remembered arriving at the Nadhoka station at the end of the trip "by the last light of evening. Everything is solid black and white—the snow banked high, the horse drawn sledges, the iced ruts in the roads, the dark figures scurrying past in the zero cold. There is a movie house showing a sea battle in the Russian Revolution. There is a queue waiting to get in, standing silent in the snow. At a great round, deserted traffic circle, on the tops of flag poles fifty feet high, great long brilliant red banners streaming in the wind. . . ."

He and Bastian had planned to go on to Kyoto and rendezvous with Gary Snyder, who was living there. Having been told that he wouldn't need a visa to go to Japan, Ferlinghetti went directly from the train to the ship, and simply walked on board with Bastian. When they came around to collect the tickets, however, Ferlinghetti was told that he would indeed need a visa; he had no choice but to get off the ship, leaving Bastian to go on by himself.

Meanwhile, his fever worsened, "and they put me in the seaman's hospital for about a week with pneumonia. No one spoke anything but Russian once you got away from Moscow. I couldn't even find out what I had for a while. Finally I heard one of them say 'pen—ee—ceel—een.' I was in there about six days. I think they thought I was a British ship captain or merchant seaman, because there were a lot of ships in the port."

When he got out he found he couldn't get a visa to visit Japan. "I would have had to go back to Moscow. There was no way to get a photo taken or anything. I tried to telephone Japan from the American Consulate, but there was no way to telephone. No way to communicate. I could have died out there and nobody would have known about it for months.

"It was a pretty depressing trip. I finally took an Aeroflot Russian airplane back to Moscow, and that's when I wrote 'Moscow in the Wilderness, Segovia in the Snow'—in the airport in Moscow."

The poem expresses both the sense of overwhelming vastness of the Russian country and the urge of the poet to somehow awaken transformative magic in it. The music of the Spanish master of guitar, Andrés Segovia, is heard on a Moscow bus radio, "in the iron-white streets / ... saying / There's a huge emptiness here. . . ." The effect of his music isn't a sudden external apocalyptic transformation, but a resonant portent of interior movement—"a thaw," as Ferlinghetti terms it. It's the kind of interior shift of consciousness the leading figures of the new counterculture, of which Ferlinghetti had certainly become one, were advocating as the way to necessary and inevitable changes in the larger society. Such a shift was the work of the artist especially, and of all creative spirits. So in the poem's conclusion, as a result of Segovia's playing,

> an ancient armadillo
> asleep for centuries
> in the cellar of the Kremlin
> raises its horny head
> opens its square third eye
> and looks around blinking
> and then at last
> unglues its great gut mouth
> and utters
> ecstatic static

Ferlinghetti's own mood was far from ecstatic, however, when he finally got back to San Francisco in March. The pneumonia still had him, and he didn't really feel right again until summer. He recovered slowly, happy to see his children, though relations with Kirby had by now reached a certain impasse. In his absence, Dick McBride, who was working on the publishing, had rented an apartment on Grant and Filbert, a few blocks from the store, to use as an office. The office part left a three-room apartment vacant, and it was set up to accommodate visiting writers and friends. In the next year Ferlinghetti began using it himself as an office away from home, and even to stay there, apart from Kirby.

At the same time, he began work on a new full-length play, *Uncle Ahab*, and on the new books City Lights would publish. Philip Lamantia's *Selected Poems*, Bob Kaufman's *Golden Sardines*, and René Daumal's *Mount Analogue* would all come out in 1967, along with a new edition of Charles Olson's *Call Me Ishmael*.

By that summer, the "summer of love," the media had fully covered and combed over the hippie culture, as they had the Beat culture a decade before, and San Francisco was swarming with part-time hippies, voyeurs, and exploiters. In the fall, on October 6, residents staged a "funeral" for the hippie movement in Buena Vista Park, adjacent to Golden Gate. The printed notice invited friends to attend sunrise services for "Hippie, devoted son of Mass Media." The service itself featured a casket filled with beads, flowers, hash brownies, and other hippie regalia surrounding a mock corpse; and the whole event was, of course, widely covered by the media. Not surprisingly Ferlinghetti avoided the funeral, having no interest in such media phenomena.

That month he wrote again to Laughlin about selling the bookstore and took a short trip south, to New Mexico, part of his continuing explorations of the time, and in part to get away from the stresses of his San Francisco life. Looking for some friends in El Rito, he stumbled upon San Francisco painter and critic Wilfred Lang, who had been a member of the Rexroth group and had known Patchen, Everson, and others at the Waldport, Oregon, CO camp during World War II. A friend of Lang's who was visiting him at the time offered Ferlinghetti the use of her nearby house while she was traveling in the East, and he eagerly took up the offer, staying there for three days, enchanted by the surroundings.

"Maybe this is the place," he wrote in his journal. "Maybe I'll never go back. Nowhere to go from here. Bring the family out? Or—? Strange, open, isolated feeling here." But he knew himself better than that, finally realizing, "I'll go back, no doubt. Too old & too late to change karmas & families. . . ."

Still, it wasn't that he was too old; and if it was too late to change, it was the call of the larger world to which he could not change his response. It was a call he had always heard, that had led him to the very person and place he was. As the Vietnam escalation continued, so did the protests, and Ferlinghetti's part in them. While he was in New Mexico, 55,000 antiwar protestors had stormed the Pentagon in the most violent confrontation with authorities yet. Ten thousand police were called out to "protect" the city, and among the 250 arrested were several well-known people, including writer Norman Mailer. Then on October 17 some 3,000 demonstrators tried to close the Oakland Army Induction Center. When police tried to disperse them by forming a "flying wedge," more than 200 protestors suffered serious injury, and 119 were arrested. Seven of them were later tried and acquitted on conspiracy charges.

But that didn't stop many of them. On December 9 Ferlinghetti joined another demonstration against the draft at the Oakland Army Induction Center along with Joan Baez's mother, Kay Boyle, and thousands of others. Wearing a black derby hat and a red scarf, Ferlinghetti arrived with the rest at dawn, planning to meet three busloads of new inductees. They were going to block the entranceway where the buses would pass.

At first Ferlinghetti didn't intend to get arrested, as many of the others were prepared to do, but, as he remembers, "Kay Boyle came up to me and said, 'I bet you won't get busted,' so then I had to."

When the buses inched forward, the demonstrators refused to move, despite orders from assembled police to disperse. One of the soldiers shouted, "Kill the hippies!" but real violence was avoided. The demonstrators moved peaceably into the paddy wagons to which police led them, and many more demonstrators followed them to the Alameda County Courthouse. They were held until the following day, when they were arraigned; sixty-seven, including Ferlinghetti, were arrested. When he called Kirby to let her know what had happened, she was so furious that he had taken such an extreme step that she hung up on him.

But he really didn't want to be bailed out, anyway. Along with the other protestors, he meant to actually serve time in jail, if necessary, to dramatize the protest to the maximum. He pleaded no contest to the charge of disturbing the peace and at the trial read a statement he had written, which spoke for many of those arrested:

"The purpose of the demonstration was to stop war. Its purpose was to block the entrance to war. The motives of the demonstrators were pure and the action was totally nonviolent. It was a legitimate expression of political dissent and I believe such dissent must not be suppressed and prosecuted in a society that calls itself free. . . ."

He was sentenced to three weeks in the Alameda County prison at Santa Rita, where he was assigned to the laundry and given work stenciling pants—he had told them of his experience with printing and publishing. He also kept a journal, parts of which he smuggled out in laundry bundles so it wouldn't be confiscated. The journal, expressing the "paranoid fear of the unknown, fear of not knowing what's going to happen to your body," and the specifics of degradation that were prison life, he published in March in *Ramparts*, a radical, counterculture magazine.

Despite the anxieties the journal expressed, Ferlinghetti remembers now that "it wasn't bad at all. In fact, I rather enjoyed it in there." His stay was eased considerably by his cellmate, a young gang member who was serving time for his part in a filling station robbery which had ended in the accidental killing of a station attendant.

"He'd been in for several years," Ferlinghetti recalls, "though he was only sixteen when he got busted. Something like thirteen years later, I heard from him and he was in San Quentin for the same crime. But he told me who to stay away from. He said, see those guys over in the corner? Don't even look at them. He took my notebook, and he put my stuff in his drawer and said, they wouldn't dare touch it if it's in here. I mean, there was real gang warfare there. He had a shiv in his boot. And he helped me smuggle out the journal when I left."

He also wrote two poems about the experience. "Santa Rita Blues," beginning "A man in jail is nothing / and his name is Nada / and he's nothing but a number / and his number is zero," was published only in a photocopy edition of fifty of the original, handwritten on lined paper, produced by Thomas Parkinson and sold at a later benefit reading Ferlinghetti did for the "Campus Draft Opposition" at Berkeley.

The other was "Salute," which he did collect in his next book. At its end he raises his "middle finger / in the only proper salute" to ". . . every prowlcar with riotguns & sirens and every riot-tank with mace & teargas . . . ," among a long list of the armed and uniformed authorities supposedly keeping peace, who, in fact, as Ferlinghetti and thousands, even millions, of others saw it, were defending the war by attacking the protestors. Finally, after eighteen days, Robert Truehaft, who was Jessica Mitford's husband and a lawyer specializing in civil rights cases in Oakland, arranged Ferlinghettti's release.

The domestic violence which had been building reached a peak in 1968. On April 4, Rev. Martin Luther King, Jr., was killed by a sniper in Memphis, setting off a wave of inner-city riots in more than a dozen cities. But at the time, Ferlinghetti was again in Paris, where he had gone in February, and was staying in Montparnasse near Jean-Jacques Lebel.

Lebel was deeply involved in the mounting student uprisings there, even though he wasn't a student anymore, and was grinding out mimeographed tracts with Daniel Cohn-Bendit and other leaders to distribute, helping to rally support against the current regime.

The movement had begun the previous fall at the Nanterre campus, in a western suburb of Paris, with a protest against traditional rules aimed at prohibiting male and female students visiting each other's dorms after evening curfew. But that was really only the tip of the iceberg of a whole complex of issues concerning restriction of individual rights. When the French Minister of Youth visited Nanterre in January to dedicate a new swimming pool, Cohn-Bendit earned national attention by publicly confronting him about his recent book which failed to address central issues of sexual freedom among the young. Then at the end of the month, rumors flew of official lists of students targeted by officials to fail exams in order to get rid of them and defuse protests, and actual riots ensued. In many ways, French students took their cue from America, with whose uprisings they were very familiar and interested, and the protest spread. During Ferlinghetti's months there, a dozen other towns had similar actions, many directed against the U.S. role in Vietnam—in the fifties the French had also tried to hold the country as a colony—and U.S. attempts to enlist French and other support in their effort.

In late March students occupied the Nanterre administration building, and by May, would occupy the Odéon in a new French revolution that would bring the country nearly to a halt with a nationwide strike idling some ten million, while ten thousand police battled protestors.

Ferlinghetti was fascinated by the mounting revolution and discussions among Lebel, Cohn-Bendit, and other leaders of the movement to whom he was close. One of the major issues, he remembers, "was whether they should have a psychedelic plank in the platform. There was a big split over this because a lot of the students realized that the French workers couldn't relate to this at all—having a platform legalizing dope. In France the workers were on the side of the students as far as political position, but they didn't understand about dope."

The point seems trivial, but reflects the social and economic class difference which runs deeper than any political common ground in France, as it does in the United States. What remained, however, was the intensity of the charged atmosphere, the sense of being at the center of a nation-shaking movement, which etched its way deeply into Ferlinghetti's experience. The detached poet, American but with French roots, not really a part of the maelstrom, but its intimate observer, was caught again in the wonder and amazement of the events surrounding him. Though he didn't write anything about the time then, twenty years later, when he found himself in Paris again, it would surface to become the background for another novel.

When he came back in March, he embarked on a reading tour in New England and the East. Then, after he returned to San Francisco, domestic violence reached another peak on June 6. Just after speaking to his supporters at the Ambassador Hotel in Los Angeles, accepting victory in the California Democratic primary, Robert Kennedy was shot by a disgruntled Jordanian Arab angry at Kennedy's support for Israel. Once more, Ferlinghetti took up the role of the public poet.

Poet David Meltzer had organized "The Incredible Poetry Reading" at the Nourse Auditorium in San Francisco for June 8, the day Kennedy was buried. The reading was to be the kickoff for a week-long arts celebration, "The Rolling Renaissance," and featured Allen Ginsberg, Michael McClure, Philip Whalen, John Wieners, Lew Welch, and Meltzer, in addition to Ferlinghetti. Meltzer had read on a program with Ferlinghetti as an intermission act for a San Francisco Mime Troop production in 1967; and this time, the Mime Troop opened the reading with a "crazed version," as Meltzer described it, of "The Star-Spangled Banner." The audience of between one thousand and fifteen hundred heard Ferlinghetti read his just-composed "Assassination Raga," about John Kennedy's assassination, to the recorded accompaniment of a sitar, the Indian stringed instrument Beatle George Harrison had first brought to Western music, and which was appearing with increasing frequency at all kinds of performances.

Both a raga and the sitar are linked with Indian spiritual practice, and Ferlinghetti's poem was intended as an affirmation of life in the face of this tragedy. The sitar itself "represented nonviolence coming through against the violence of the language and the assassination," Ferlinghetti explained later. "The sitar kept coming through like the voice of peace and reason." In the performance, recorded and released by Fantasy Records, the sitar's affirmation was set against a lyric describing the funeral train's passage: "And sitar sings & sings nonviolence / sitar sounds in us its images of ecstasy / its depth of ecstasy / against old dun & death. . . . And the funeral train / the silver train / starts up soundlessly / at a dead speed / over the hot land / an armed helicopter over it / They are clearing the tracks ahead of assassins. . . ."

The assassination assured the nomination of Hubert Humphrey at the Democratic convention the last week of August in Chicago, but not without a massive wave of protest by demonstrators who gathered in the city parks near the convention site. Police and National Guard heavily outnumbered the protestors, and Ginsberg and many other major literary and political figures participated in demonstrations there, witnessing the violence that filled the streets.

At the time of the convention, however, Ferlinghetti was out of the country again, on his way to Mexico. Just as he had been in Paris earlier in the year, at the center of events leading up to the general strike of May, he witnessed in Mexico the major upheavels in Oaxaca and Mexico City that were encouraged in part by the impending 1968 Olympics scheduled for October. The government was trying to assure a peaceful atmosphere for the games, but students were equally eager to take advantage of the international spotlight and focus attention on the huge economic disparities in Mexico and on the plight of impoverished millions.

On September 10 Ferlinghetti noted in his journal (published in 1970 as part of *The Mexican Night*), "I go to the occupied University of Mexico campus in late afternoon—with some poets and editors of *El Corno Emplumado* [a political and literary quarterly edited by Margaret Randall and others]—and pass through the barricades into the buildings held by the students, like Cuba 1960 with young cats in fatigues guarding the entrances & chicks with rifles. A calm prevails today. In the Med School the students have embalmed the bodies of some of their comrades killed by the government of the people. The army is a mile away, cooling it for the Olympics. Soon it will happen. It does. Still Che Guevara goes on, through the jungles."

The very day he made that entry, however, Che Guevara, former ally of Castro and the Latin American symbol of guerrilla revolution for millions, died in the jungles of Bolivia. And on October 2, ten days before the Olympics opened, some five hundred students attending a political meeting in the Tlatelolco Plaza in Mexico City were surrounded and killed by special government troops. Though neither Guevara's death nor the massacre of the students was the "happening" Ferlinghetti's journal foresaw, the term expresses clearly the sense of apocalyptic change that was so much a part of the times. It was the very spirit that helped stimulate the travels, and the poetry itself. If the great revolution never happened in quite the way Ferlinghetti and Ginsberg and others imagined, the ferment of which they were part was still very real. And the forces that spawned those hopes, and the waves of activity surrounding them, didn't end any more suddenly than they began. Nor did Ferlinghetti's involvement with them.

A body, in shades of gold, and streaked, lies on a white ground. Face, waist, knees, are all blocked by heavy, wide gray stripes. They cross two lines, not quite parallel, that run on either side of the body, over the arms. The title gives it away: *The Death of Neal Cassady at San Miguel de Allende.* They're railroad tracks, under the body, and we're looking up: the white is sky, spotted with blue.

"How's that for vérité?" Ferlinghetti said when he showed the 1987 painting at his Hunter's Point studio.

In February 1968 Ginsberg's and Kerouac's friend, the driver of Ken Kesey's Merry Prankster bus with its destination sign that read "Further," had walked out of a party where he'd been mixing booze and barbiturates. Wearing only a T-shirt, he collapsed "in the rain at night along the railroad tracks, counting the ties to Celaya, this year, still high on life, he never walked but ran to wherever he was going, and so arrived there first. . . ."

Ferlinghetti had written the description in March 1969 when he was in San Miguel de Allende assembling and editing Cassady's writings. City Lights published the first edition of *The First Third* in 1971; a subsequent edition was almost twice as long, as more and more of Cassady's writing turned up from the hands of various old girlfriends who had typed sections for him.

Then a year and a half after Cassady's death, on October 21, 1969, Jack Kerouac died in St. Anthony's Hospital in Orlando, Florida, of hemorrhaging esophageal varices, a result of his alcoholism. The two deaths seemed to mark the end of an era.

The month Kerouac died, Ferlinghetti was on a reading tour in

Minneapolis, Chicago, and Hartford, Connecticut, where he served a week-long residency at Trinity College. In Buffalo on the way, he met Ginsberg and Robert Creeley, then rode with them to the upstate New York farm Ginsberg had bought, where they stayed while Ferlinghetti went on by himself to New York City. Staying alone there at Ginsberg's Lower East Side apartment, he recorded briefly in his journal an extreme of the recurring estrangement he'd always felt intermittently, and to which his currently difficult family situation certainly must have contributed.

When he got to Hartford, strangely, no one called him about Kerouac's death—he only read about the funeral, which took place in nearby Lowell, Massachusetts, in the newspaper. The oversight by his literary friends to call could only have added to the general estrangement he felt, and stands as yet another example of the separation he felt from the Beats. Reporters later approached him for his response, but he resisted the public spectacle their presence tended to make of such a tragedy.

"I don't like funerals," he told them. "I've been asked by all sorts of big publications to write something about Jack. I can't do that. . . . They should have done something for him two years ago when he needed it."

What could have been done for Kerouac in 1967 is open to question; and Ferlinghetti has of course written many elegies for assassinated public figures and for literary friends. Finally, eighteen years later, he did write about Kerouac on the occasion of the dedication of the Jack Kerouac Memorial in Lowell.

"There is a garden in the memory of America," begins the second of the nine-part "The Canticle of Jack Kerouac," a poem built with the sprawling Whitmanic vision that unites Kerouac and Ginsberg with Ferlinghetti in their restless traveling across psychic as well as physical spaces. After the opening, it goes on to see Kerouac's

> *. . . old wood house*
> *in Lowell*
> *As the world cracks by*
> > *thundering*
> *like a lost lumber truck*
> > *on a steep grade*
> *in Kerouac America. . . .*

Ferlinghetti's refusal to dwell on these deaths underlined the personal and intellectual vitality that still propelled him and others whose lives had been involved with Kerouac and Cassady. For those two, and the Beats of which they had become symbols, the story may have been over in a strictly personal sense, as Ginsberg wrote in his own "Elegy for Neal Cassady":

> *Lament in dawnlight's not needed,*
> *the world is released,*
> *desire fulfilled, your history over,*
> *story told, Karma resolved,*
> *prayers completed*
> *vision manifest, new consciousness fulfilled. . . .*

But for Ferlinghetti, for Ginsberg, for the whole literary and social revolution of which they were part of the vanguard, the "story" had become the cultural movement which was "the Sixties." Though the decade was nearly over, the energy was far from exhausted, and continued its social upheavals at least through the first half of the seventies—even beyond the end of the Vietnam War in 1974.

In the summer of the previous year, Ferlinghetti had sent his new manuscript of poems, *The Secret Meaning of Things*—a title which first occurred in a journal entry noting that the discovery of that secret meaning is the function of poetry—to New Directions. Beginning with his most recent poem, "Assassination Raga," it also contained five other longer poems he had written in the previous three years, all of them the result of travels away from San Francisco. "Bickford's Buddha" describes scenes in Harvard Square while he was there for a reading; "All Too Clearly" was written on a visit to Southern California; "Through the Looking Glass" describes an airplane and LSD adventure; then "After the Cries of the Birds" and "Moscow in the Wilderness, Segovia in the Snow" complete the collection.

In an extensive 1969 interview, he argued that the book was "generally not political at all," and in the narrow, explicit sense that is true, certainly in comparison with poems like "Tentative Description . . ." or "One Thousand Fearful Words for Fidel Castro." But if the poems don't address specific governmental issues, they do engage directly the larger social and political context in which they were written. The urge toward transcendence, animated by psychedelics, by Buddhism, that was so much a part of the youth movement's response, and opposition, to prevailing cultural values, is undeniably a political stance. Though some of the poems, like the somber "Assassination," stuck to the left margin—an adherence to sober convention that seems appropriate to its subject—

most spread across pages in the open form Ferlinghetti had been using since *Pictures*. Now, however, besides the painterly reasons that had influenced the choice of form in the first place, such openness had become a characteristic mark of the very cultural and intellectual openness the work sought to embody.

When the book came out in March 1969, Ferlinghetti was near the height of his popularity. *A Coney Island of the Mind*, in its nineteenth printing, had sales of over half a million. *Starting from San Francisco*'s sales were also well into the hundreds of thousands and still accelerating. *Her* continued to sell steadily, and Ferlinghetti was considering a new edition of *Unfair Arguments*. Constantly in demand to read, hundreds, even thousands, filled auditoriums wherever he appeared. And like *Coney Island*, the new book went into a second printing even before official publication.

Still, despite this popularity and his importance in the prevailing counterculture (or perhaps because of it), *The Secret Meaning of Things* got little favorable notice in the American mainstream or trade media. *Library Journal*, one of the leading periodicals which reviews books for libraries, was one exception, with writer Jerome Cushman saying, "The language of Ferlinghetti's poetry is so plain and unadorned that the reader is surprised to find himself in a state of mild shock when the poem's fervor comes through with a zap. The passion of 'Assassination Raga,' first read the day Robert Kennedy was buried, is almost primeval in its intensity. Ferlinghetti . . . is so involved in today's milieu and his writing is reinforced by a sound literary heritage and an electric reach toward the center of things. . . ."

But the more academic *Virginia Quarterly Review* was typically harsh in its criticism: "Those of us who remember the late 50's and the shock of the San Francisco Beats will find in this book something like the law of diminishing returns on word magic. . . . Ferlinghetti's early anti-rhetoric and anti-convention has become a rhetoric itself called upon to make amends for a dearth of emotive force, intellection or passion. There is a point beyond which 'bad karma,' 'dharma groove' . . . and the 'Atman' begin to sound more silly than profound and embarrass rather than inspire."

Such dismissals by academics, however, were more than balanced not only by sales but by one of the foremost recognitions that any book could receive from the literary establishment. The following year, *The Secret Meaning of Things* was one of the five annual nominations for the National Book Award in poetry. Though it didn't win, the honor was a major recognition of importance by that establishment which had always derided and ignored him and other exponents of such accessible, populist poetry.

The attention he had been receiving continued to grow, especially in Europe. In 1968 he also received notice that he was the recipient of the Premio Internazionale di Poesia Etna-Taormina, an international prize sponsored by the Sicilian government, awarded every three years to one or more poets from different countries. Celebrated "since the days of Virgil," according to the New Directions publicity release at the time, previous winners included Dylan Thomas, French poet Jules Supervielle, and Italian Nobel Prize winner Salvatore Quasimodo. The prize provided the occasion for another trip to Europe, this one to extend for better than two months.

He left in early December, traveling alone, as usual, and during the journey, he felt between days of exhilaration the same spasms of loneliness and lostness that dogged him regardless of any public acclaim. Early in the trip, he recorded the experience of a profoundly sensual vitality:

". . . as if as middle age progresses my own body develops more & more of a solitary hunger to be close & in contact with other bodies, a sort of runaway voluptuousness, a runaway sensuality, even licentiousness, for everybody & everything in sight, or within reach. . . . Though with men, it's not the body thing at all, yet I still feel great affection & openness to certain male friends, including ones I haven't seen for many years. . . ."

This sensual awareness extended, not surprisingly, to the larger world as well, where at times, at least, it seemed to take on the intensity of a religious experience: "A sense that the whole universe & creation is whirring around & throbbing together, all living & dying parts of it, animate & inanimate alike, all being & existing together, as parts of one huge sentient organism, the leaves on the trees or the brown leaves on the ground & men's and women's bodies all quaking together, no end to it, no end, no end to it all, 'no end to the withering of autumn flowers,' and no beginning either, all wrapped up in one huge Breath of Being. Om. Back to some source, some silence of silences where all ends and all begins. . . ."

But in Ostia just five days later, he noted that ". . . lost as I still am in this Italian Dantesque landscape at night, I asked whatever supreme power there is in the sky 'for a sign.' God, give me a sign, I said, using the word as much as a curseword as for a deity."

Still, in his speech accepting the prize, not surprisingly he focused on that transcendent moment and seemed to incorporate the experience into his larger view.

"I am asked what is the function of poetry today," he said. "It is to make the Revolution. That means not just a political revolution among the students, but a revolution of the spirit, of the interior life. . . ."

It was an urgent concern, not just of poets or young people, but of most who were vitally involved with the newest directions, on the front edge of the culture. Ferlinghetti went on to say in the 1969 interview that he was spending more and more time at his cabin at Big Sur. Like many, he was drawn to the idea of a simpler, rural life; and because of his popularity, it had become impossible to get any respite from the constant demands his San Francisco life made on him.

Michael Brunette, a carpenter friend of Gary Snyder's who lived near Snyder outside Nevada City, California, had built a ten-by-twelve-foot Japanese teahouse for Ferlinghetti near the Bixby cabin. Brunette had learned Japanese-style carpentry from some Japanese carpenters who had come from Japan to erect a small temple that had been given to a Buddhist commune near Snyder's cabin. For Ferlinghetti he trucked down ponderosa pine ridgepoles from the high country and built the teahouse on the edge of a stone pool, with construction techniques that didn't use nails.

Ever since he had known Ginsberg and Snyder, Ferlinghetti had been aware and interested in their deepening involvement in Eastern spiritual philosophy and practice. By the mid-sixties those interests had become a cornerstone of the youth counterculture, and Ferlinghetti's own involvement with them had likewise become progressively more serious. In the teahouse Ferlinghetti kept a tatami mat for meditation, and "I did a lot of chanting," he said recently, "as most dope smokers and LSD consumers were doing in the sixties. I did a lot of chanting of Hare Krishna before the Hare Krishna mantra became such a cliché. It was a really beautiful mantra to sing; and the Great Paramita Sutra and other mantras."

But of all the gurus—self-styled and otherwise—who either capitalized on those interests or made themselves available, Jiddhu Krishnamurti, centered in Ojai, California, near Santa Barbara, was the one Ferlinghetti "got the most out of." Grounded in Buddhism, Krishnamurti's particular teachings struck a strongly sympathetic chord with Ferlinghetti's own anarchist philosophy.

He had been discovered by two Western spiritual seekers in 1911 when he was still a child, and groomed to be the "vehicle" of the next "World Teacher." When he grew up, he traveled throughout his native India, Europe, and the United States, finally settling in Ojai in the twenties.

During his years as a teacher, he founded schools in India, in England, and in the United States, and headed the "Order of the Star," which the two who had discovered him had established. Then at a world theosophical congress in 1939, believing that the kind of clerical bureaucracy which made him a "head" was counter to the true spirit of his own Buddhist insights, he dissolved the order completely. He also, incidentally, came to influence painter Jackson Pollock through a mutual acquaintance.

"He avoided any kind of formal church or hierarchy or labels," Ferlinghetti explained. "He eschewed the label 'Buddhist' even. He rejected being a master, he rejected being a leader . . . I really admired that."

At his own readings, Ferlinghetti began using an autoharp with his poetry, incorporating both the spiritual and the secular temper of the counterculture. Both Ginsberg and Bly had used musical instruments with varying success; and of course, Ferlinghetti had read with jazz accompaniment in the late fifties. As a poet who had always valued the largest possible audience, he was well aware that most young people were much more interested in visual and oral forms than in traditional books.

"Who is reading books of poetry these days?" he said in the 1969 interview. "The rock generation certainly isn't . . . say under the age of twenty-five. . . . The whole revolution of the sixties was psychedelic and visual and oral: the poster trip and the rock trip . . . the book wasn't it. Maybe now it is Zap Comics. The amount of Zap Comics we sell at the bookstore is enormous."

Yet another bookstore clerk was in fact arrested for selling the new political and sexually explicit "underground" comics, which police judged obscene. Again, however, the case was dropped by the courts.

Ferlinghetti himself had no musical background, but the autoharp was easy to play. Further, as he pointed out then, "it is an indigenous American instrument. It's not like using the sitar or tamboura," both Eastern instruments other performers had begun using. Though Ferlinghetti's own work is less bound to Whitman and American roots than to European, especially French, sources, he found the Eastern influences even more alien, and the incorporation of the American instrument more fitting.

He became interested specifically in trying to develop what he called an "American Mantra" (a mantra being a Buddhist or Hindu prayer, chanted or sung to create a transcendent religious state in the chanter) "with American English words as opposed to singing Sanskrit or other unknown tongues," as he explained it in an introductory note in *Open Eye, Open Heart*, the 1973 collection where he published some of these mantras. They are of varying lengths, but all are emphatically rhythmic, many repeating key words or phrases throughout in slightly varying contexts.

> *Sun Sun*
> *Ah sun Om sun*
> *Sun Sun Sun*
> *Great God Sun*
> *Still riseth in our Rubiyat*
> *and strikes and strikes*
> *And strikes the towers*
> *with a shaft of light!*

begins "Big Sur Sun Sutra."

Fantasy Records released an album of Ferlinghetti chanting and singing with the autoharp, but looking back twenty years later, he views this experiment, like his readings with jazz, "a disaster. . . . It was a great act of generosity on [Fantasy's] part . . . I'm no musician, and it was horrible on my friends. Because it was really awful to hear, but I thought I was wonderful . . . I had the nerve to get up on stage with it." He laughed. ". . . I turned myself on anyway."

The effort to address and integrate the external and internal—the politics of the real world, and the realizations of the new consciousness— continued as his work vibrated between the two poles. In the spring, after his return from Europe and the March journey to Mexico, he read again with Robert Bly at another Resist antiwar benefit in Santa Barbara. The event was emceed by Kenneth Rexroth and featured rock music as well—an example of the uneasy marriage of music and poetry about which he reflected.

Though he saw these new combinations as a way to "bridge the gap" between the fifties and the sixties, "the single unaccompanied voice couldn't stand up to a rock group," he reflected more recently. "I mean, it's murder to come on stage after a good rock group as a single unaccompanied voice." In the 1969 interview he said, "I didn't get on until one A.M. I was part of an enormously long variety show program, and I had to follow Mad River. I did one long poem with a taped raga backing up my voice. That was really murder."

At the reading, Bly read the long, mystical-surrealist antiwar poem he had been working on and reading in various stages for some time, "The Teeth Mother Naked at Last." Particularly taken with the poem, Ferlinghetti told Bly after the reading, "You know, you're crazy—" and asked if he could publish it. They agreed to issue it first as a broadside, distributing thousands of free copies to draft-resistance centers. Then the poem was printed and sold as a pamphlet, and in the Pocket Poets series, and eventually a final version was included in Bly's 1973 collection, *Sleepers Joining Hands.*

At the same time, Ferlinghetti had some moments in Montecito, just outside Santa Barbara, to reflect on his personal life—the other pole. That March he had turned fifty, certainly a major milestone, inspiring "A Phoenix at Fifty": "At new age fifty / turn inward on old self. . . ." The experience, at least at the time of composition, was one of determined rebirth, as the title suggests, in the presence of "pure desire made of light." In confronting the inescapable fact of mortality, his attitude is vigorously optimistic. At the conclusion, partly as the result of a helicopter which has appeared,

> *the blown light batters thru*
> *lids and lashes*
> *I burn and leave*
> *no ashes*
>
> *Yet will arise*

Then a little later that spring, he began another long work as explicitly political as anything he had yet done. Written the May and June after Richard Nixon's inauguration as President, the prose of *Tyrannus Nix* became a scathing attack against Nixon and the policies which carried on the Vietnam War and encouraged police violence against dissenters: "Old Slick Dick in you we finally see no face at all behind the great Seal of the United States We see an index of night. . . ." Further on, he wrote, "I heard you plainly tell them on TV to get a little tougher to get a little rougher on campus and the next day they murdered one of us. . . ."

The "murder" was the May shooting of young James Rector in Berkeley by an Alameda County sheriff. Rector had apparently been an uninvolved bystander caught in police suppression of the ongoing demonstrations surrounding the establishment of People's Park that spring. The property had been a vacant lot that the University of California owned, which students and habitués had converted by themselves into a park. When the university began assuming control of it, ostensibly to build a soccer field, and motivated by Governor Ronald Reagan's campaign pledge to "clean up Berkeley," students and sympathizers rebelled, refusing to leave. Police eventually dispersed them, and the university put up an eight-foot-high steel mesh fence around the lot; but when more than 2,000 protestors marched from a rally to "take back the park," the confrontation turned violent. Police and deputies used tear gas and shotguns; over 100 protestors were hurt, one blinded, and another killed by deputies' buckshot. The police violence caused more and more of the Berkeley community to come to the support of the protestors, and confrontations continued until June, ultimately highlighted by a peaceful Memorial Day march that drew some 25,000 to 50,000. During that demonstration, marchers carried green flags made from Girl Scout uniforms while Quakers passed out daisies to guardsmen who put them on their bayonets and in their rifle barrels. Faced with such community opposition, the university finally abandoned its plans, leaving the park to its original users.

As a result of People's Park, Ferlinghetti published "Green Flag" as the third edition of the *Journal for the Protection of All Beings,* edited by two of the People's Park protestors. On the back cover Ferlinghetti wrote, "This anthology of poetry by a mob of beautiful poets, some famous, some infamous, some unknown, grew like grass out of the People's Park Movement in Berkeley in May and June of 1969, the poetry itself symbolizes Green Power at its nonviolent best."

His own polemical *Tyrannus Nix* wasn't in fact intended to be a poem, but a "populist hymn" in the spirit of Vachel Lindsay, Carl Sandburg, and others—writers Ferlinghetti had become familiar with as an undergraduate. Still, as narrowly political and didactic as the piece was, his internal side came out in the end with his hope that "the Lotus might yet open and open into the very stoned heart of light The void of serenity might yet prove not too strange for the mind of man We are daily faced with the Miraculous And the air is electric with hate And the air is alive with love and we are charged with loving You too."

One June evening, when Ferlinghetti called James Laughlin about the book's production, Laughlin went on to tell Ezra Pound about it. Laughlin reported that Pound "produced a broad grin." Despite the old poet's disengagement from contemporary affairs, Ferlinghetti's tract seemed to have called up some sympathy to the caricatures Pound improvised in his World War II broadcasts from Italy, however misguided they were.

At the time, Bantam Books became interested in printing the book in mass-market form and wrote to New Directions about the possibility, but Bantam never took it on. Laughlin suspected that "someone there in the top management probably loves Nixon and put the veto on the book. Naturally the editors at Bantam wouldn't report that, but would give another reason. . . ." When New Directions brought out the book in November, in a long, narrow format in Ferlinghetti's own hand printing, not surprisingly, like all of Ferlinghetti's work, it sold well—ultimately some 45,000 copies.

On June 8, 1969, as Ferlinghetti was completing *Tyrannus Nix*, Nixon announced an agreement with South Vietnam President Nguyen Van Thieu to institute a policy of "Vietnamization" of the war. The idea was that the Vietnamese would begin to take over more of the fighting, and the United States would begin to reduce its massive military presence— over a half million American troops were in South Vietnam by that spring. But the agitation against the U.S. presence there, and against other per- ceived establishment injustices, would continue to grow before it began winding down with the war itself.

In 1969, besides People's Park in Berkeley, demonstrations saw nine- teen hundred National Guardsmen fight with students at the University of Wisconsin, an auditorium burned by demonstrators at the City College of New York, four hundred state police called to quell students at Harvard, and black students at Cornell seizing the administration building, among the most widely covered uprisings. And in the spring of 1970, on May 4, four students at Kent State University in Ohio were killed by National Guardsmen in another massive wave of protest over the sending of U.S. troops into Cambodia.

But even as Ferlinghetti continued to be one of the most sought-after figures by college audiences, filling auditoriums with his performances, his own difficulties with his marriage deepened. Then in September 1969 the death of North Vietnam's leader, Ho Chi Minh, provided yet another opportunity for a demonstration in Berkeley against U.S. involvement in Vietnam, this one in the form of a "funeral" for the deceased leader. Ferlinghetti went to read a Yevtushenko poem at the event, and the occasion resulted in a poem of his own which mixes his personal and political sides more fully than anything he had written.

"Enigma of Ho Chi Minh's Funeral" is more definitely surrealist than much of his writing at the time, a direction no doubt inspired partly by the times themselves, where the seemingly unreal events of the war and the pursuit of expanded consciousness textured every day. Though its title and Ferlinghetti's decision to include it among the "Public and Political Poems" of the *Open Eye, Open Heart* collection suggest strongly political content, the poem itself rings strikingly a portentous, personal note, and is finally about the relationship between the political and the personal.

> I am walking down the middle
> of Telegraph Avenue Berkeley
> in the middle of the surrealist enigma
> which is Ho Chi Minh's funeral . . .

the poem begins, and goes on to describe the poet's reading of a "post-revolutionary poem by Yevtushenko," which asserts that "Truth is no longer truth / when the Revolution incidentally / sets fire to a loved one's roof. . . ."

It is a surreal dream image that suggests the way politics and political involvement can affect—and damage—one's personal life. When at the end of the poem "I run over my family / accidentally," the painful personal implications are unavoidable.

Even from the early days, Ferlinghetti and Kirby had seemed to friends and acquaintances not well matched. Though Kirby's quick, lively intelligence made an interesting contrast to Ferlinghetti's shy, quiet, even taciturn manner, the difference didn't seem to work as a complement. Beyond the first several months of teaching, she had never been able to find any job, activity, way of life—anything—to satisfy her; and her dissatisfactions often appeared to turn into antagonism toward her husband. Though she didn't have any literary ambitions, Ferlinghetti's own satisfactions and successes must also have provoked some jealousy at his ease in the world.

In 1970 Robert Bly came to Inverness, on the coast just north of San Francisco, to spend a year. He remembers a drive with Ferlinghetti and Kirby when the two men were simply having fun, making jokes about the oysters they were eating. Kirby sat stiffly, refusing to join in at all. "It was as if she couldn't stand it that he was having so much fun," Bly said.

According to one mutual friend who has known them both since their first years in San Francisco, Kirby's sister, who was permanently bed-ridden, her father, who was deaf, and the liberal conscience of her mother, all combined to instill "a load of guilt" about what she did have. And she wanted badly to have a child, which she hoped would make her happy, but she and Ferlinghetti had been unable to conceive through the fifties. Aside from that one determination, she seemed unable to make any decision and stick to it. Expressed regularly in a volatile temper, her unease, combined with Ferlinghetti's commitment to the frontiers of the new consciousness and his immersion in the rapid cultural ferment, put more and more distance between them.

He usually asked Kirby to come with him on his travels, but since the

Nerja adventure, she had always declined. The children were very young, of course, which would have made things difficult, but even as they grew, she chose not to go; she was subject to severe allergic reactions, and troubled as well by her own brand of restlessness and dissatisfaction.

"There were many places where he just wanted to make the scene, and it just wouldn't have worked to bring his wife along," a mutual friend speculated. Ferlinghetti and the people around him "were deeply involved in literature and had little to do with anything but experimental writing. Kirby was just a complete alien to that atmosphere and those people. . . . Then it became the psychedelic sixties and Bixby Canyon, and Lawrence was going off to all kinds of places, and then it became a serious rift. . . . They were experimenting with drugs at that time . . . they were floundering around, they didn't know what was going to happen, but they were going to do it . . . and Kirby was cantakerous and pissed off because he was doing it, and she was a millstone around his neck."

For Ferlinghetti, the friend recalls, it seemed "his whole mind, his whole interest was in that phase of his development, that experience that he would be able to use, and the family, the wife and the kids were not really that immediately important to him."

Though Kirby did try some of the psychedelic drugs later, at the beginning, "when they started taking acid," she said recently, "I just lost contact with him. I just wouldn't go. I wouldn't smoke grass."

Ferlinghetti, however, holds no rancor, and takes a longer view.

"She's an uprooted southerner," he explained. "She comes from that old southern culture where a woman is brought up in the genteel tradition. . . . She's just very generous and kindhearted and gullible. It's almost as if she needs a guardian angel to take care of her. She had no use for [that tradition] when she was growing up. She revolted against having a coming-out party, and against the cotillion and the country club and all that. She had rejected the South."

But as she grew older and became a mother, her upbringing apparently came to the fore, conflicting with the rebellious streak which she had earlier shared with Ferlinghetti.

"Being an uprooted southerner, she really needs her roots," Ferlinghetti went on. "In San Francisco she didn't have that, so she was much more dependent on me. When I left, it was more disastrous than it would have been for someone who didn't come out of that kind of culture."

Ferlinghetti had begun spending more time in San Francisco at the Filbert Street apartment, as the situation became more complicated. And in addition to the land at Big Sur, back in the late fifties he had bought another lot in Bolinas, a small, protected coastal community just north of the city. The land was 100 feet square—five 20-foot-square lots. In the flush of the late sixties back-to-the-land rural consciousness, this location, commuting distance from San Francisco, was a place he could imagine living. These land purchases seemed to grow in part from the very homelessness of his childhood. The desire to put down roots, to have a place—or places—to which he belonged in the world had been formed early and continued to pull at him. Even in the eighties he has expressed some desire for a place in Mexico, where he has so often visited; a place in Arizona, a place in Hawaii—all landscapes which attracted him strongly at different times and for different reasons. On the one hand, it seems the sort of idle conversation we all pass; but as with other ideas which remain merely daydreams for others, for him, at least in the case of Bolinas and Big Sur, it became fact.

In the late sixties he arranged to have a house built on the mesa at Bolinas, a three-bedroom, flat-roofed redwood house on stilts, with a big fireplace to warm the living room. By the time the house was finally ready, however, he and Kirby were virtually separated, and for three years or so, at the beginning of the seventies, she moved out there by herself, with Julie and Lorenzo. During the sixties he had gone off for various trips, and "he came back several times," Kirby remembers. "The time he went to Russia, he was gone for months." And in 1968, when he went to Sicily, Kirby thought he was leaving for good. "He said he wasn't ever coming back," she remembered. "But he did. I guess he felt obligated."

His own childhood as an orphan and foster child was something whose pains he did not want to impose on his own children, and when he was gone, he simply missed his family. Though he never actually lived with them in Bolinas, he was a frequent visitor.

In March of 1972 these problems were clearly on his mind as he took Lorenzo, now nine, on a month-long trip with Allen Ginsberg to Australia, where he and Ginsberg had been invited to read at the Adelaide Festival of the Arts. On the way they stopped first in Oahu and visited Michael Weiner, an ethnobotanist and psychedelic specialist at the University of Hawaii who was an acquaintance of Ginsberg's. Weiner's concern that scientists were becoming too isolated from the larger culture led to his own interest in literature, and he and Ferlinghetti became friends. A year later Ferlinghetti again took Lorenzo with him to visit Weiner for a week of camping and fishing; and when Weiner and his family moved a few years later to Fairfax, just north of San Francisco, the friendship continued.

After a week with Weiner and his family, in which they also visited the main island, Ferlinghetti, Lorenzo, and Ginsberg went on to Fiji. There, along with three to four hundred other white tourists, they witnessed the fire-walking ceremony at Koraleva by the Begu tribe. Two nights later Ferlinghetti spent a restless night in Nadi, kept up by the noise of traffic and of others at the hotel "between dreams of the breakup of my family . . . all night. . . ."

These personal confusions contributed to another twist at the festivities surrounding Adelaide. Though Ferlinghetti was certainly not a "womanizer," his position as artist and celebrity, as well as his striking good looks, had been drawing women to him for years wherever he went. But his dedication to his family, rooted in his own early abandonment, and the traditional moral virtues with which the Bislands had sought to imbue him, along with his own high profile in San Francisco especially, led him to keep any groupies, or even more substantial attractions, at arm's length. It isn't surprising if in other places, however, given his distance from home and the relations with Kirby, he was occasionally drawn to women he met.

Now, during the difficult working-through of his own confusions, he was drawn into a brief affair with a woman he met in Adelaide, with whom he spent parts of the next week. He was never one to indulge his own pleasure at the expense of others, however, especially his family, and he was always sensitive to the feelings of all involved. He took very seriously his role as father. Thus, though Lorenzo remembers most of the trip in great detail, he has no memory at all of her, nor does Ginsberg.

After the stay in Adelaide, where he and Ginsberg were joined by Voznesensky, and thousands jammed the readings, they went on to Melbourne, where another reading was scheduled. Between the two stops, Ferlinghetti and Lorenzo went off to the outback, where they stayed with another acquaintance, an Australian publisher and editor who had a large sheep farm. The friend had a son Lorenzo's age, and Ferlinghetti took the two boys for a four-day jaunt on a paddle-wheel houseboat he rented on the Murray River, Australia's longest inland waterway, fishing and enjoying the scenery and the surroundings. The double-decker boat, driven by an old VW engine, plied the switchback river between its dramatic cliffs which were dotted with exotic pink cockatoos. It also gave Ferlinghetti a chance to be captain again, a role he relished since his war experience, though at one point he managed to get lost; they didn't have a compass and wound up back where they had been the day before. But there was no real hurry to get anywhere.

When they returned to Melbourne, he and Lorenzo shared a suite adjoining one rented for Ginsberg, and the two poets, along with Voznesensky, read at the Town Hall there. Though Melbourne is a much more conservative city in general, every "outsider," everyone who was attracted by the counterculture, hippie spirit, came to the huge reading, filling the hall to its capacity of several thousand.

At the event some Russians demonstrated against Voznesensky as a representative of the Soviet Union, protesting against dictatorship and censorship and asking him what he thought about Aleksandr Solzhenitsyn. Ginsberg asserts that the Russian really couldn't respond openly, as he was almost certainly shadowed by the Soviet secret police, but Ferlinghetti and Ginsberg defended him, and the reading went on. Afterward, Ginsberg and Voznesensky went off to Darwin Land in Central Australia, while Ferlinghetti and Lorenzo spent the next two days wandering around Melbourne, before going to Sydney for two days, and another reading there.

Before going home, he and Lorenzo went deep-sea fishing off Grand Kepel Island, near the Great Barrier Reef off the east coast of Queensland, where they caught a seventeen-pound, two-foot golden trevally, an incident Ferlinghetti recounts in his journal with an ironic comparison to Hemingway. They spent a couple of days in the tropical landscape there, collecting shells on the long white sand beaches and taking a Land-Rover to see some of the old houses.

Then they went on to New Zealand, and after the seemingly idyllic days in Australia, some of the familiar shadows from home surfaced again. Struck by a Maori proverb about death and rebirth, he wrote in his journal, musing amid seemingly wild alternatives:

> Shall I disappear in Bali next year & take a Balinese wife? Shall I rent a houseboat in Sausalito, or buy a sea-going fishboat and sail Polynesia? Should I move to New Orleans or Santa Fe? Shall I give up poetry and concentrate on great prose-poetry novels? Shall I take up painting again in earnest? Shall I go into monumental sculpture and try some of those myriad ideas I've always had for same? Shall I cut my hair or let it grow longer and tie it in a perruque? Shall I return to my "wife & family" and stay home with the kids? All these are serious ideas, which I am actually at this moment capable of realizing—but incapable of resolving; incapable of choosing among them, I will no doubt do what is always done by default; thus we continue strangely

and blindly along some inexplicable course, in a direction which somehow has been set by decisions unconscious, by predilections we are not even able to articulate or recognize as prime movers, where we go and for what reasons as deep a mystery as existence itself . . . An open-heart sandwich impossible to eat.

On the way back he and Lorenzo stayed for a week in Tahiti, at a beach house an editor he knew made available along with a Jeep. He went snorkeling and visited the Musée Gauguin, noting that, ironically, there wasn't one original painting by the French master who had forged his art about South Pacific subjects.

When he got back to San Francisco, none of the confusions had been resolved, of course, though it had been an idyllic journey. He took another brief trip to Mexico in May, making some notes toward a new travel journal and writing the poem "Carnaval de Maïz," contrasting the poverty of the third-world peasants with American complacency; but Ferlinghetti himself felt far from complacent.

By the end of the year the publishing office on Filbert Street had been moved downstairs into the storefront, and Ferlinghetti was living almost completely in the small three-room apartment upstairs. Besides the kitchen, he had a study and a bedroom, with only a simple mat on the bare floor for a bed. For the next three or four years, then, when Kirby and the children lived in Bolinas, Ferlinghetti frequently spent time with his family there, and then Lorenzo lived for a time with him on Filbert. Though the going back and forth didn't necessarily make for an ideal domestic arrangement, he stayed close to his children, making the best he could of these difficult terms. And as his domestic life changed, so did his poetry, slowly turning more personal, more inward, as he grappled with his new circumstances at the onset of middle age, and the 1970s.

Walking down Grant Avenue one day in the spring of 1971, Ferlinghetti ran into the woman he had met with Philip Lamantia in Paris six years before. Soon after that meeting, Nancy Peters and Lamantia had become steady companions, living and traveling in Europe through the late sixties. After returning to the United States, Peters added a degree in library science to a comparative literature degree from the University of Washington and worked for a year at the Library of Congress in Washington, D.C. In 1970 she came to San Francisco on vacation, liked the city, and decided to quit her job and find a way to live there.

Learning she had worked at the Library of Congress, Ferlinghetti told her about a current City Lights project. They were trying to put together a bibliography of Allen Ginsberg's by now voluminous published writings, and there were last-minute problems with organization. Some supplementary indices were needed to make the bibliography complete and usable—could she help?

Peters had been working with Donald Allen on the *Collected Poems* of Frank O'Hara just after her move to San Francisco, and she was pleased to have more free-lance work before finding a job as a librarian. Then, just a few days after she started working at City Lights, Ferlinghetti's editorial assistant, Jan Herman, got an offer to go to Germany.

"He said, 'I'm going to leave tomorrow,' " Peters recalls, " 'and here's how you do this job. The whole idea is, Lawrence wants to see as little as possible of the mail. Just take care of everything and don't bother him. That's the way he most likes it. And when he comes in, you can give him a summary of what's going on.' Jan showed me the files and waved to some old cardboard cartons and shoe boxes of manuscripts and records in closets and kitchen cupboards. When Lawrence next came to work I said, Jan's gone and I'm here now until we decide what to do next. He gazed at me in a remote sort of way and said, 'Oh, fine.' I've been here ever since."

Shig Murao was still managing the bookstore single-handedly with great style, and Peters began assuming the same role at the Grant and Filbert publishing offices in the corner storefront and apartment. From 1967, when the offices first moved there to accommodate the increasingly large volume of City Lights Books, through 1969, twenty new books came out, and in the next three years, nineteen more, along with several broadsides and short pamphlets, all helped greatly by the new organization Peters brought to the press. Among some of the most prominent were Kerouac's *Scattered Poems*, the Cassady collection, Ginsberg's *The Fall of America*, Los Angeles writer Charles Bukowski's *Erections, Ejaculations, Exhibitions, and General Tales of Ordinary Madness*, Diane DiPrima's *Revolutionary Letters*, and Voznesensky's *Dogalypse*.

The Kerouac poems had been collected mostly by Ann Charters, Kerouac's first biographer, from various magazines where they had first appeared in the fifties. The book also included a section of the *San Francisco Blues* manuscript which Ferlinghetti had originally turned down for publication, a decision Ferlinghetti came to regret. He felt that City Lights ought to have more Kerouac on its list, but Kerouac's family has not permitted him to publish a larger, hundred-page manuscript of Kerouac's poems, which he is still holding. When Ferlinghetti was in Kerouac's hometown of Lowell, Massachusetts, in 1978, he called Kerouac's third wife, Stella Sampas, to get permission to publish "Pomes All Sizes," Kerouac's title for his manuscript. She was "coldly" uninterested, according to Ferlinghetti's journal of the conversation, referring him to the New York literary agent who handles Kerouac's work. When Ferlinghetti told her that the agent was interested in money while "we're interested in poetry," she said she "didn't want to get into that." Ferlinghetti went on to tell her that he had put flowers on Kerouac's grave, and she said, echoing Ferlinghetti's own statement to the press after Kerouac's death, "I appreciate you putting flowers, but why didn't you take care of [Jack] too?"

Bukowski, whose work has gone on to sell as well as Ginsberg's, and so help in no small way to support City Lights' publication of important but less popular writing, first came to Ferlinghetti's attention in the sixties through his poetry, which had appeared widely and in some of the most prestigious underground literary magazines of the time. His tales of Los Angeles working-class life, of odd jobs, racetracks, whiskey, and women, captured a world that Ferlinghetti thought significant, in a distinctive and important voice. The Bukowski collection that City Lights published was assembled by Gail Chiarrello, who had also been working for the press and had collected some of his stories from various underground magazines and newspapers where they had first appeared. Ferlinghetti accurately predicted that Bukowsi would become popular and sought to publish more of his work, but Bukowski remained loyal to John Martin, who had founded Black Sparrow Press and initially published Bukowski's work.

In September 1973 City Lights brought Bukowski to San Francisco to read to a packed house at the Telegraph Hill Neighborhood Center, as part of the City Lights Poets Theater. The theater had been formed in 1971, growing out of conversations between Peters and Ferlinghetti, and largely through the work of Joe Krysiak, a theater aficionado-playwright-producer of sorts, as well as graphic designer, who worked at the store as a book packer.

"Lawrence and I wanted City Lights to sponsor important events, to introduce poets of international stature and to be involved in benefits for things we believed in," Peters said. "But the store was too small."

Krysiak had a studio at the Project Artaud People's Hall, a converted warehouse at the edge of the Mission District, and one of the first co-op living-studio spaces for artists. For the readings Krysiak designed striking posters as well as sets and staging, and the hall was consistently filled to its capacity of some two thousand.

The first Poets Theater readings, by Russian poets Andrei Voznesensky in October 1971 and Yevgeny Yevtushenko in February 1972, were terrific successes. The Russians read in a dramatic style that delighted the audience, Ferlinghetti writing later that they "stood like athletes used to performing in huge stadia and gestured dramatically." In a later, 1979 *New York Times* review, John Russell echoed the description of Voznesensky's distinctive style, writing that his "consonants had the ring of cavalry on cobblestones" and "even silence had its heartbeat."

Ferlinghetti had always found Yevtushenko ironically aloof and patrician, given his proletarian sympathies. During his visit to San Francisco, the Russian poet traveled by limousine and stayed at the Sir Francis Drake Hotel in Union Square, one of San Francisco's oldest and finest, "holding court and ordering the hotel staff around and complaining," according to Peters.

"He was horrified that he was to read in a warehouse," she went on, "and he demanded a great concert hall. We had to explain 'cultural differences' to persuade him that in the U.S. a factory warehouse was a politically appropriate place for a poet to read. And that American poets aren't in the elite class as they are in the Soviet Union, so the Opera House was in any case out of the question."

Nonetheless, his performance, like Voznesensky's, was hugely popular, and years later Ferlinghetti remarked that at least he came to the post-performance party.

The younger Voznesensky, on the other hand, was more personable and accessible, and Ferlinghetti felt more comfortable with him from their first meeting at Spoleto in 1965. After that meeting, in the interests of cultural exchange and understanding across "the obscene boundaries," as Ferlinghetti had put it in his journal then, he had invited the Russian poet to read in San Francisco in 1966, in a program cosponsored by rock promoter Bill Graham at the Fillmore Auditorium. Ferlinghetti read the translations between sets of the Jefferson Airplane, and despite the rock-music echoes and atmosphere with which the poetry had to compete, Ferlinghetti's popularity and Voznesensky's reading style made their appearance a great success. During his October visit he stayed at the Filbert Street apartment for a week or more, sleeping on the mattress on the floor and sampling American bohemian literary ambience. After reading in a few more cities, he joined Ferlinghetti in Las Vegas, where they both had been invited to read at the University of Las Vegas. Planning to meet Voznesensky there, Ferlinghetti went from the airport to a modest motel near the outskirts of the city where he had made reservations for the two of them. When he arrived, however, he found that Voznesensky had left a note saying, "I'm not staying at this dump, I'll be at Caesar's Palace."

"Lawrence was quite shocked," Peters recalls, at the Russian's eager immersion in the height of capitalist decadence. And his shock grew when he went to Caesar's to find Voznesensky ensconced in the bathtub, where he was on the phone to Moscow describing his amazement at the capitalist decadence.

It turned out that the whole extraordinary affair came about because someone connected with the university was married to the manager of Caesar's and had arranged for the poet's accommodations there.

Though the specific incident was never preserved in a poem by either of them, the whole adventure occasioned "Las Vegas Tilt," which Ferlinghetti terms "a real documentary poem," as it recounts other highlights of Ferlinghetti's trip from his takeoff in San Francisco, concluding with Voznesensky's try at a slot machine.

The long poem takes a predictably discouraging view of the place and its meaning for the American dream. "THE FATE OF THE WORLD / DEPENDS UPON / THE WAY WE LIVE . . . ," Ferlinghetti writes at the beginning of the poem, quoting from a sign on the way to the San Francisco airport. Then, in the dizzying kaleidoscope of Las Vegas that the poem describes, he sees "The end of the American dream . . . on the Street That Never Sleeps . . ." as " 'the extraordinary adventure of white America' / roars on. . . ." It is ". . . a scene from Dante . . ." at whose end we "await the final / deluge jackpot landslide / of earth and life / in which," the poet reminds us, "the fate of the world / depends upon / the way we live."

That "way we live" seems ominously destructive in the view of the poem, and its pessimism is deepened in many of the poems he was writing at the time, reflecting his personal life as well as his view of political conditions. In Vancouver the previous March, he had read with Bly and Voznesensky, and five hundred copies of a broadside of "A World Awash with Fascism and Fear," written about the same time, were given away. Completely without any of the humor, or ironic undertone, or balancing force that all his other public poems contain, it is probably the most unremittingly negative view he ever published:

> *This land is awash with fascism & fear*
> *And the jails cry for freedom*
> *Let us not deal with the obvious*
> > *exemplars & assholes of fascism*
> *We will not name them with new free publicity*
> *We all know where certain fat cats are at*
> > *Their medals*
> > > *give them away. . . .*

Despite its claim in these opening lines that it will not name "the obvious exemplars," the poem goes on to list current places and people that were sources or victims of injustice, and is a clear example of one extreme of feeling that events at the time precipitated in many people. The Vietnam War still dominated the news, and though American troops were withdrawing, the "light at the end of the tunnel" that government officials kept talking about was still feared by increasing numbers of Americans to be that of an oncoming train, as a contemporary joke went. The poem also alludes to the situation in Greece, where a brutal coup in 1967 had overthrown the democratic government. The new regime had executed thousands without trial and ruthlessly tried to suppress all individual liberty and expression. Many artists and writers had fled to exile and aided the formation of a Greek resistance.

In April 1972 City Lights Poets Theater sponsored a benefit for the Greek Resistance at Fugazi Hall on Green Street in North Beach. The benefit brought together writers from Greece with writers from America as well as other countries. Andrei Codrescu, Diane DiPrima, Fernando Alegría, Kay Boyle, and more than a dozen others read, along with Ferlinghetti, who read his "Forty Odd Questions for the Greek Regime and One Cry for Freedom."

"Where do we catch the boat for Plato's Republic?" the poem asks in a characteristically ironic allusion to Greece's history as the ancient cradle of democracy. And in the next line, he underlines the point: "Is it true that your great Greek tragedies and tragi-comedies are now being performed daily in police stations?" Toward the end he asks, "Does *Zei* still mean 'he lives' in your language?"—an allusion to the film *Z*, by Costa-Gavras, whose title refers to a popular candidate assassinated during the election campaign aborted by the coup. For better than a year, the movie drew turn-away crowds in major cities all over the country, who were stirred partly by the still high political awareness Vietnam had brought. Outraged at the U.S. government's at least tacit support of the repressive Greek dictatorship, the film's horrors were also seen as a cautionary tale relating to the United States' own domestic circumstances.

Adding to the series of gloomy events both public and personal which seemed to be accumulating, Ferlinghetti and City Lights had earlier that year marked another death closer to home, which occasioned another large Poets Theater performance. In late January 1972, Kenneth Patchen, one of the poets whose passionate pacifist and anarchist stances had been a model for Ferlinghetti even before he came to San Francisco, and particularly influential in his first decade there, died in Palo Alto, where he had spent the last decade of his life. Patchen had moved down there to be closer to a hospital with the most advanced treatment for his degenerative paralysis, and as the disease progressed he became understandably more isolated.

In addition to a large body of beautiful lyric poems, at the heart of Patchen's work were an equally large number that spoke to contemporary political and social circumstances. He had published a dozen volumes since 1936, and a *Collected Poems* of nearly 550 pages in 1967, but, like Ferlinghetti himself, had received little attention from the critical establishment. Now, after his death, City Lights organized a memorial reading at a smaller theater on Mason Street that Krysiak had booked.

There, Ferlinghetti first read "An Elegy on the Death of Kenneth Patchen." Quoting from Patchen's poems, Ferlinghetti emphasized his belief in the importance of Patchen's vision as well as his dismay that he had been so unheard:

> . . . *he spoke much of love*
>   *and never lived by "silence exile & cunning"*
>   *and was a loud conscientious objector to*
>   *the deaths we daily give each other*
>   *though we speak much of love*
> *And when such a one dies*
>   *even the agents of Death should take note*
>   *and shake the shit from their wings*
>   *in Air Force One*
> *But they do not. . . .*

Bukowski's reading in late 1973 was the last of the Poets Theater, and for Peters and Ferlinghetti is memorable for Bukowski's girlfriend getting drunk and kicking out the panels in the door of the publishing office. But that scene had little to do—at least by itself—with the decision to abandon the theater.

"It was great fun," Peters said, "but we were putting an awful amount of time and energy into it. Krysiak wanted to direct some Eugene O'Neill plays, and we were all burnt out by the *Sturm und Drang* of clashing egos. I never wanted to organize another multi-poet event. Then, too, lots of new reading spaces were springing up."

The same year, Ferlinghetti's *Open Eye, Open Heart*, his longest collection, which includes the Patchen elegy, came out from New Directions. Divided into four sections, including the final "American Mantra & songs," the book comprises a full range of the personal and public poems he had been writing since the mid-1960s. The first section, containing the most personal poems, begins with "True Confessional," another of the "autobiographies" in the manner of the first "Autobiography" in *Coney Island*. It is followed by "Mock Confessional," a more satiric view of the genre, which invents parts of a life, as Ferlinghetti sometimes did during interviews in the late sixties. Both were written in late 1971 and early 1972, when his final separation from Kirby was imminent.

The first, especially, though not without humor, is much more somber, and purely interior in its portrait, than the "Autobiography" of fifteen years earlier. In it he pictures himself completely caught up by other forces,

> *a wind-up toy*
> *someone had dropped wound-up*
> *into a world already*
> *running down. . . .*

The pessimism of such a fatalistic view is relieved at the end, however, by insight characteristic of the spirituality of the time, which he had incorporated into his own view and work. There, his

> *. . . blue blue eyes*
> *. . . see as one eye*
> *in the middle of the head*
> *where everything happens*
> *except what happens*
> *in the heart*
> *vajra lotus diamond heart*
> *wherein I read*
> *the poem that never ends*

Though the "Mock Confessional" which follows, in many ways a more complex poem, is suffused with his signature ironies, it is hardly a light-hearted poem. Skipping from event to event like the earlier "Autobiography," it plainly declares some of the profound contradiction fragmenting his life at the time:

> *It seems my personal life is a complete fuck-up*
> *though I'm a raving success in the field*
> *While I'm catching the high fly*
> *a worm has succeeded in eating*
> *a hole in my soul*

But the end here, as in "A Phoenix at Fifty" and several other of the personal poems he wrote in these years, does strike a hopeful note of optimistic perseverance:

> *. . . my metamorphosis*
> *may not be done*
> *though now I am "old." . . .*

Neither of these "autobiographies" discovers any new answers, but they do exhibit an emotional dimension and a determined faith in the future running deeper than most any poems in his earlier books.

184 • Barry Silesky

Several other of the seventeen poems in that section pick up frequent Ferlinghetti concerns—sexual desire, the mythic "eternal" woman, and ironic observations of people in various locations. The fifteen poems in the second part all come from various, mostly European, trips, including the "Pound at Spoleto" prose poem, three from the Trans-Siberian adventure, and others from his 1965 Europe trip. The third section is made up of fourteen "Public & Political Poems," though some, particularly "Enigma of Ho Chi Minh's Funeral," have a distinctly nonpublic aspect as well.

Again, as with *The Secret Meaning of Things*, the book was largely ignored by the mainstream press, though *Secret Meaning* itself went on to sell nearly eighty thousand copies. The academic *Virginia Quarterly Review* again had nothing but harsh words for the work, saying, "There is a poetry which pulls moments apart and extends them into a different dimension to find their meaning, and this is not it. Rather we have a few genuine poems, several good mantra phrases, and a score of warm images from a show-and-tell life."

But J. M. Warner in *Library Journal* was as lavish in his praise as *Virginia Quarterly* was harsh in its criticism: "At fifty years of age, Ferlinghetti is still as dynamic, verbose, alarming, charming, and unsettling as when he began writing poetry. . . . His rhythms are rough, colloquial to the point that reading his poetry aloud is absolutely essential to get at the source of his meaning and the sense of his metamorphic content. . . . Big Sur, Las Vegas, Vietnam, London, Kenneth Patchen—Ferlinghetti shouts it, chants it, rails it, and either wins you over or revolts you. All with common language that in his context becomes often surreal and unerringly hits your eye and heart."

By the time the book came out, Ferlinghetti's divorce from Kirby was nearing its final stages, and many of the poems he was writing were understandably personal as they grappled with these circumstances. Though the distance between them had been building for a decade, Kirby's anger made the separation increasingly rancorous. Exacerbated by drinking and by pills, according to several accounts (though Ferlinghetti, typically, insists such characterization is unfair to her), her rancor persisted long after the divorce was final. Several observers remember an incident in the mid-seventies when the *San Francisco Bay Guardian*, a weekly arts and entertainment newspaper, published an edition featuring Ferlinghetti with his picture on the cover. One evening Kirby walked into the bookstore where a stack of the papers was sitting on the front counter, lit a match, and set the whole pile aflame.

For his part the sense of loss and alienation that such a trauma occasions came out in his poems. "Great American Waterfront Poem" is one of the most direct records of this. Another prose poem, he wrote it at the Eagle Cafe, a small, old, casual waterfront café decorated with ship regalia on the Embarcadero near Fisherman's Wharf. Ferlinghetti notes that the waterfront is the "Beginning of end and end of beginning," then goes on to remember "the first poem I ever wrote in San Francisco twenty years ago just married on a rooftop in North Beach overlooking this place." He looks at "The phone booth where I telephone It's All Over Count Me Out" while he sips a beer and waits for the lawyer to "call me back at noon" with "the final word on my divorce from civilization."

However traumatic it may have been (and Ferlinghetti, again with characteristic reticence, objects even to the use of the term), the divorce from Kirby was hardly a "divorce from civilization." Certainly the alienation he experienced as a poet and artist who all his life seemed to be apart and separate—first from the "normal" families he saw around him, then from the "normal" lives and values Americans lived by through the 1940s and 1950s—was immeasurably intensified, but his response had never been withdrawal. Rather, it was, as it had always been, broader and deeper engagement.

In January 1973 a cease-fire was finally signed in Vietnam, and in August, when bombing of Cambodia stopped, so did U.S. combat in Southeast Asia. It was April 1975 before the last U.S. helicopters flew out with the last U.S. officials while desperate refugees clung to the runners and fell to their deaths trying to escape, but after almost fifteen years, more than fifty thousand American deaths, and the worst domestic upheaval since the Depression, if not the Civil War, the Vietnam War was finally over. What ensued, however, was no dreamy tranquillity. In 1972 five men associated with Nixon's reelection committee were arrested for breaking into Democratic National Committee headquarters at the Watergate Hotel in Washington; two years later Nixon would resign under threat of imminent impeachment.

Ferlinghetti responded by adding a paragraph to *Tyrannus Nix* in 1973, recognizing that Nixon had turned out "to be beyond our wildest 'paranoid' fantasy of the depths of your deceptions." And beyond American borders, there was also no shortage of significant issues to be engaged, which Ferlinghetti continued to pursue in the next years.

The 1974 *City Lights Anthology*, a larger-format version of *City Lights Journal*, reflects several of these. The benefit reading for the Greek Resistance spawned a section of nine "Greek Poets Today" as well as Harold

Norse's poem "Greece Answers," which addresses the repression there. The anthology also contains poems by jailed Iranian poet Reza Baraheni; by the late Chilean poet Vicente Huidobro; by Isabelle Eberhardt, a young European who had lived among the Moslems in North Africa; by Jean Genet; and a new translation of Rimbaud's *A Season in Hell*. Besides the writing from other countries, "black power" leader Huey Newton has work included, Ginsberg contributes his record of the meetings with Ezra Pound, and several other writers whom City Lights published or who had been associated with City Lights and San Francisco are represented— Jack Micheline, Jerry Kamstra, Charles Bukowski, Gail Chiarello, Robert Creeley (some of whose contributions had been written at Ferlinghetti's Big Sur cabin), and Richard Brautigan. The issue concludes with a large section of work by "The Surrealist Movement in the U.S.," featuring an essay by Philip Lamantia and poems by nearly two dozen others, including Nancy Peters.

The issue also contains an essay by Herbert Marcuse, a Marxist theoretician whose books *Eros and Civilization* and *One Dimensional Man* had become cornerstone texts for the counterculture. Marcuse's essay "Marxism and Feminism" addressed the new women's liberation movement, placing it in a socialist framework and emphasizing its importance as a revolutionary movement. And after it is an excerpt from Diane DiPrima's long feminist poem, "Loba," and several more poems by women.

Ferlinghetti, ever the anarchist and revolutionary sympathizer, supported the women's movement, which gained strength beginning in the late sixties, though he had come of age and lived most of his adult life at a time well before the traditional roles of women began to change. Still, like most men of his generation, and many younger, he wasn't always aware of his own prejudices, nor able to overcome them. His own view of women, as expressed in *Her* and in his poems, was heavily conditioned by the idealization of the feminine that the women's movement protested. That kind of idealization, many believed, encouraged the treatment of women as aesthetic-sexual objects because it didn't admit the very range of human power and possibilities women had been historically denied.

His poem "In a Time of Revolution for Instance" recounts a characteristic anecdote at a café, where "three very beautiful" people, two men and a woman, come in. The poet is keenly aware of the difference between their apparent circumstances and his own: "they looked like they might be / related to the Kennedys and / they obviously had no Indian or Eyetalian / blood in them" while the poet himself "felt like Charlie Chaplin eating his shoe." He finds the woman very attractive, however, and concludes, *"in a time of revolution for instance / she might have fucked me."*

When he first read the poem to Peters, the final line was "I could have fucked her." Peters told him that this was exactly the attitude that enraged the women's movement. She warned him that reading this offensive line in public would ignite hostility from politically conscious women. Ferlinghetti nonetheless read the original version in Berkeley, and as Peters predicted, a number of women in the audience were incensed. A group of them went so far as to charge the stage, attacking Ferlinghetti with curses and fists. Forced to retreat off stage, he was visibly upset at what he felt was a misunderstanding of the poem.

After some thought, he decided to change the line to that published in *Open Eye*. Peters didn't feel the reversal to "she might have fucked me" "worked very well," as she put it, but Ferlinghetti was happy with the revision, and on reflection, it is clear that the violence in that line—which in the reversal is committed by "her" and not the male—is in the nature of revolution. Nonetheless, presumably to back even further away from charges of sexism, he revised it again for *Endless Life*, his volume of selected poems that came out almost ten years later. In the new version, he concludes, "we might have made it," the euphemism making "willing and equal participants" of both characters, as critic Michael Skau terms it.

Peters is also quick to point out that "for a man of his generation, he's been unusually open to the changes the women's movement has brought. In his personal relationships with women, he's honest, gentle, loyal, and generous. Quite extraordinary. He's a man who genuinely likes women, enjoys being in their company, and is capable of real friendship."

Ferlinghetti's own contribution to the anthology was a brief record of a journey he took in early February 1974 with his daughter, Julie, on horseback to the Green Gulch Ranch of the San Francisco Zen Center. There, Richard Baker-Roshi, the spiritual leader of the center, presided over a memorial to Alan Watts, who had been one of the foremost popularizers of Zen Buddhism to American audiences. He had died in October 1973, and Ferlinghetti rode to the hundredth-day celebration in honor of his passing. He later wrote that Watts had been "a brilliant speaker, . . . [who] was also known for his wild laughter and was a friend of many poets."

At the time, Ferlinghetti himself had begun to speak against what he called the "spiritual authoritarianism" infecting so many of the spiritual movements that had sprung up since the late 1960s. He was attracted to

Watts and Zen for some of the same reasons he was attracted to Krishnamurti; it was a discipline not overburdened with authoritarian rituals, and saw enlightenment as a fundamentally individual matter. In the journal Ferlinghetti notes that his sixteen-year-old dog, Homer, had also died recently, and in another journal he recorded that in the same month, Julie's dog had been run over and died. It was a year of loss on several fronts; and another major loss occurred in 1975.

Anne Waldman's long poem "Fast Speaking Woman," published by City Lights that year, helped vault her to national attention, and as part of the publicity surrounding the effort, she came to give a reading at a small theater near City Lights. The morning of the reading, however, Shig Murao told Ferlinghetti he had to go to the hospital. For several months he had been less than his usually energetic self; he had fallen once or twice, he seemed to some to tire more easily, to be distracted.

Ferlinghetti took him, and there Murao remained for some three weeks, recovering from a stroke he had suffered, brought on by an undiagnosed diabetic condition. Forced to deal directly with the store for the first time in more than a decade, Ferlinghetti came to realize that for several years it had been falling into deeper financial difficulties. At the same time, he was concerned about the tremendous workload that Murao had been shouldering. Joe Wolberg, who had been working at the store, took over managing while Murao was in the hospital, and made some changes Ferlinghetti approved to cut down book thievery and otherwise tighten operations.

Then, while Murao was recovering at home, Ferlinghetti told him what he had done. Murao was shocked. Though he knew that Ferlinghetti officially owned three quarters of the store to his one quarter, and that the monetary investment had been Ferlinghetti's, he had always been treated as an equal and believed the store was the cooperative, community center it had seemed for twenty years. That his partner would take such measures without consulting him at all seemed outrageous. Ferlinghetti believed, however, that he was making the situation more amenable for Murao by lightening his load, and helping the store at the same time. His idea was that Shig be a "majorduomo," as Ferlinghetti put it, and leave the packing and lifting and more physically demanding day-to-day work to Wolberg. The problem was that Shig saw such a move to share authority as a demotion, a reduction of responsibility that implied a lessening of his capabilities. And Ferlinghetti had done it without even consulting him. For Shig it seemed a question of honor.

"Lawrence writes his poems with no one standing over him and telling him how to write," Murao said later, "and that's how I ran the bookstore, without any outside help." If he could not come back and fully resume the responsibilities he had before his stroke, he would not come back at all.

Ferlinghetti was tremendously saddened by the impasse. Much more than just an employee, even a valued one, Murao had been a close friend. But some reorganization was clearly necessary to keep the bookstore afloat. After several months Murao turned the negotiations over to another bookseller to arrange for Ferlinghetti to buy him out. And when he heard about the conflict, even Ginsberg got involved and tried to mediate, but to no avail.

"I came sometime after the stroke," Ginsberg recalls, "and neither side really wanted to talk about it. It took some time for me to realize that there was this enormous split. And I was sort of heartsick because I knew both and was still dealing with both, and to this day I still stay with Shig when I go out there.... I felt karmically indebted to both because of 'Howl.'

"Larry made any number of attempts to placate him, get him back, apologize even, but Shig wouldn't have any of it. Perhaps an ingrained cultural difference, or Shig's neurosis, or Larry's ...

"But Shig was part of the basic culture of the store," Ginsberg went on. "Mainly I tried to get Shig to talk to Larry a little, and relayed messages from Larry that he regretted having moved Shig that way, that he didn't mean an insult.... Larry thought he was doing Shig a favor because he was working too hard. And Shig felt Larry was acting unilaterally—that Shig had an interest, was a partner, but hadn't been consulted. And had lost face."

Ginsberg well understood that profitability was far from Murao's main interest for himself. Not that he hadn't been a good manager, but "he was in it partly for the merit of it being kind of a Bhuddist, communal, post-sixties social service operation," as Ginsberg put it, "not so much devoted to making money, but as to maintaining a community center. Larry was trying to tighten the reigns on the business side. He was quite well meaning, thinking that he was relieving Shig of overwork.... But Shig interpreted it as Larry being selfish and trying to seize control of the store and shunt him aside."

The result, sadly, was that Ferlinghetti was forced to agree to another separation. For $32,000, he bought out Murao's share of the store and Wolberg took over management.

"To me it was like a divorce between parents, that kind of a traumatic shock," Ginsberg says fifteen years later. "The world was no longer stable."

It was not a tremendous amount of money for a quarter of a thriving business, but the business was less than thriving at the time. And though the store did better for a while, eventually Wolberg's offhand manner and declining interest caused its own problems. In October, when Ferlinghetti took another trip by himself to Mexico, the difficulties of the last three years were certainly much with him. Traveling without any baggage, he rode buses to Mexico City, then to Puebla, Xalapa, and Veracruz on the Gulf Coast. Stopping in Cuernavaca, he wrote a poem that mourns yet another loss, the death of Chilean Nobel Prize–winning poet Pablo Neruda two years before. This elegy exhibits that touch of the surreal, reported in flat, straightforward language, which is characteristic of both Ferlinghetti and Neruda. It begins with the kind of marvelous proposition that suffuses much of Neruda's poetry, and twentieth-century Latin American literature in general:

> *On the coast of Chile where Neruda lived*
> *it's well known that*
> *seabirds often steal*
> *letters out of mailboxes. . . .*

According to the poem, they do it because they want to learn the secrets contained in "The General Song of Humanity," which is the poem's title, and echoes the title of Neruda's last published volume, *Canto General*, which is also his largest.

> *But when they stole away*
> *with Neruda's own letters*
> *out of his mailbox at Isla Negra*
> *they were in fact stealing back*
> *their own Canto General*
> *which he had originally gathered*
> *from them. . . .*

". . . Now that Neruda is dead," the poem concludes, and there are no more of his letters, the birds are on their own: "they must play it by ear again— / the high great song / in the heart of our blood & silence."

It is, of course, not just a description of the circumstances of imaginary birds written two years after a great poet's last song had been written, but a metaphor which tries to encompass the nature of the loss to all of us. Its title suggests that the "song" which has been lost is a song which both belongs to and somehow expresses all of us; that is, the loss is not simply diffused and abstracted by collective application, but is equally particular and personal—an individual loss that not only the birds but, by clear extension, each of us has also suffered.

Given his own circumstances, it is more than appropriate that Ferlinghetti would write such a poem. Divorced, alone in Mexico, both his wife and his business partner of twenty-plus years gone, Ferlinghetti once more expressed eloquently his own immersion in "The General Song."

12

Our long national nightmare is over," Gerald Ford had said to Congress on August 9, 1974, when he was sworn in as President. With Nixon's resignation and with the last Americans finally gone from Vietnam April 29, 1975, the national sense of relief at the end of more than a decade's lingering trauma was almost palpable. Like the country itself, and the culture of which the poet was "antennae," Ferlinghetti found himself turning inward in the first half of the seventies, occupied with adjusting to his own new circumstances as he moved back to North Beach, separated from Kirby, and then finalized the divorce. On the one hand, such adjustment is always eased by some continuity; and for Ferlinghetti the bookstore, the publications, and especially writing were central ongoing activities. But equally to the point, ease and insularity were never states with which Ferlinghetti felt very comfortable. His immersion in "The General Song" continued to lead him outward in new directions. With no single issue dominating the political fabric, Ferlinghetti's efforts in the second half of the seventies and through the eighties were directed at an array of separate issues, many of them local, which caught his attention.

Even as the country exhaled and sought to lean back at the final withdrawal from Vietnam, he launched a new sortie against what he feared was the withdrawal of artists and poets into narrow self-concern. It was a pendular swing he'd detected again in the more personal, insular writing that had always been favored by academic critics and the mainstream eastern press, and the similarity with the writing climate of the forties and fifties seemed striking.

His response, in February 1975, was a new polemic:

> *Poets come out of your closets*
> *Open your windows, open your doors,*
> *You have been holed-up too long*
> *in your closed worlds. . . .*

His second "Populist Manifesto" makes a direct assault on the quiescence of too many poets, challenging them to

> *Stop mumbling and speak out*
> *with a new wide-open poetry*
> *with a new commonsensual "public surface"*
> *with other subjective levels*
> *or other subversive levels.*

On the one hand, the poem could be seen as a hearkening back to the urgency and excitement of the 1950s, when the poets of the San Francisco Renaissance first burst on the scene. Ferlinghetti was in his mid-fifties now, and a little nostalgia would certainly have been understandable. When Ginsberg was mugged near his New York City apartment the previous December, he'd responded in his "mugging" poem with the Buddhist "Om Ah Hūm" Mantra and, in his own "Manifesto" in January, asserted the virtue of simple "Awareness—which confounds the Soul, Heart, God, Science Love Governments and Cause & Effects' Nightmare." But Ferlinghetti was never one to dwell on the past or on the detailed exposition of interior life, despite some forays in that direction tracked by his "American Mantras" and a few other poems of the previous three or four years. It wasn't that he thought personal, introspective poetry universally weaker; rather, he continued to believe that poets, like anyone else, had a social responsibility as well, which responsibility they far too often ignored. Proclaiming "The hour of *om*ing is over," his "Manifesto" is a claim for the importance and vitality of the spirit of rebellion against complacency and conformity, a spirit which for him is the very lifeblood of poetry.

Nor did the poem represent a lone voice in a static, self-satisfied wilderness. Just as he had throughout his career, Ferlinghetti struck a chord in a wide audience. First printed as a broadside, the "Manifesto" was distributed free at a benefit reading he did for the United Farm Workers of America at Lone Mountain College in San Francisco in April. He went on to broadcast the poem on KPFA radio in San Francisco that month, and to read it at "Walt Whitman Day" at Rutgers university in Camden, New Jersey, in May. In the following six months it was picked up and published by nearly a dozen newspapers and magazines, including the *Los Angeles Times* and the *New York Times*. Its message, like so much of Ferlinghetti's work, reached beyond America as well—in the same period the poem was published in England and Yugoslavia and translated into Spanish, Italian, and French.

The poem became the last, and the most publicly political, of the 1976 *Who Are We Now?* which otherwise stands as his most introspective collection. The title, which is the opening line of the first poem in the book, "Jack of Hearts" (itself the title of a Bob Dylan song on Dylan's 1974 *Blood on the Tracks* album), expresses the sense of uncertainty and disorientation which has pervaded much twentieth-century poetry from the surrealists to the Beats, and which was also sharpened by Ferlinghetti's own situation.

". . . who are we ever," the poem asks after the opening question,

> *Skin books parchment bodies libraries of the living*
> *gilt almanachs of the very rich*
> *encyclopedias of little people*
> *packs of players face down*
> *on faded maps of America*
> *with no Jack of Hearts. . . .*

For most of its four pages, then, it offers descriptions of the missing "Jack":

> *. . . the one who'll shake the ones unshaken*
> *the fearless one*
> *the one without bullshit. . . .*

And

> *the one the queen keeps her eye on*
> *Dark Rider on a white horse*
> *after the apocalypse*
> *Prophet stoned on the wheel of fortune*
> *Sweet singer with harp half-hid*
> *who speaks with the cry of cicadas*
> *who tells the tale too truly*
> *for the ones with no one to tell them. . . .*

The dedication to Dylan suggests that the heroic, surrealistic Jack may be Dylan, but insofar as Dylan is a poet—and Ferlinghetti certainly agreed that he was—the "Jack" is also an archetypal figure: at times muse, at times an embodiment of Kerouac, at times a holy figure, all echoing the Ginsberg-like "He" in the *Starting from San Francisco* poem. And by these associations with poets, "he" also, of course, suggests the poet Ferlinghetti himself. On the other hand, the "we" of the poem hope the Jack will somehow save them from the dismal state of the opening lines, thus including the author with the general mass of humanity who is seeking the Jack. It is that unavoidable association which puts the poet squarely amid the lost, needy multitude.

In another half dozen poems the themes of loss and disorientation are even clearer, as well as the quest for "a new beginning." "Great American Waterfront Poem," "People Getting Divorced," "Lost Parents," and "The Recurrent Dream" all speak directly to these subjects. "Alienation: Two Bees" and "Director of Alienation" also seem related to the same impulse, though their depictions of disorientation, of being out of place, are cast in a more universal context, and are a characteristic experience in many Ferlinghetti poems. In "Director of Alienation," for instance, the poet is wandering in that temple of bourgeois culture, Macy's department store,

> *and thinking it's a subterranean plot*
> *to make me feel like Chaplin*
> *snuck in with his bent shoes & beat bowler*
> *looking for a fair-haired angel*
> *Who's this bum*
> *crept in off the streets*
> *blinking in the neon*
> *an anarchist among the floorwalkers*
> *a strikebreaker even*
> *right past the pickets*
> *and the picket line. . . .*
>
>   .   .   .   .   .
>
> *Look at this alien face*
> *in this elevator mirror*
> *The Tele-tector scans me*
> *He looks paranoid*
> *Better get him out*
> *before he starts trying on the underwear. . . .*

196 • Barry Silesky

In April 1976 a crowd of some three hundred at the Little Fox Theater on Pacific Street saw Ferlinghetti appear in a Chaplin-style derby with a card attached on which he had written "Director of Alienation" and read the poem. The occasion was a benefit for the revived *Beatitude* magazine, organized by Neeli Cherkovski and Raymond Foye, two younger poets who had come to North Beach like many before them to be a part of the bohemian ambience and creative ferment that had marked the neighborhood since World War II. And with the sympathetic alliance Ferlinghetti always felt with ordinary people, with those not privileged, of which both the Chaplin derby and the poem are representative, he repeated the performance again outside for free, to the delight of the hundred or so who could not get in.

On his own and living in North Beach again, Ferlinghetti befriended many of this new generation and encouraged the revival, an involvement which might again be ascribed to a nostalgic impulse. Or it might be taken as a desire to help Cherkovski, who had become his biographer. The biography project had come about soon after Cherkovski moved up to San Francisco in mid-1975. Poet Harold Norse, whom he'd known in Los Angeles, introduced Cherkovski to Ferlinghetti at the Trieste, and though Ferlinghetti wasn't especially interested in Cherkovski's poems, they began seeing each other on the street, then occasionally eating together at Little Joe's or one of the other casual eateries Ferlinghetti continued to frequent. Very soon afterward, Cherkovski also met former radical Jerry Rubin at the Trieste, with whom he discussed his idea of writing a book on Ferlinghetti. Rubin loved the idea and introduced Cherkovski to his agent, who echoed the enthusiasm, and sold Cherkovski's proposal to Doubleday, the major trade publisher. They recognized Ferlinghetti's importance and popularity over the previous twenty-five years, and Cherkovski went to work on the book, which ultimately came out in 1979 as a hardback. Ferlinghetti's popularity, however, had continued slowly to decline after the sixties, and though the new biography did a "yeoman's job," in Cherkovski's own words, of covering the essential facts of Ferlinghetti's life, it was made somewhat brief by the publisher. Further, it was never published in paperback for the more budget-minded audience to which Ferlinghetti more often appeals.

Still, despite whatever allegiance he might have felt with Cherkovski—and they did spend a good deal of time together over those three years, Cherkovski even living in Ferlinghetti's Filbert Street apartment for a month or so in 1978 when Ferlinghetti was gone—or any nostalgic impulse, Ferlinghetti's appearance for the new *Beatitude* had much more to do with his long-standing support for such independent, community-based, "antiestablishment" enterprises.

"Lawrence is a warm, kind, and caring person," Cherkovski said even recently. "A quintessential community person—community in the old sense. He loves the idea of neighborhood, it seems, and he's really managed to re-create a little Montparnasse kind of slice of French bread in North Beach with the bookstore. For a while in '75–'76, it seemed like he was just one of the gang. I think he made a lot of the younger poets feel they were really doing something worthwhile."

He had for years appeared at various benefits to aid important political causes, and the values of independence and of accessibility to and alliance with the ordinary and the outcast which *Beatitude* promoted in both its incarnations were exactly the values Ferlinghetti had supported since his first political awakening. As early as 1969, in *Tyrannus Nix*, he had written and spoken against writers and magazines accepting support from the National Foundation (now the National Endowment) for the Arts. Formed in 1965, that source of government funding for the arts had grown rapidly in the early seventies to become a significant source of income for many writers, and especially for literary magazines, whose number had been burgeoning. Ferlinghetti's objection to accepting such help was rooted in the idea of "guilt by complicity, chez Camus," as he termed it many times.

"Many American poets," he had written in *Tyrannus Nix*, "do in fact help the government in sanctioning a status quo which is supported by and supports WAR as a legal form of murder: witness the number of avant garde poets and little presses who have in recent years accepted U.S. grants directly from the National Foundation of the Arts or from its conduit, the Coordinating Council of Literary Magazines and Little Presses, making it clear that the avant garde in the arts is not necessarily to be associated with the political left. See [Herbert] Marcuse's 'repressive tolerance,' that is, the policy of tolerance and/or sponsorship as a self protection against violence; or as Susan Sontag recently put it, 'Divesting unsettling or subversive ideas by ingesting them.' The State, whether capitalist or Communist, has an enormous capacity to ingest its most dissident elements."

And in another 1969 interview, he said, "The first thing a poet has to do is to live that type of life which doesn't compromise himself. It seems to me that taking government grants and living on them is compromising himself before he even starts writing."

It was, he admitted, a "purist position" which was not above criticism, most pointedly from those who argue that if government grants are used to further opposition to the very government policies which threaten free expression and a free society, such use is more than justified. But Ferlinghetti continued—and continues—to maintain and promote the opposition of artists to accepting government arts funding, and City Lights Books has continued to exist entirely independent of any such funding.

In 1976 he also distributed a sixteen-page pamphlet, five hundred copies of which he photocopied himself, under the imprint of the "Anarchist Resistance Press." The second page underlined his populist sympathies with its note, "Anything in this pamphlet may be reproduced by anyone interested"; and the following page announced that "Anarchist Resistance Pamphlets will be issued from time to time, as the situation demands it." The pamphlet included four overtly political poems along with two letters to Stanley Kunitz, consultant in poetry to the Library of Congress in 1975.

Though it stood in the tradition of so much of the mimeographed literature of the sixties, the pamphlet was not a nostalgic look backward, a clinging to the past, but an affirmation of Ferlinghetti's ongoing commitment to political values he had long held. The letters were a rejection of an invitation to read at the Library of Congress in Washington, and along with the poem "A Banquet in the Suburbs of Empire," they speak directly to that idea of the "complicity" of poets who seek or accept government grants in the destructive policies of government. Specifically Ferlinghetti mentions in the letters the Vietnam War and the assassination of Chilean President Salvador Allende, accusing the United States of financing Allende's overthrow through the CIA. It was a fact widely believed by the political left from the time of the event, though only acknowledged by government officials some years later.

The other major direction toward which Ferlinghetti's public attention was turning, along with many, was the ecology movement. Rachel Carson's 1962 best-seller, *Silent Spring*, had first sounded the alarm, and by 1970, concerns about environmental destruction had blossomed into the first "Earth Day," in which an estimated twenty million people participated in some way. Many of the sixties counterculture helped fuel the movement and were experimenting with various versions of living on the land, individually and in communes—homesteading, squatting in tipis, abandoned cabins, or other transient structures in rural areas all across the country. For Ferlinghetti the land in Bolinas, and especially the cabin at Big Sur, allowed him rural retreats intimate with nature, and the time he spent at both places regularly, and increasingly through the late sixties and seventies, kept him in close touch with the spirit of that movement.

His 1973 "Alaska Pipe Dream," a prose poem written in Montreal and published in the *New York Times*, was the first poem in which he directly addressed the issue of environmental threat. A cautionary tale warning of the consequences of the pipeline that was being built to carry oil from Alaska through Canada to the United States, the poem imagines "the world's largest Oil Spill" killing wildlife across Alaska and Canada "so that the St. Lawrence dripped both oil and animal blood into the water supply of the City of Montreal." It goes on to deride Canadian officials who termed the pipeline an "Internal American Matter" with which they need not concern themselves. Though its targets may not be precisely accurate, in light of the disastrous Valdez oil spill off the Alaskan coast sixteen years later, his anticipation, if not prophetic, was certainly clear-sighted.

Many more of the poems he wrote in the mid-seventies also confronted the mounting environmental crisis, including the "Populist Manifesto" in its lines,

> *The trees are still falling*
> *and we'll to the woods no more.*
> *No time now for sitting in them*
> *As man burns down his own house*
> *to roast his pig*
>
> .   .   .   .
>
> *Mayakovsky's Moscow's burning*
> *the fossil-fuels of life. . . .*

And though the 1976 "Wild Dreams of a New Beginning" can be taken as a reflection of his own personal situation, in its physical focus on renewal it is unmistakably larger, speaking more dramatically than any earlier poem to the environmental issue. Articulating the dream shared by many of a return to a pristine, preindustrial civilization which might follow some kind of apocalypse, the poem envisions "a Pacific tidal wave a mile high" which

>   *sweeps in*
> *Los Angeles breathes its last gas*
> *and sinks into the sea like the* Titanic *all lights lit*
> *Nine minutes later Willa Cather's Nebraska*
>   *sinks with it*

At the poem's conclusion,

the washed land awakes again to wilderness
the only sound a vast thrumming of crickets
a cry of seabirds high over
in empty eternity
as the Hudson retakes its thickets
and Indians reclaim their canoes

That summer he spent nine days cruising the northwest coast from Sidney, British Columbia, through Puget Sound to Anacortes, Washington, with his son, Lorenzo, then three days camping by the Deschutes River in Oregon. And in August 1977 he spent another week camping with Lorenzo in the same area. Both trips afforded him new, firsthand experiences of an unspoiled environment, whose increasing scarcity was becoming more apparent, and affirmed his continuing close connection to his children.

By the mid-seventies Ferlinghetti's popularity, like that of so many of the counterculture heroes of the previous decade, had faded somewhat, at least by the measure of book sales. In 1970 *Coney Island* was reprinted in an edition of 125,000; though demand for the volume has kept up through the eighties (with nearly a million copies now in print, counting foreign editions), the quantities have declined steadily. And the same is true of the other books that were so popular through the sixties. Still, he continued to draw huge audiences wherever he read, and to mobilize people.

For him the very act of writing constituted a public act on a larger scale than for most, as it invariably led to publishing and performing for a large audience. But at the same time, he also took advantage of opportunities to do more—as in the 1967 Oakland protest that led to his stay in Santa Rita. Besides benefit performances (as for *Beatitude*), there came frequent letters to major newspaper and magazine editors, and his highly visible participation in other important efforts. During the mid-seventies he appeared at several readings to benefit the United Farm Workers of Cesar Chavez; and he read and spoke in favor of a California initiative to stop construction of nuclear power plants.

Over the years these public stances had gradually accumulated a stature for Ferlinghetti even in the official world he had been criticizing for twenty-five years. The bookstore, its publications, and Ferlinghetti himself, independent in every sense of the word, had become something of an institution in San Francisco; and ironically, given his continually critical, gadfly role in the life of the city, the government itself decided to recognize and honor him. September 1977 was declared by official municipal proclamation "Ferlinghetti and City Lights Month" as part of the Civic Art Festival. The first time a poet, as opposed to a visual artist, had ever been so honored, the proclamation noted his contributions to the "cultural life of the community as poet, publisher, and bookstore owner." Beginning on the twenty-first and lasting for a month, the Capricorn Asunder Gallery of the Art Commission exhibited his paintings, and photographs of him and his past.

No doubt flattered, Ferlinghetti was, however, not one to forget his own warnings about government's enormous capacity to "ingest its most dissident elements." In accepting the honor at a civic ceremony, he offered ten suggestions for civic improvement. One was to tilt Coit Tower, the San Francisco landmark atop Telegraph Hill in North Beach, so that it would emulate the Tower of Pisa and become a greater tourist attraction. On a more serious note, he proposed that the city award an annual "poet laureate" a free "poet's cottage" in Fort Mason for the year. This was an idea he had discussed with Nancy Peters while they were walking through Fort Mason, an area full of former Navy barracks and abandoned housing units, which is now a part of the Golden Gate Recreation Area. Equally serious was another proposal to tear down the Embarcadero Freeway along the waterfront and convert the area to a park. Though none of these have occurred, Ferlinghetti continued— and continues—his agitation for a more human face for the city, and the country.

The crew of the *James Bay* also were certainly aware of the audience Ferlinghetti reached when they invited him to join the final leg of their journey to the whaling areas off the Pacific Northwest coast in October. The ship belonged to Greenpeace, the international environmental organization, and their purpose was to save the whales which were rapidly being exterminated by unregulated whaling. The voyage they undertook aimed to disrupt the whaling industry there and to attract more publicity and adherents to their cause. Ferlinghetti accepted the invitation and sailed with them in October 1977. While on the ship he recorded a dream of

> *Moby Dick the Great White Whale*
> *cruising about*
> *with a flag flying*
> *with an inscription on it*

"I Am what is left of Wild Nature"
And Ahab pursuing in a jet boat with a ray gun
and jet harpoons and super depth charges
and napalm flamethrowers and electric
underwater vibrators and the whole gory
glorious efficient military-political-
industrial-scientific tech-
nology of the great-
est civilisation the
earth has ever
known
devoted to
the absolute extinction and
death of the natural world as we know it. . . .

The "Greenpeace" poem was one of a series he wrote during those 1977 journeys to the Pacific Northwest, recording the landscape and his experiences there. In 1978 he published them in a small City Lights collection titled *Northwest Ecolog*, a term coined by Ginsberg to title a 1970 poem, combining the Greek-based "eclogue"—a shorter, pastoral poem (usually a dialogue between two shepherds)—and "ecology." The poems of Ferlinghetti's ecolog constitute a sort of journal of his trips to the Northwest, containing meditative descriptions of the landscapes, mixed with his typical, sharp-edged observations of people and circumstances.

He was also accompanied on the Greenpeace voyage by the woman who had been instrumental in introducing him to the beauty of the Northwest, and who had also played a key role leading to the city's public honoring of his contributions. He had first met Paula Lillevand in 1974, though she had in earlier years been a North Beach habitué and a close friend of Shig's—they had gone out together, in fact, before Ferlinghetti met her. Originally from Seattle, she first came to San Francisco in 1958 and had two daughters of her own. After going back and forth to Seattle in the sixties, she settled again in San Francisco in 1971, and three years later, with a professor she knew from Lone Mountain College, the small women's college which was her alma mater, she was working to bring both Ginsberg and Ferlinghetti for readings.

A few months before the fall 1975 reading, Ferlinghetti came to a dinner with her and others involved in the event, and, at least as she remembers, the attraction was immediate. Blond and very attractive, the thirty-four-year-old Lillevand shared Ferlinghetti's political commitment and his preference for a simpler, less materialistic life. At the time, she was living in Pacific Heights but the next year moved again to North Beach, and "we were constantly together," she recalls. "We were both single parents, and one of my children was having a difficult time. Lawrence stood by and helped me and gave moral support. We also both had ex-spouses who were like children themselves, so we created a family environment and took on all the teenagers. We would go to Big Sur, take whatever kids were around; we'd cook dinners, I gave parties, we just had a great time. . . ."

On New Year's Day, 1978, Ferlinghetti left the Filbert Street apartment he'd lived in for more than four years and set up housekeeping with Paula and her daughters nearby on Francisco Street, just a block from the Chestnut Street apartment Ferlinghetti had lived in with Kirby when they were first married. When Kirby got tired of the isolation at Bolinas and moved back to an apartment in the city, Lorenzo moved in as well and commuted to high school. Then the next fall, Julie moved to Francisco Street also, having decided to attend the Convent of the Sacred Heart High School in Pacific Heights.

The new family gave a settled warmth to Ferlinghetti's days, though domestic problems with the children were sometimes difficult. Paula's daughters were two and three years younger than sixteen-year-old Julie, and relations among them were not smooth. At the same time, one of Paula's daughters was especially wild—there were late night calls and trips to the police that Ferlinghetti attended with the devotion he continued to bring to family matters.

Paula's domestic, maternal side appealed to him, and as Peters remembers, "she had a wonderful ability to make a home." Though the furnishings were spare, even spartan by some standards, "when you walked in the front door, everything was always freshly scrubbed and polished, and delicious odors of Norwegian pastries were wafting from the kitchen. Family was important to Paula."

Also in January of that year, City Lights Books made a move. Despite its reputation and relative success, literary publishing has never been a great profit-making venture, and a rent increase on Filbert Street forced City Lights' to move the offices back to the store. At the same time, City Lights needed larger warehouse space for the growing list of publications. Craig Broadley, who had been managing the billing and shipping operations of City Lights' publishing, wanted to move to Oregon with his family to begin a vineyard; so they formed the Subterranean Company in Eugene, which continued distributing City Lights books along with other independent publications. When Ferlinghetti moved out, Philip Lamantia took over a room in the third-floor apartment for use as a studio, with City Lights using the rest of it as an archive for rare books and for storage.

Then in June, City Lights celebrated its own landmark as an institution. The twenty-fifth anniversary of the bookstore was marked by a party at the nearby Old Spaghetti Factory, with its beautiful disorderly garden in the back. Several hundred people came—artists, the Bay Area literary community, journalists, old bohemians, readers, and bookstore regulars, among them Herbert Gold, Ed Dorn, Robert Duncan, Bobbie Louise Hawkins, David Meltzer, Jack Micheline, Janice Blue, and Bob Kaufman.

"It was a beautiful sunny day," Peters remembers, "and there was a splendid feeling of community and reunion. People were greeting old friends they hadn't seen for years. Enemies were reconciling, embracing. Everyone drank lots of wine, and much credit goes to Paula Lillevand, with her flair for entertaining, who created an extraordinary feast, huge tables of food, et cetera. It was a landmark event. And it was, sadly, among the last bright days for the Spaghetti Factory and its poetry readings, as it was soon sold along with the rest of the block to developers who began the gentrification of Grant Avenue."

Kaufman and Blue were among the neighborhood poets whose work Ferlinghetti chose to include in another edition of *City Lights Journal*, the fourth, which he also published in 1978, listing himself as editor Mendes Monsanto. The pseudonym, his aunt Emily's surname, demonstrates again not only the playfulness but the refusal to be cast and pigeonholed and "institutionalized" in the way such recognitions as the 1977 proclamation and the twenty-fifth anniversary might promote for some. It also suggests the importance of continuity in preserving that element of family remembrance, in the midst of a life marked by the loss of family.

The new edition of the *Journal*, itself another mark of continuity, was mainly divided among writers who were largely "unknown," some of whom had San Francisco connections and some Ginsberg selected from the poetry workshops at the "Jack Kerouac School of Disembodied Poetics" at Naropa Institute in Boulder, Colorado; some old familiars (Ginsberg, Kerouac, Corso); and a group of writers from overseas.

Among the foreign writers was Victor Jara, the Chilean folksinger who had been killed during the 1973 coup, and Breyten Breytenbach, an Afrikaaner who was a political prisoner in South Africa. Ferlinghetti's reading of Breytenbach's poetry in 1977 inspired him to write "White on White," a poem addressing the pervasive racism not just in South Africa, but throughout the world.

Ferlinghetti's own contribution was another call to arms. Published first in January 1978 in a San Jose newspaper, his "Adieu à Charlot" ("Goodbye to Charlie," as in Chaplin, who had died in December), also subtitled the "Second Populist Manifesto," urged poets—the "Sons of Whitman sons of Poe / sons of Lorca & Rimbaud / or their dark daughters"—to "take back your land again / and the deep sea of the subjective."

By "subjective," a concept which became a central point of reference for him in future years, Ferlinghetti meant—as the poem says—"the Little Man in each of us / waiting with Charlot or Pozzo"; that is, that essential humanity which hears "the thunder in the blood / to remind you of your selves," and "whoever is most beloved . . . whoever makes your heart pound / the blood pound." It is the private version of "The General Song of Humanity," the voice of interior spirit and energy. Ferlinghetti was always very careful when explaining the idea to make clear he was not advocating a poetry of interiority, of private feelings and personal psychic states. In fact, it is just that sort of poetry which he protested most adamantly as leading to a solipsistic dead end. Rather, he saw the subjective as that deep-rooted, visceral life force, attention to which can lead to "fresh objective revelations and observations," as he described the central object of his poetry in a 1980 interview. The subjective is that force opposed to the mechanistic, institutional power of the modern state.

"The poet is the bearer of the subjective. He is the natural born enemy of the state," he proclaimed in a 1984 interview, one of several in which he made that provocative statement. The point is apparent; while government governs by imposing norms on behavior, it is the poet's function to transgress the norm and promote the iconoclastic alternative which represents true progress. And Ferlinghetti, always the promoter of the iconoclastic, continued to carry its banner.

In November he took up his public role as San Francisco's de facto poet laureate when the city was stricken by one of its greatest tragedies. On the twenty-seventh of that month, a frustrated, desperately crazed city supervisor, Dan White, walked into the City Hall offices of Mayor George Mosconi and shot him to death. He then walked a few feet down the hall and did the same to Supervisor Harvey Milk, the first publicly gay activist for gay rights to be elected to such high office. Amid the quickly mounting hysteria which followed these murders, Ferlinghetti composed "An Elegy to Dispel Gloom," published two days after the assassinations in the *San Francisco Examiner*.

> *Let us not sit upon the ground*
> *and tell sad stories*
> *of the death of sanity,*

the elegy begins, finally concluding that "such men as these do rise above / our worst imaginings." A few days later a letter from City Hall thanked Ferlinghetti personally for the elegy, which they assured him helped maintain calm in the city in the face of the tragedy.

If his national popularity had declined some since the beginning of the decade, and his focus was more often toward local and regional issues, the force and breadth of his continuing appeal across the country was demonstrated dramatically during a visit to Madison, Wisconsin, in early April of 1979. On March 28 another environmental disaster dominated national attention when a series of malfunctions at the Three Mile Island nuclear power plant outside Harrisburg, Pennsylvania, brought on America's worst nuclear accident. In Madison for a week-long stay as poet-in-residence at the University of Wisconsin, Ferlinghetti responded immediately: "Flying low through the Harrisburg fallout," his new poem began, and concluded ". . . even though they know a snowjob when they see one

> *in the wilds of Wisconsin*
> *or wherever the hard rain falls*
> *they go on swallowing the snow-white lies*
> *following each other head-to-tail*
> *to the dim plutonium shores*

On April 7 he published "A Nation of Sheep" in *The Madison Press Connection*, a small, alternative newspaper, and read the poem on a local FM station. The station went on to broadcast the poem continuously, inspiring a spontaneous response—students at the university began to march with candles and to carry on a candlelight vigil at the state capitol there. That event in turn inspired Ferlinghetti to extend the poem and write a new ending incorporating this dramatic event.

> *I see them walking with candles*
> *up State Streets to capitols*

I see their candles flickering
against the white night
flickering up capitol steps
to the chambers of power wherever. . . .

A few hundred people carrying on a vigil is not the same as half a million marching in Washington for a cause, and it doesn't necessarily have any visible effect on those "chambers of power." But it articulates a strong public emotion, and so provides an outlet when there is none for public sentiment. It is the Greek idea of *katharsis*, articulated by Aristotle—the release of emotional tension through art. And a month later Ferlinghetti's expression reached a much larger audience when his poem was published in the *New York Times*.

Thus, though the decade ended for him, as for the country, much more peaceably than it began, it was not a peace of lassitude or ease. While the emotional grounding of his work had deepened, the passion of his public voice continued to sound with the same urgency.

"In my end is my beginning."

The final line of "East Coker," the second of T. S. Eliot's *Four Quartets*, has long been famous for its universal echoes. Though Ferlinghetti has certainly not come to his "end," and daily resists the role of the "good gray poet" idling out his twilight, in our sixties, memory is longer; and as the lines of that poem, which he carried with him through World War II and in his early years in San Francisco, suggest, the impulse to complete the cycle, to return, is for many so compelling as to have the force of inevitability.

He touched that ground in late 1976 with "The Old Italians Dying," the first of several poems he would write in the coming decade with similar notes of remembrance. The lament is not only for old Italians but for North Beach itself, originally their neighborhood and a whole way of life. By the time the poem was written, much of the area had been bought up by Hong Kong businessmen, other foreign capital, and young, affluent speculators, a change he had described even more directly a year earlier in "The Groovy Chinese Invasion of North Beach San Francisco." Having become heavily touristed and increasingly gentrified and expensive, much of the old bohemian ambience Ferlinghetti had found there twenty years before was largely gone. "The Old Italians Dying" doesn't mourn any lost Bohemia, however, but focuses on the disappearance of the older, traditional life which had given the neighborhood its character. It was a change that was happening in neighborhoods of several older cities, from New York's East Village to Chicago's Old Town, so that the poem, like so many of Ferlinghetti's, extends beyond simply local concerns to take in a whole segment of American life.

"For years the old Italians have been dying / all over America," the poem opens, suggesting in its second line that larger scale. It goes on to create a litany of specific images describing the people and the neighborhood, then turns at the end to face the reader:

> *You have seen them sitting there*
> *waiting for the bocci ball to stop rolling*
> *waiting for the bell*
> > *to stop tolling & tolling*
> *for the slow bell*
> > *to be finished tolling*
> *telling the unfinished Paradiso story*
> *as seen in an unfinished phrase*
> > *on the face of a church*
> *as seen in a fisherman's face*
> *in a black boat without sails*
> *making his final haul.*

The emotional reaches here seem to manifest that quality of the subjective which he'd been talking about for several years, perhaps more clearly than anything he'd yet written. And though the poem has some familiar touches of humor in the caricatures it sketches, the final images represent a new chord for Ferlinghetti in their tone of pure elegiac pathos.

Then the following April he spent three weeks at a beach cabin on Anasquam inlet at Cape Ann, Massachusetts, north of Boston. The visit provided a chance to be next to the sea again, immersed in a landscape that had inspired poets from T. S. Eliot to Charles Olson. It was the particular ground for Eliot's third quartet, "The Dry Salvages"—which is, as Eliot announces in his epigraph, "les trois sauvages—a small group of rocks . . . off the northeast coast of Cape Ann, Massachusetts." There Ferlinghetti worked on a poem he had been trying to write off and on for years. This time he succeeded, completing in the fall "The Sea and Ourselves at Cape Ann," which strikes again those subjective chords.

This one explores his own lifelong fascination with the sea, beginning with his memory of himself "when as a boy I came here / put ear to shell / of the thundering sea. . . ." It goes on to conjure other poets—Charles Olson, Robert Creeley, Eliot—who shared something of that fascination, "yet none could breathe / a soul into the sea. . . ." Then after recalling his experience "as a man much later" when he "made a landfall in the gloaming / sighting from seaward in convoy," he finds "the sea still a great door never opened. . . ." At the poem's end "we sit / 'distracted from distraction' / . . . in parked cars." The bittersweet of this conclusion, though less pronounced than that of "The Old Italians Dying," is nevertheless undeniable in its evocation of loss—in this case, of that spirit of wildness and mystery that the sea embodies, to the insularity of our "parked cars."

These two poems lead off *Landscapes of Living and Dying*, the collection New Directions published in 1979. About the same length as *Who Are We Now?* the book is itself a return, as some reviewers commented, to familiar Ferlinghetti territory. Many of the poems offer snapshots of surroundings, mostly away from San Francisco, generally caught with characteristic wry wit and inescapable political overtones. The more directly personal poems of *Who Are We Now?* are absent, and the public voice rings as stridently as ever in "Nation of Sheep," "White on White," "Adieu à Charlot," and "Rough Song of Animals Dying." But those subjective notes which sound so strongly in the first two add greater emotion to several others as well, and pervade the whole collection.

The tide of literary taste had turned in America's increasingly visual culture, however, as the political climate moved steadily back toward the more conservative right. Ronald Reagan's election to President in 1980 seemed to mark the final end of any lingering "sixties spirit," and the social concern that had enlisted so many in that decade and even through the seventies. At the same time, accompanying that political shift was a corresponding aesthetic shift toward introspective, personal poetry. A new formalism was sweeping critical taste, marked by the quiet tones, square stanzas, and other traditional poetic devices that had dominated the forties and fifties, and which critics praised. Not surprisingly the poetry audiences originally built by the new oral poetry of the Beats and of others through the sixties, of which Ferlinghetti continued to be a major exponent, shrank as well. Thus, the book's sales continued to reflect the decline in Ferlinghetti's readership—New Directions printed only ten thousand, the smallest number of any Ferlinghetti book. Still, it is important to remember that any poetry book in America rarely sells even five thousand copies, and usually fewer than fifteen hundred. And Ferlinghetti continued to be one of the most popular performers of his work, consistently filling halls at readings all over the country.

As the 1970s turned into the 1980s, his days were as filled as ever with the business of City Lights publishing, with reading tours, with writing, with his relationships with Paula and his children, though the children were older now and needed less attention. Then another major project arose which also demonstrated that impulse toward return, though in this case it was not so much a personal return. As Ferlinghetti approached the age of sixty at the end of the seventies, and the great surges of social, political, and literary movement of which he'd been part ebbed away, he saw a chance "to give his account of the city's literary life during the years he was a part of it," as Peters put it.

"Lawrence's concept for the book originally was to have it as a photographic book with pictures that would have some kind of extended captions," Peters describes the origin of *Literary San Francisco*, which grew out of conversations between them about the swelling archive of photographs City Lights had been collecting. "But as we got going there seemed to be more and more to be said. And it was Lawrence's chance to write his memoir, as it were, of the fifties and sixties, about KPFA and the conscientious objectors who were here that became known as the San Francisco Renaissance, the literary scene as he found it here, about Rexroth's importance in San Francisco literary history, and then the coming of the Beat Generation and the significance of the *Howl* trial."

As they got going, it seemed hard to begin in midcentury without continually going back to earlier events and people; ultimately they decided the book must go back to the city's beginning. Ferlinghetti, however, wasn't interested in doing that research, so Peters took it on and wrote the first half of the book, covering the early years until the twentieth century, while Ferlinghetti wrote the second half. They never saw each other's work until the deadline date, but both were pleased with the result.

The finished book, 136 pages of photographs and text in 8½″ by 11″ "coffee table" format, stands, like all of Ferlinghetti's work, as part informal, personal document, but equally a public document. And because the San Francisco literary life, of the fifties particularly, continues to have such national impact, making the book far more than a local scrapbook, the major trade publisher Harper & Row decided to copublish it with City Lights. Upon its publication, city officials recognized its importance with the issue of another "City Lights Day" proclamation, and there was a celebration for the event in the San Francisco History Room at the Civic Center. With all this fanfare, the book did brisk business following the 1980 publication, but as major publishers do, Harper soon let the book go out of print. City Lights, however, is planning to publish a new, updated edition in the early nineties.

At the same time he was involved in this and other projects, he became more and more engaged in the pursuit of another old interest he had taken up again in 1977, when the city had honored him by displaying his paintings at the Capricorn Asunder Gallery of the city's Art Commission.

Because he had stopped painting in the mid-sixties when writing, publishing, and public appearances in the political and spiritual movements of the counterculture simply took over, old paintings had been displayed. But Peters had begun going to the free weekly figure-drawing classes at the San Francisco Art Institute, which offered an open studio to anyone on Friday, with a model. Ferlinghetti became interested and decided he'd like to go also; he joined the Art Institute and began going—at first, only occasionally, but soon never missing a Friday session. He attended free classes at Fort Mason as well, where he drew under the watchful eye of artist Ethel Guttman, whose ex-husband, Marty Snipper, Ferlinghetti had known in the fifties when both had studios in the old Audiffred Building.

In 1979 Michael Bowen, an artist and acquaintance from the sixties, called him about cosponsoring an art show at Fort Mason of "visionary" artists. Ferlinghetti first thought Bowen meant artists with some kind of coherent "vision" or viewpoint—social, political, or otherwise—but Bowen had in mind the vision of psychedelic days, with its images of the fantastic. Though Ferlinghetti didn't think it right to be a "cosponsor," he did exhibit in the show, his first real art exhibit. The criticism one visitor wrote in the show's book of collected comments rankled, however: "Why don't you stick to what you know, Larry," the critic wrote. Familiar with Rexroth's painting, with Patchen's illustrations for his poems, he hated the idea of being thought a poet who merely happens to paint and gets attention for it only because of his renown as a poet. And as he continued to develop his artistic career with greater and greater intensity through the eighties, he has insisted at every opportunity on separating his visual art from his writing.

His new career took another step forward in 1983 with the help of artist Maurice Lapp. They'd met while Lapp was painting North Beach street scenes, and they'd occasionally gone off together to paint in more secluded places around the city and up the coast. By the early eighties Ferlinghetti had produced a huge collection of drawings and decided he wanted to do something with them. He spent an afternoon with Lapp, who helped him choose fifty for "Leaves of Life: Fifty Drawings from the Model," which he published at City Lights.

All are nudes, about two-thirds women, most gestural studies executed simply in charcoal or enhanced with a wash. Ferlinghetti wrote his own introduction for the book and, as with his editorship of the most recent *City Lights Journal*, signed with his lost family name of Mendes Monsanto. Besides an element of playfulness, the use of the pseudonym emphasizes again the separation he wants to ensure between his drawing and painting and his writing.

The large claims the brief introduction makes for the work also might be taken as tongue-in-cheek, but they articulate a serious aesthetic viewpoint:

"The tragic sense and a sense of joy in life meet in these studies of the human figure by Lawrence Ferlinghetti," he wrote. "The touch is light and sensitive yet curiously profound, for one feels here sometimes that the hand knows something the mind cannot know.

"Those connoisseurs of idiocy who pretend there is great emotion and thought in currently fashionable high art will not find Ferlinghetti's drawings to their taste, for there is far too much of both here, disturbing the deep non-objective sleep of the rootless cosmopolitan unpenetrated by either passion or despair."

The brief, pseudonymous introduction also provided an occasion for him to make his own concise statement about the current state of art as he saw it:

"The high function of art as the locale for fathoming man's fate seems to be mostly forgotten these days. But when one comes to consider that the decay or regression of modern art may be traced to the deterioration or fragmentation of the Image (in every art) we begin to see how valuable drawing such as this may be."

Though the affirmation of the value of figurative art is a complete turning away from the abstraction of his early art, and in that sense is a new departure and not a return, such an aesthetic also reflects a move back to more traditional form. It is the kind of movement that is often seen in artists of all disciplines, whose youthful experiments give way to a deeper engagement in more traditional values. But most significant, the introduction further underlines the seriousness with which he approached this new work.

Soon after he began drawing again in 1977, he had begun to paint again as well, using acrylics. Within a year he had abandoned them, like many painters, tired of their plastic, synthetic quality, which lacks the depth of oils. Then he began hanging occasional paintings in the bookstore, and in a July 1981 interview with the *San Francisco Examiner*, he talked about his new vocation:

"It's a kind of arrogance, a presumptuousness, I suppose, to put up my own paintings. You get to a certain age, a certain stage, and it doesn't matter. If I fall on my face, I really don't care. It took me twenty years to get back to painting. There's a lot that can be said in painting that can't be said in poetry. I feel I have more to say as a painter. Today there's a mass of information being thrown at everybody and essentially it doesn't mean anything. I'm working toward a new symbolism in painting. Actually I'm hoping to start a movement, a new symbolism, to make sense of the mass of information most people find bewildering. Art should bring some order out of chaos."

Though "the new symbolism" didn't gain much adherence, nor his paintings take the art world by storm, or by anything like the enthusiasm with which his poetry was greeted in 1958, and is still widely greeted, his passion for painting has continued unabated. For the time being, he had decided not to give any more public readings in San Francisco, and when asked, asserted that it was his way of protesting against Ronald Reagan and his policies. But it was also part of his effort toward his new career. Though he still gave as many readings as ever around the country and at festivals in Europe and Mexico, more and more he wanted to talk about his painting and put it before a larger public.

He didn't pursue the usual route of aspiring artists who carry their work to various art dealers and galleries to find someone to represent them, and besides the 1977 exhibition, and an informal show at a beer and pizza restaurant a few years later, he didn't find much recognition for his painting. In 1983 he did serve as judge for a student show at the University of Texas–El Paso, but he didn't have a formal show of his own until 1985, when Ethel Guttman decided his work merited an exhibition at her gallery. She called it "The Painted Word," capitalizing on Ferlinghetti's identity as a poet, and ran the exhibition of his paintings from mid-October until mid-November.

"I'm not worried about being recognized as the greatest painter," he said to an interviewer at the time. "I get high doing it. And if people you like like it, that's enough; that's all that's important." Nonetheless, he was clearly interested in testing his painting with a larger audience and gaining attention for it.

Meanwhile, he was again forced to turn his attention back to the store. After Shig's stroke and unfortunate departure, Joe Wolberg had at first done a good job managing, but after a few years, Wolberg began to lose interest in the job, let the store's inventory of books decline, and spent less and less time on the job. In 1983 he left to work as a publicist for United Artists. Ferlinghetti asked Peters to become a partner in the business and to take over the management of the bookstore as well as oversee publishing.

"At the time," she remembers, "we had almost no quality stock, the inventory was way down, and we had $100,000 in bills that no one had any idea how we were going to pay. Theft had become a tremendous problem. We had had the reputation—for years—as the place to come to steal books. Then, too, no one who's ever worked here had much of a business background, including myself. Lawrence and I and whoever went to the accountant once a year would sit there and the accountant would tell us what went on, usually that the gross margin looked devastatingly dangerous. We'd sort of gaze out the window, and Lawrence would suddenly jump up and say, 'Well, are we done for this year?' and we'd zoom out the door. No one knew what 'gross profit margin' meant. As long as we weren't too far in the red, no one much cared."

But now City Lights was too far in the red. Peters set about changing that at once, and perhaps saving City Lights itself.

"Basic, I think, was installing that machine," she said, referring to a security device shoppers pass at the front counter. It immediately made a difference.

"But what really turned the store around," she went on, "was the energy and talent of the people already working here—Richard Berman, Paul Yamazaki, Bob Sharrard, Gent Sturgeon. They were experienced bookmen—literate, politically informed—who were just waiting for a chance to help bring the store back to life."

Peters and the staff began rebuilding the inventory "to let people know that we were again stocking the kinds of books that City Lights had been known for earlier—classics of literature, avant-garde writing, poetry, and serious politics. We also began developing in-depth special subject sections: third-world literature and history, jazz and blues, cultural theory, green politics, and commodity aesthetics." And she began organizing author book signings and other events in the store again, a feature that had helped make City Lights a literary center and that had almost stopped entirely. Now, she said in 1989, "We've been growing steadily, with around fifteen percent a year growth in sales."

Ferlinghetti is quick to say he is "very grateful to everyone at City Lights for making it a great bookstore," and emphasizes Peters's contribution. She was the one "most responsible for the turnaround of the store," he said recently, "although it was a great team effort."

Thus, with the store in Peters's capable hands, Ferlinghetti could again pursue his new art without the distraction of business. Despite his hopes, however, his painting remained largely a secret to most of his literary audience. He continued to write as well as paint, and as might be expected, it was his writing, both past and present, which continued to gain him the most attention. If he had become less popular in America in the last decade, he nevertheless remained one of the few really well known American poets in Europe, and invitations to international festivals brought him back there nearly every year through the eighties.

In 1979 he received an invitation to read at the First International Festival of Poets in Ostia, Italy, that summer. The sponsoring organization included Fernanda Pivano, the Italian scholar, longtime translator, and promoter of the Beats since the fifties. Daughter of an aristocrat, former student and close companion of poet Cesare Pavese, Pivano had championed Hemingway and Steinbeck during Mussolini's time, and in Italy, "our work became famous because of her translations," according to Ginsberg.

Ferlinghetti planned his first trip back to Europe in ten years, and at the end of June, set off with Paula for Rome, where they stayed for a few days before the festival. They visited the Vatican, as she had wanted to go to see the Pope, and Ferlinghetti, with his longtime critical view of organized religion, went along, but separate from her, taking in the scene and writing a poem about it. Then they traveled up the ancient Appian Way, before heading down the few miles to the beach town of Ostia, just west of Rome.

Ginsberg, Diane DiPrima, and Gregory Corso were also there, along with Yevtushenko, who visited with Paula and Ferlinghetti on their balcony one evening, one of the rare occasions when the Russian wasn't accompanied by a translator who, Paula and others believed, served as a monitor for Soviet officialdom. The festival itself was right on the beach, and Ferlinghetti remembers it as "the Italian Woodstock," attended by some twenty thousand hippies. But unlike the American version, which was largely a celebration of life-style and values, the heavy hands of politics shaped this one.

Ginsberg, characteristically, was one of the first drawn into the political machinations, as he and Peter Orlovsky were visited their first day by a group claiming to be anarchists and modeling themselves after the Beats. They wanted to set up a soup kitchen for people who were poor, so Ginsberg and Orlovsky contributed money for their efforts. But during the festival the supposed Beat anarchists continually disrupted the readings, saying poetry wasn't important but food was, and shouted down Yevtushenko's reading. In the process they mounted the stage, which wasn't designed to hold large numbers, and it began to splinter. When the time came for the Americans to read the next day, Orlovsky, in a white suit, took control of the microphone, lifted the giant iron soup kettle off the stage, then handed the microphone to Ginsberg, who asked those of the audience who wanted to hear poetry to be quiet. All but a couple dozen or so in the crowd of some five thousand fell silent, which made Ginsberg suspect that the small group of "anarchists" were very likely CIA provocateurs.

"How could they be so supposedly in tune with Cassady and beatniks, and at the same time be such a small group and try to shut us up?" Ginsberg said. Further, he went on, "according to Pivano and others, the new Communist organization in the city hadn't been able to organize any cultural festivals without radical disruption." Though Ginsberg's suspicions may have seemed to some farfetched, other CIA disruptive activities against political and cultural groups they thought anti-American had been brought to public attention. That CIA provocateurs should shout down the Russian, Yevtushenko, and try to shout down such "dangerous radicals" as Ginsberg and Ferlinghetti was certainly in keeping with attitudes and tactics that had in the seventies been publicly revealed. But finally the reading went on, including a belated performance by Yevtushenko, and the huge audience was delighted.

The poetry celebration at Ostia also led Ferlinghetti to another project he completed several years later. On the beach one day he was accosted by a group of reporters who asked him what he thought of Pier Paolo Pasolini, the radical Marxist Italian poet, novelist, filmmaker, and polemicist, who had been murdered there four years before. He hadn't read much of Pasolini, but he began to look for more of his work. The melancholy tone pervading many of his poems, combined with vivid imaging and a deep sympathy for the dispossessed, appealed to Ferlinghetti, and when he found that no English translations of Pasolini were available, he resolved to do the work himself. When he got back to San Francisco, he contacted Francesca Valente, who worked at the Italian consulate there, and the two went to work translating a selection of Pasolini poems from his various books. In 1986 the project was completed and Ferlinghetti published *Roman Poems* at City Lights.

After the festival he and Paula traveled to Spoleto and there met two Italian filmmakers who said they were doing interviews. The four liked each other, and the Italians invited the Americans to travel with them. They stayed at a villa in Luca which the family of one of the filmmakers owned, then went on to Tuscany. After this idyll, Ferlinghetti and Paula went to Paris, where they stayed with Jean-Jacques Lebel, and Ferlinghetti again wandered that so romantic ground that had attracted him since his youth, and which still had such powerful appeal.

Throughout the trip Ferlinghetti kept his journal and wrote more than three dozen poems about the adventure. A year later New Directions published them in a limited, hardback edition of 250 copies, all signed by Ferlinghetti, titled simply *A Trip to Italy and France.* Containing eleven "Canti Romani," eight "Canti Toscani," and twenty-one "Paris Transformations," most are rooted in characteristic anecdotal observation, particularly the "Canti Toscani," while the "Canti Romani" combine their observations of the present with the shadows of Dante and the sense of history pervading the Roman streets.

The "Paris Transformations" are especially rich with past associations at the roots of Ferlinghetti's life, and that sense of nostalgia and tenderness which suffuses much of the writing he has done about that city. The first poem, in fact, with its litany of Paris streets embedded in the center, is a veritable paean to the nostalgia the city generates in him:

> Gare du Nord to Montparnasse
> Rue de la Roquette and Place Voltaire
> Place Léon Blum and Père Lachaise
> Les Halles and tour St. Jacques
> Saint Sulpice and Cherche Midi. . . .

And at the end, "The map of Paris / stamped upon my brainpan."

The final "Transformation" strikes another new note for Ferlinghetti, taking that sensation of passing time, the root of nostalgia, to its inevitable end:

> For years I never thought of death.
> Now the breath of the eternal harlequin
> makes me look up
> as if a defrocked Someone were there
> who might make me into an angel
> playing piano on a riverboat.

Here the somewhat comic and absolutely temporal last image adds a mystery that raises the brief poem above the sentimental pathos inherent in its subject and gives a sudden depth. This deeper, emotional tone in his work was something Ferlinghetti addressed directly while in Rome for the Fifth International Poetry Festival in late August and September 1984. In capital letters, in his journal he wrote: "I am arriving at a new definition of an aim for writing = Poetry is / should be: '*Life perceived with passion.*' " He went on then to note the poems of his which he felt had achieved this aim—number 1 of *A Coney Island of the Mind* ("In Goya's greatest scenes . . ."), "The Photo of Emily," and "The Mouth of Truth."

"The Photo of Emily" is another in the series of autobiographical poems he had written since the *Coney Island* Oral Message "Autobiography." Based on the one old photograph he has of his "French mother," the melancholy of this poem is deep and unbroken:

"She wore a cloche hat," Ferlinghetti begins the remembrance. Midway through the poem, amid the biographical detail repeated and inserted in a fragmentary way, she is standing on "A dark bridge . . . her face in shadow." The fragmentation of the composition echoes the way Ferlinghetti's biography has come to him, and his own discontinuous sense of his past. The poem ends with the nine-year-old Larry Ferling Monsanto, whom he remembers and imagines, running off "into the dark park of those days / by the Bronx River" and never seeing her again "except in the back of old boutiques / peered into now again / with haunting glance / in the Rue de Seine."

The other poem he cited as an example of "life perceived with passion" is another imagined character sketch, of a woman he saw in 1983 on the streets of Rome when he was there for the Fourth International Poetry Festival. The mouth belongs to a woman he imagines is "some secretary" to whom "the boss was beastly tonight" who

> *. . . trots along on her too high heels*
> *She has smart rhinestone glasses*
> *and silk pants very well cut*
> *She has a sweet face*
> *spoiled by lipstick*

Though far from the "eternal woman" Ferlinghetti regularly idealized, she nevertheless embodies something transcendent in her slick, imperfect, aspiring chic, and becomes its voice:

> *when she's asleep on her back*
> *by the open window*
> *by the tree with its leaves like lips*
> *the lower lip so sensitive*
> *will quiver*
> *the throat utter some deep sound*

the tongue mute messenger
with its speechless truth
To whom will she tell it
in what dream
and what "dark dove with flickering tongue"
pass below the far horizon
of her longing?

It is not that Ferlinghetti's earlier work didn't include poems with this sort of romantic imagination; but now they seemed to come more often and with more personal resonance. And the playful poems of earlier years, while not entirely absent, seemed less frequent.

In Paris Lebel continued to sponsor the international festivals he began in the sixties, now called "Polyphonix," and Ferlinghetti was one of the most popular guests almost every year through the eighties, reading to audiences of several hundred to a thousand and more. During the same years, Italian festivals brought him to Milan, to Tuscany, to Rome, and drew equally large or even larger audiences. Other festivals, in Amsterdam in 1981, in Mexico City in 1982, saw the same kind of interest. All of them attracted larger audiences than any for poets in the United States, and with them, the kind of media attention seemingly reserved here for rock stars or national political candidates.

One of Ferlinghetti's most exhilarating moments came in Amsterdam in October 1980, when more than a thousand came to the "One World Poetry Festival" to see him, Ginsberg, McClure, and others. For the final evening's reading, he emerged on a high balcony dressed in scarlet bishop's robes and read "Loud Prayer," his parody of the biblical Lord's Prayer from *Coney Island*. After he finished, as he described it in his journal, "the globe of the world was lowered, with spotlights on it, to wild rock music as naked male and female bacchantes danced around it, and the crowd danced and roared as the world descended to the dance floor and cracked open, and a great python actually was lifted out of it, out of white sulphur flames, and the great snake wound around the neck and arms of a naked native black dancer who whirled and writhed with it to the heavy rock beat on drums. Then, as the fires had been extinguished and the serpent taken out (the Earth cleansed of Evil) the globe closed up again and ascended again in the night skies."

He described the whole week-long festival as "a fantastic outpouring of creative energy, a great flowering of it, rushing together from around the earth—for a brief few days and nights of intense creation, a wild concentration and outburst of the creative imagination at its most flaming lyric stage—in all the arts. . . ." But such intensity of feeling rarely lasts as long as that week in Amsterdam, whether for Ferlinghetti or anyone. And such adventures were not always unconditionally joyous for him, nor did they make for anything like a utopian life in the day-to-day experience.

In September 1984 Ferlinghetti recorded "one of the worst insults to poetry and the most contemptuous attitude toward it that I have ever encountered. . . ." The first was at Assisi, Italy, in summer 1983 when a man there "threw a coin on the ground and facetiously asked me to recite. The second was last night at the biggest theatre in Rome, the Teatro Augentina (to which I had been invited to read poetry after a play) when they forgot to announce that I would read after the play, and the audience left."

Such inadvertent mishaps happen to anyone, of course. More serious are the problems of personal isolation which most artists confront, almost necessarily. And in Ferlinghetti's case the isolation is probably intensified by the estrangement from family which is so much a part of his very identity. He invariably traveled alone, as much by choice as by incidental circumstances; and alone, between stops, between those moments of exhilaration, he found himself shadowed and regularly overtaken by the loneliness that had never been far from him.

That loneliness was given new occasion in 1980, when his life with Paula wound to an end, though in no dramatic burst. By then the children, who had been so much at the center of their lives, were nearly grown— Julie was nineteen now and gone, Paula's daughters were seventeen and sixteen—and Paula was beginning to worry about her own future.

"I was so happy with Lawrence for a long time," she said, "but I began to think, what's in it for me? I wanted to get married, and he said, I don't believe in marriage. I laughed, and said, listen, you were married for twenty years."

And from her point of view, his new involvement in his painting also divided them a little further.

"I thought he was wanting a lot of praise," she said. "I think he's kind of gotten a little more silly about liking compliments and lapping it up. Never before had I seen him crowd-please. He'd always been so gracious. But when he took up painting, he just went off a bit, because he fell in love with painting, and that was fine, but it was a new love, and . . . it didn't happen overnight, but I began to be critical, and we began to part."

It wasn't that Ferlinghetti was afraid of obligations—his devotion to his work, to his children, to all his responsibilities, has been clear over the years, and if anything, sets him apart from any "flaky poet" image that has surrounded the Beats and other artists. Further, his commitment to Paula for several years and his help with the difficulties of her children underline this. But Paula's increasingly critical attitude and perhaps the residue of his difficult experience with Kirby (though he refuses to acknowledge that these were the factors, or discuss any of the reasons) had to make Ferlinghetti reluctant to marry again.

Late that year Paula moved just two blocks away to an apartment of her own. They remained on friendly terms, talking regularly on the phone, spending holidays together, but Ferlinghetti was again living alone.

On June 14, 1982, "Bloomsday"—the anniversary of Leopold Bloom's 1904 wanderings about Dublin in James Joyce's *Ulysses*—Ferlinghetti celebrated the anniversary by wandering the San Francisco streets alone. That night, imitating the characters in *Ulysses*' "Nighttown" chapter, he got drunk, and again noted in his journal a sense of vague desire and some of the same confusions about his personal direction that had always been part of him.

He dropped in on a birthday party for writer Kay Boyle at a Polk Street restaurant and found himself seated next to feminist Kate Millett. As a "libertarian anarchist," he was fully behind the movement for equal rights for women, but his initial attitudes had been formed at a much earlier time, when a more traditional view of women prevailed. The archetypal idealization of women in *Her* was a strong part of his thinking; and in part, the birthday gathering simply stirred his old appetite for controversy. Perhaps expecting some lively discussion, he told Millett, "Some men have a hard time destroying their old classic illusions of eternal woman."

But Millett surprised him. "Maybe you shouldn't," she said.

Again in Oaxaca, Mexico, in August 1982, after a festival in Mexico City, he wrote that "loneliness is still a curse. Still, the people that singly wanted to come on this trip with me must understand: I have to be alone on trips like this. Or else they are not trips like this."

Though he was no longer living with a woman companion, he was, as always, with people a good deal of the time, at work and socially; and he went on to meet and see other women throughout the decade. But in December of 1982, in notes toward the idea of a novel, he wrote that "in the mid-sixties a man (and perhaps a woman) loses a certain drive, an anima, if you will, a libidinous hunger . . . the love-hunger, though loneliness still remains an eternal problem. This loss of *feeling*, this simple lack which suddenly presents itself like a passive void, an emptiness—is something not even recognized at first. It takes a few years for it to sink in: 'suddenly' one no longer *feels* as much, in human relationships, in love. Love itself would seem to be suddenly less, the feeling for love, the feeling of love for another diminishes strangely—not just for one other but for all others—as if the whole thing had been a great ruse—the whole construction of Platonic love or romantic love based on a huge illusion, on an actual, bestial, animal sex urge, which now suddenly evaporates or dries up, and all feelings of 'love' with it. 'Affection,' perhaps not. Nor 'loneliness.' "

As a note for a novel, it is not to be taken as a literal description of a permanent state of mind, but such sensations do not come *sui generis* either; the note must be seen as a reflection of at least one aspect of his general outlook. Still, this lessening of feeling, of the libidinous "love-hunger," didn't lead him into any seclusion, and even as his mid-sixties turned into his late sixties, he never went long without a woman companion.

Besides sporadic problems of isolation, also like so many artists, he was afflicted by occasions of self-doubt about the value of his own poetry, despite its popularity. In 1981 New Directions published his selected poems in a volume titled *Endless Life*, including at the end three new poems; one of them, "Retired Ballerinas, Central Park West" (which the *New York Times* published), is a portrait of artists in declining circumstances, striking again that more emotional, melancholy note.

This time, however, some of the major review organs gave the retrospective collection a far more positive assessment, on the whole, than any of the individual collections which it represented, and a much more positive valuation particularly than his last two or three. The *New York Times Book Review*, still the most prestigious national book magazine, took up this collection, the first by Ferlinghetti it had highlighted in twenty years. Joel Oppenheimer seemed almost to apologize for previous assessments by others in his praise: "What was curious about Ferlinghetti for many of us," he wrote, referring to Ferlinghetti's position in the 1960s, "was that he was indeed magnetic in the flesh and in recitations, but the poetry seemed lacking on the page. We were wrong. Here, in *Endless Life*, is assembled the poet's own choice of his work from the last twenty-five years. We can see the range of these poems spread out on the page and they still hold. . . ." Ferlinghetti, Oppenheimer went on, "learned to write poems, in ways that those who see poetry as the province of the few and the educated had never imagined. That strength has turned out to be lasting. The poems have 'Endless Life.' "

Though the doubts Ferlinghetti may have had about his work do not seem to have come with the intensity and persistence that have tortured some, neither were they a burden from which he could entirely escape. In Paris, in September 1984, he recorded it in a short journal-poem:

> *Woke at three in the morning*
> *and reread my Paris poems*
> *from all these years abroad*
> *and wrote this afterWord*
> *to this little pile of words*
> *of my life*
> *which all add up to*
> *one small syllable*
> *in the eternal dialogue,*
> *ephemeral condensation*
> *of everything ever thought*
> *or sought or seen*
> *and turned to dream,*
> *to ash in a pipe of hash*
> *to ash of hashish*

At the very time he expressed this spasm of personal insignificance, he was staying at his old friend George Whitman's "Tumbleweed Hotel"—the term Whitman gave to the spare living quarters over his Shakespeare & Co. bookstore—for a reading and book signing of his new collection of poems, *Over All the Obscene Boundaries*. At 120 pages it is his second longest collection, comprised almost entirely of poems from his European travels, including most of the poems from the 1981 *A Trip to Italy and France*. And many of those who have known Ferlinghetti and followed his work feel it is his best collection ever, in terms of the craftsmanship and depth of the poems. The language is denser and more complex than in most of his earlier work, and the greater emotional resonance heightens the intensity of many. At the same time, the collection displays the full range of Ferlinghetti's interests, well evidencing his playful, ironic side as well. Though there are fewer directly political poems than in any collection since the 1968 *The Secret Meaning of Things*, poems like "The Generals—A Naive Dream," "He with Beating Wings," and "Fable of the So-called Birds," to mention the most direct, certainly evoke characteristic political themes.

Neither did these years see any diminution in his political involvements. In 1981 he collected some of his recent polemics in *The Populist Manifestos*.

The small volume reprinted the first two Manifestos and included both a prose and a verse version of the third, "Modern Poetry Is Prose," and a 1980 interview with Jean-Jacques Lebel, in which Ferlinghetti discusses his poetics and the relation between poetry, meditation, and politics.

In late January 1984 he again took his political interests a step further, traveling to Nicaragua to spend a week observing firsthand and reporting on conditions there under the five-year-old Sandinista regime that the United States government under Reagan was trying to overthrow. Ferlinghetti had met Nicaraguan poet Ernesto Cardenal some years before the Sandinistas took power, when Cardenal had visited San Francisco. Educated at Columbia University, he had studied with Trappist monk and poet Thomas Merton at Merton's Kentucky monastery, and been ordained as a Catholic priest. Now he was Minister of Culture for the new revolutionary government, and he accompanied Ferlinghetti and photographer Chris Felver while they toured the country.

During the week, they visited a wide variety of sites—a small military museum in the capital of Managua, the newly built resort of Pochomil on the Pacific Coast, two poor towns near Managua where the revolution had its earliest and strongest base, Lake Nicaragua near Cardenal's hometown of Granada, a sugarcane plant, an "open" prison farm where prisoners worked under minimum security, the Costa Rican border area, where the war with the U.S.-sponsored "contra" forces was going on, and Solentiname, the island in Lake Nicaragua where Cardenal had built a chapel and founded a revolutionary religious community. On his own one afternoon, Ferlinghetti went to the offices of *La Prensa*, the opposition newspaper, where he had a long talk with the distinguished poet and editor Pablo Antonio Cuadra about the political situation and the role of artists and poets there, a conversation he also carried on with Cardenal and other officials he met.

He also gave a poetry reading, with Cardenal doing the translations, to a half-full amphitheater of mostly students, poets, and some U.S. "militants of various sorts." There he read his anti-Reagan poem, "Tall Tale of the Tall Cowboy," but even the smaller crowds than he had been used to at other international festivals didn't reduce his enthusiasm.

While there, he met several other Nicaraguan poets and officials, and on his last day was paid a visit by Daniel Ortega, the head of the ruling junta. Ortega seemed to him "another young intellectual whom I might have met in some graduate school in the States—nothing dictatorial or militarist about him, despite his immaculate uniform—another very good looking gentleman. . . ."

The visit echoed in many ways Ferlinghetti's 1960 trip to Cuba, another country whose revolution had sparked much hope among artists, intellectuals, and civil libertarians that some kind of new model state might come into being. In Nicaragua Ferlinghetti also found "a humane revolution—at least it would seem so on the surface," as he said to a CBS interviewer there (which interview was, not surprisingly, never aired). Though he had no sense that he was being restricted, he realized that he was "on a guided tour"; that what he was shown was not necessarily random or even representative. In that sense his visit was more programmed than his Cuba tour had been; and the years may have made him a little more skeptical.

Still the philosophical anarchist, he was keenly suspicious of all doctrines, sensitive to the contradictions they invariably seem to engender. Later in the fall, when he was at a festival in Rome where Cardenal also appeared, he noted, "It would seem the ultimate paradox . . . that a Catholic priest like Ernesto Cardenal . . . is embracing an atheist political ideology. Thus the liberated ideologues in the Latin American Church appear to be embracing an ideology which *may* lead to *economic* liberation but at the same time leads to enslavement of the mind [emphasis Ferlinghetti's] . . . poverty of the body gained at the expense of poverty of the mind."

More recently, however, he said the note represented "generally an uninformed and ignorant view of what I later learned to appreciate as Liberation Theology, as practiced by Latin American priests such as Father Cardenal." He went on to emphasize that the 1984 comment "really had repressive Stalinism in mind" and that "communism is showing a different face in 1989."

Despite his suspicions then, however, nothing he saw or heard in Nicaragua then or later led him to doubt the motives of the revolution and its leaders, and their earnest desire to improve social and economic conditions, rather than to profit themselves or enhance their own power. When he returned, he wrote up his journal entries and in the fall published at City Lights the account of his visit, as *Seven Days in Nicaragua Libre*.

When he visited again in the summer of 1989 with Lorenzo, for the tenth anniversary celebration of Somoza's overthrow, his experience reinforced his sympathy with the Sandinista regime. Except for a brief trip to Pochomil, he spent nearly a month in and around Managua. Lorenzo is fluent in Spanish, and Ferlinghetti speaks it well enough to have long conversations, through which he found that the many he spoke with on buses and in the street generally supported the Sandinista government.

He also appeared on a panel with Eduardo Galeano and more than two dozen other writers from all over the world, and exhibited City Lights books at the week-long book fair which drew five hundred publishers from forty-four countries. Then in honor of the "Day of Joy," he read a new poem he had written for the occasion. In his public, visionary voice, "Nica" celebrates "a new wind rising . . . through the jacarandas / through the coffee fields," and proclaims

> *a new breed of* norteamericanos
> *is also arising*
> *in "the dawn's early light"*
> *new* norteamericanos
> *who aren't like Reagan & Abrams &*
> *North*

but who instead are

> *the sons and daughters of Whitman*
> *Whitman who called all men "comaradas"* . . .

The poem was translated into Spanish for the performance he gave during the celebration, where he read it in English while the Spanish translation was read afterward. Needless to say, it was enthusiastically applauded by Nicaraguans at the performance, and was published in the Nicaraguan literary newspaper, *Ventana*.

The spring following the 1984 visit, his politics pushed him even further, when in May he joined with writers Alice Walker, Maya Angelou, Jessica Mitford, and others in a protest against the racist apartheid policy of South Africa. The protest was directed against the University of California, which, like many American universities, had money invested in South Africa. The demonstrators were urging the withdrawal of university investments from that country, and their action took the form of a blockade of University Hall. For the second time, Ferlinghetti found himself arrested, along with several others, in a political action. Unlike the occasion at Oakland in 1968, however, he was not jailed, but released with the others.

The summer following, in 1985, Ferlinghetti's longtime involvements in politics joined with his rediscovered passion for painting, and his affinity for Europe, especially France, to begin another major project. He arranged with the American Center in Paris to get a studio at the Cité

Internationale des Arts in the center of the city. He made a trade with Jean-Jacques Lebel, to use Lebel's apartment in Paris and have access to his lodge in Normandy, where he could paint the French landscape, while Lebel and his thirteen-year-old son lived at Ferlinghetti's apartment in San Francisco. Ferlinghetti, however, wound up doing very little painting at all.

"I kept running into people I had known in Paris in '68," he said, "which started me thinking about the novel [*Love in the Days of Rage*]. Then I really got wrapped up in research on it. I went to the Musée de Pompidou where they have a big library of periodicals, and I could look up on microfilm all the French periodicals for the student revolution of '68. So I spent all this time reading issues of the newspapers and magazines of that time from January '68 through that summer."

Once he got started, he established a routine. "Every morning I would wake up and go swimming in a pool from which you could see the Panthéon while you were swimming. I worked out the plot of the novel while I was doing my laps. Then I would go to one or another café and write in a spiral notebook for two or three hours. Then I would go down to George Whitman's bookstore around noon or one o'clock and run into people."

He finished a draft of the novel there, but it was still some distance from being finished. He had begun writing the novel in French, "but when it got down to the nitty-gritty, I couldn't make it in French anymore. So after a few chapters that broke down and I started in English in first person singular in the voice of the woman. But that didn't hold up either. It was too risky to do that. I can't really think of anyone who's brought that off well—a man writing in the voice of a woman. So I gave that up. The third version was in third person singular. So it begins, 'The last time she saw Paris. . . .'

"That's a variation of the famous line, 'The last time I saw Paris . . .' by Elliot Paul, one of the great expatriate books that all the Americans, such as myself, were reading in Paris after the Second World War."

Even in third person singular, however, the novel had a ways to go. Nancy Peters read the draft when he completed it and suggested some substantial changes, mainly the deletion of some of the anarchist banker's theory conversation, which had been taken directly from the book's model, Fernando Pessoa's *The Anarchist Banker*. She also suggested that the woman main character, from whose point of view the story is told, but who doesn't say much, would be more believable if she were developed as a painter than as an English professor, as Ferlinghetti had originally pictured her.

At the same time, Ferlinghetti sent the draft to New Directions, which, for the first time ever, turned down a Ferlinghetti manuscript. Longtime editor Griselda Ohanasseian felt, like Peters, that the narrative needed work and that the abbreviated treatment of the characters made them unconvincing. For his part, Laughlin, still a strong believer in his mentor Pound's banking theories, found the anarchist economics unpalatable; to Ferlinghetti he suggested the book would be improved by having a social credit banker.

After another draft he sent the manuscript to E. P. Dutton, which brought it out in late 1988. Reviews in this country were mixed, though the *New York Times* reviewer decided that "even with its flaws, this short novel is haunting." And in England major review media generally praised it. The *Weekend Telegraph* of London pronounced it "beautifully, stylishly written, and unforgettable," and the *London Times* liked its "seductive and refreshingly innocent" style. The *London Literary Review* writer offered some qualification to her enthusiasm, but more than compensated, saying that "although the plot is thin and the style occasionally careless, Ferlinghetti makes up in atmosphere and excitement: the narrative rushes breathlessly across the page, capturing the wild idealism of the time; ideas, sometimes surreal, swarm through the long, rhythmical sentences, occasionally rising to prose poetry." Readers liked it enough that a year later the first fifteen thousand hardcover printing had sold out, a second printing was issued, and the paperback scheduled for the next spring.

The questions of political commitment and its ramifications which drove the novel came up again the very fall after he had written the first draft in Paris. He was invited to an international festival held in October 1985 in Graz, Austria. The same idea of "guilt by complicity" which made him oppose artists' accepting government grants led him to want to decline the invitation as the Austrian president, Kurt Waldheim, had been implicated in Nazi atrocities during World War II. Ferlinghetti felt that his presence there would connote tolerance, if not approval, of Waldheim and Austria when many felt that Waldheim, and Austria if it tolerated him, ought to be excluded in the strongest terms from the international community.

Ferlinghetti discussed the invitation with his old friend, Reinhard Lettau, a radical German academic and writer, who had also been invited. Lettau, who was also Jewish, argued that they should in fact attend, as the festival was sponsored by opponents of Waldheim, and their presence would publicly support that opposition; they could organize a public protest there. Ferlinghetti finally agreed and in September went to Europe for the second time that year.

At the beginning of the visit, he met Lettau in Austria, and though they weren't able to organize a protest, they did circulate a statement opposing Waldheim and gave interviews expressing their views. As Ferlinghetti had feared, however, that opposition was never heard; neither the statement nor any of the interviews were ever published, and as far as he could see, their presence appeared to publicly accept, if not support, the legitimacy of Austria's and Waldheim's history in world politics. All in all, the experience reinforced his views about the importance of opposing even the appearance of complicity in such circumstances.

The following summer of 1986, Ferlinghetti went to Europe yet again to do some more research on the novel, and to appear at two more international festivals. That July, he traveled to the World Congress of Poets in Florence and read with Gregory Corso, among others. Then he took trains through Italy and down to Cogolin, in southern France, near Nice, for the other festival. And afterward, he traveled west to Bordeaux and on to Portugal where he visited the Portuguese poet André Shan-Lima.

He returned to San Francisco after that trip to finish work on another project that he and Peters had been discussing off and on for some time: an annual review, combining the thrust of *City Lights Journal* with the *Journal for the Protection of All Beings*. Gradually their discussions had led to a commitment to undertake it, but not as a hit-or-miss project.

"We swore we would get one out a year if it killed us," Peters said.

They decided it would be an annual and the format would be different. They settled on a slightly oversized, rectangular 7½″ by 9½″ book with a color illustration on the cover and a new name: *City Lights Review*. When the first issue came out in 1987, however, its contents were no sudden departure but brought together, like the previous journals, the full range of Ferlinghetti's interests. Politics, art, literature, ecology, joined in an international anthology—more than half the contributors, many of them widely known, were from outside the United States, predominately Europe.

Major articles discussed anarchism, the relation between politics and the avant-garde, and the threat of nuclear war. There was more fiction here than in previous *City Lights Journals*, and a number of younger writers, but many more familiar, recognizable names—Henri Michaux, Reinhard Lettau, Federico García Lorca, Philip Lamantia, Marie Ponsot, James Laughlin, Ernesto Cardenal, Allen Ginsberg. Subsequent issues contain focuses on the AIDS epidemic, on media and propaganda, and on green politics.

To that first issue, Ferlinghetti contributed, as he had done persistently, yet another agitation for change. Titled "A Modest Proposal to Change the Names of Certain Streets in San Francisco," this one grew from the *Literary San Francisco* project; it was a formal document to be presented to the city Board of Supervisors, proposing the renaming of fifteen city streets after famous, deceased writers who had been important in the literary life of the city.

It seemed an unlikely possibility, no matter how worthy, destined to languish in the kind of utopian backway where such speculative, "fringe" agitations are relegated. Ever since the city's month-long tribute to his work in 1977, however, Ferlinghetti had been increasingly a presence in civic affairs. Though naming streets after writers may have seemed mainly a symbolic gesture, he knew well that symbols bear important messages; and as the recipient of a "Golden Gadfly Award" from a local journalists' organization in 1986, he took his civic role seriously. He was not willing to see the proposal easily dismissed.

It's early rush hour in San Francisco, and the traffic all up and down Columbus Avenue and Broadway is heavy, both people and cars, invisible faces breathing hurry through the flat December twilight. A block and a half up Columbus from City Lights Bookstore, in the front window of the Caffe Puccini, Ferlinghetti sits by himself with a cup of coffee and an open newspaper. Even sitting down, he seems tall, the lines of his strong chin clear through the trimmed white beard. A thick, tan L. L. Bean sweater protects against the ubiquitous San Francisco chill; his pants are brown corduroys. At seventy he's as thin as ever, as fit as ever. Michael McClure remembers swimming with him in Rome a half dozen years ago.

"Except for the gray hair on his head and body, he's terrific," McClure says. "He's taken care of himself. He looks good in the swimming pool. Where we've grown up watching people chain-smoke themselves and booze themselves and meth themselves to death, there's a level of animal integrity that has continued, grown, and flowered."

The clean-shaven, fiftyish man at the table next to him is a local artist. Ferlinghetti introduces me and tells me they have been talking about painting.

"I'm not writing at all now," Ferlinghetti says. "I'm just not interested in poetry. I'm only interested in painting."

It's not entirely true—he has written an occasional poem over the last two or three years, and he's begun another novel—but it's impossible to overstate his dedication to painting; he works at it for several hours just about every day. This year (1990) he has his first one-man show (except for Ethel Guttman's local 1983 exhibition and another small one at U.C.–Santa Cruz in January 1990), coming up at Berlin's internationally noted Springer Gallery. It's a real breakthrough into the kind of attention he's wanted for his painting, and the gallery has sent a curator to San Francisco to choose the dozen or so canvases that will be exhibited.

"In the European tradition the artist is expected to do more than one art," he goes on. "Like William Blake was an engraver. In this country you're supposed to stay in one field. I even got a hostile letter—an anonymous letter." He's referring to the critical comment at the 1979 Fort Mason exhibit. "The guy said, why don't you stop trying to make it as a painter on the strength of your reputation as a poet? And that's what I want to avoid. I want the painting to make it on its own."

He emphasizes the point he's been trying to make to everyone since he took up painting again.

"I don't want to be thought of as illustrating my poems, which is what Kenneth Patchen did. I feel that these poets who were *also* painters were just that—they were poets who were also painters. They never studied drawing. I want the drawing to make it on its own. We're talking about a separate activity that takes years to develop."

Despite his proclamation about the importance of drawing, however, and the time he has spent at it, Guttman feels "he basically doesn't know what drawing is all about. But," she goes on, "there's an emotional need." When he worked in her class in the late seventies, she explains, "he would attack this piece of paper until it was destroyed, basically, trying to translate what he was seeing. And all I could do for him was to get him to gain control over the medium. For some reason, he'd do things I've never seen anybody do. He would destroy the front of the paper and then turn it over and work on the reverse image.

"He didn't like working with charcoal, he liked working with inks, with a lot of water. And if he didn't like what he was getting, he'd take water and wash it out, and then do it again, and then wash it, and then again until the paper got absolutely saturated."

His painting, Guttman says, also ignored conventional methods. "There's never any pre-preparation. He never makes a formal sketch, he never defines or corrects or rearranges anything. And he has no judgment of his own work. He can't say, well, compositionally this is bad, maybe I should get it off center. I think he's involved with what he wants to say, and he gets it down, and once he's got it down, he's satisfied."

But most observers agree that assessments comparing his drawing or painting with conventional technicians are inappropriate. George Krevsky,

234 • *Barry Silesky*

a collector and associate at one of the major San Francisco galleries, says, "Ferlinghetti's drawings are not the drawings of a Michelangelo or da Vinci. Nor would I compare him to Rembrandt, Matisse, or Picasso as draftsmen. But his unique eye and skill as an artist . . . that's what is evident. His sensitivity toward human beings, toward people, comes through. In terms of vision, in terms of color, in terms of what the technology of this point in history is saying, I think that's important in his art. Is he a better or worse draftsman than Julian Schnabel or Jennifer Bartlett or some others? Andy Warhol was trained as a commercial artist and draftsman. He was a very fine technical commercial artist. That's not what we're talking about with Ferlinghetti. We're talking about a very fine, sensitive artist, using paint and canvas to mirror the human condition consistent with the way he portrays progressive ideas on the printed page. At this stage in Ferlinghetti's life, I'm hoping that we're going to see a burst of a whole new palette of color that will add to the fabric of what history thinks of the man."

Painter, collector, and publisher Gibbs Smith is also enthusiastic about Ferlinghetti's painting, calling him "one of the best expressionist painters today." Echoing Krevsky's comments, Smith emphasizes that "many expressionists aren't careful drawers. That isn't the point. I feel that he might be a good draftsman if he wanted to be, but that isn't what he wanted to do. I think he's a very good painter, and I hope to acquire more of his paintings."

The talent that Krevsky and Smith describe is echoed by Maurice Lapp as well.

"I think his work has a real power," Lapp says, "a kind of gutsy, primitive power, a force which is not what you think of when you think of an academically trained painter. You could liken it to forms of German expressionism. Its real strength does not derive from a classical body of information. It's intuitive, it's visceral, and he uses color in an emotional way."

Guttman also agrees that despite any seeming technical shortcomings the force in his work is undeniable.

"When he came to class, he drew this repeated figure of his ex-wife. He'd draw the model, and by God, what would appear? His wife. You can't in a situation like that say, look, you didn't get the model, the model's so-and-so and so-and-so. He's in a world by himself. All his painting those four years had a haunted quality of loneliness and emptiness, and a single figure always.

"But I don't judge his work the way I judge most work. He does something else to me, he really does. A lot of people felt his work wasn't up to par as a total piece," she says of the show she had of his paintings in 1983. "I felt the great thing with Ferlinghetti is he had something to say and he said it, and there were no bones about it. He conveyed the message if you were willing to look."

Guttman saw some more recent work at his studio and felt the power that attracted her earlier very much present. Describing another painting dominated by the single human form, she noted, "What he got across was this lone figure in this tremendous space. And he was alone. You got a tremendous feeling of loneliness. I don't know if he meant it, but you got it."

Ferlinghetti finds characterizations which emphasize his "loneliness" inaccurate and (to use the term with which he labeled them after reading an earlier version of these pages) "puerile." Though his own travel journals specifically record a sense of loneliness at times, it is important to note that those feelings aren't dominant. Much more apparent to all who know him, even superficially, is his energy and vitality. Still, as various others have described it, the sense of aloofness, privacy, isolation, of being separate, always, is a central part of his character. Above all, he is a man with his own agenda.

In almost the same breath, however, most of these same people also emphasize his unpretentiousness as well as the graciousness and consideration he shows toward everyone. He is, one suggested, a gentleman in an age when such courtesies have become nearly as much an anachronism as the term. Both the qualities of separateness and of consideration seem to be rooted in his upbringing with the Bislands, who themselves were apparently distant emotionally, but whose aristocratic background emphasized the values of courtesy, of generosity, and of community service, which Ferlinghetti so completely embodies.

Some of these characteristics, along with others that are much a part of him, are apparent as well in the place he lives, where we meet the next day before going to his painting studio. The apartment is the first floor of an old wood-frame two-flat house. The burnt-red paint covers the address numbers on the entry door set back underneath a brick archway, so it's easy to miss them at first. Inside, the look, the furnishings, everything else, is equally unassuming.

In the small entryway his interest in art is present from the very first, in the two works which hang on the wall, one by him and one by Hassel Smith. Along with that interest, his distance from the political mainstream is announced by the small Cuban flag next to the closet.

The living rooms, up a steep flight of stairs, which he takes two at a time, are far from opulent; some might call the place barely middle class. A typical San Francisco flat, he says, though nowadays even a modest apartment in San Francisco is more expensive than comparable housing in most any American city. Roomy, old, a little cluttered, it is devoid of most decoration, except for the unframed posters hung on nearly every wall, including the bathroom. It is generally quite well ordered, but not especially clean. No dust balls cluster along baseboards, no bags overflow with garbage, but the surfaces don't quite shine; and the place feels just a little dingy despite the light coming through big dusty windows into all of the rooms. It seems very much the place of a man living alone.

The rooms all open from a hall which runs the length of the apartment. At one end is a large kitchen, and what is there suggests that he is a man with some care for his health. No chips, cookies, or other junk food are in evidence; but a bowl of bananas sits on one table. A juicer, an old toaster, and an Osterizer are on the other, while a few potatoes and a couple of cloves of garlic sit on a shelf. On others, there are a few cookbooks that had belonged to Julie and some cereal she once bought.

Ferlinghetti's affection for dogs and his more recent affection for cats are both in evidence. In the refrigerator, mostly empty (he is leaving town soon), there are a half dozen or more bottles of medicine for a dog, and the entry to the pantry at the back of the kitchen bears the announcement "*Chien méchant et perspicace*" (bad and shrewd dog). This, despite the fact that there is no dog here these days; it died some months ago, and Ferlinghetti has not bothered to clean out all its traces, more likely because of neglect than sentimentality. But the cat's litter box and food are kept here near the back door. The cat itself is, however, like many cats, nowhere to be seen in company.

As anyone would be, he is justifiably proud of his accomplishments, and the apartment has plenty of posters as souvenirs of his celebrity. In an alcove in the hallway next to the bathroom, a framed certificate dated April 3, 1975, signed by Major Joseph Alioto, cites Ferlinghetti's and City Lights' contributions to San Francisco and proclaims Lawrence Ferlinghetti Day. In the front room a poster announces "Ferlinghetti Reads Painting Poems, April 5, 1985." And the bathroom is decorated on every wall with posters announcing his readings.

One friend asserts that choosing the bathroom for such decoration is "a comic, self-deprecatory gesture," and that seems likely. It's an aspect of the genuine wonder which energized his well-known early poem "I am waiting . . ." and has continued to be a central part of his outlook. Leaving a recent party at the fancy hilltop apartment of the head of the local Goethe Institute, Ferlinghetti caught himself in the full-length mirror in the hall on the way out and did a reflexive double take, grabbing his felt hat in perfect imitation of Charlie Chaplin. It was an act, of course, but the "Who's that?" he asked aloud was a genuine question—a question he's been asking all his life.

As in everything of Ferlinghetti, there is a sense of moderation throughout his apartment. None of the walls are lined with the rows and rows of books that often surround and emphasize the literary occupation of those whose life it is. Rather, what is here is what is used, what is valued and of current interest. A few volumes are stacked on the small shelf near the bed: *Hooplas for Odd Occasions*, poems by James Broughton; *Blue Highways*, by William Least Heat Moon; volumes by Gabriele D'Annunzio, Gabriel García Márquez, Carlos Fuentes, Richard Ellmann, Plato, as well as French, Italian, and Spanish dictionaries.

Across the bedroom is one of the four other bookshelves in the apartment, some three feet wide and five or six feet high. The top shelf holds foreign editions of Ferlinghetti's books. The others, in no apparent order, are eclectic, reflecting his interests in literature, in publishing, in politics, in art, in the spiritual life. There are old copies of Joyce's *Portrait of the Artist as a Young Man* and *Finnegans Wake*, and Pound's *Cantos*, all books which were important in Ferlinghetti's education. Next to them are two books of typefaces, the collected works of Marx and Engels, Tarot cards, Suzi Gablik's book of art criticism, *Has Modernism Failed?* and a biography of Marcel Duchamp by Robert Lebel, the father of his "best French buddy," as Ferlinghetti calls him, artist Jean-Jacques Lebel. There is a Bible, the Bhagavad-Gita, Wallace Stevens's selected poems, *The Palm at the End of the Mind*, both Ann Charters's and Gerald Nicosia's biographies of Kerouac, the Viking Portable *Dante*, Mary McCarthy's book on Renaissance art, *Stones of Florence*.

The study is next to the bedroom, and the main thing that sets it apart from the rest of the apartment is the light—five bay windows about the table in front make this room noticeably brighter than any of the others. A three-foot-high plant and the old Royal manual typewriter are the only objects on its surface. It seems a comfortable place to work, though he's spent less and less time here since he began painting again. Asked whether he's ever thought about a word processor, he laughs.

"I don't even have a Selectric," he says. "I never learned to touch-type; I still just hunt and peck. But I can do it pretty fast."

The rest of the room displays the same qualities of surface order over casual neglect that mark the rest of the place. The table next to the door is completely covered with files, records, a small stereo. The files, he tells me, have to do with *Literary San Francisco*. Nine or ten cartons are stacked on the floor along one wall, a couple of the top ones open. They are filled with more files and journals and memorabilia, dating back to World War II, none in any order. They are here on the floor because an agent is coming to inventory them and arrange their sale (which was made to the Bancroft Library).

In the corner across from the door, there's a rolltop desk, its surface clear. The top shelf holds an old second edition of *Webster's New International Dictionary*, and above that, on the wall, a huge print of Gauguin's *Tahitian Women*. On the wall adjacent are photos of a sidewalk entrance to the Paris Métro, of City Lights, and of Ferlinghetti wearing one of his felt hats, standing at a microphone with a poster of Mexico on the wall behind him.

He sits down at the table, takes off the glasses he has been wearing while browsing through his mail, and begins to answer a question about his relationship with Allen Ginsberg, whose new writings, after more than thirty years and eleven books with City Lights, are now being published by the trade giant Harper & Row.

"Well, it's logical," he says about the development. "City Lights has always been ready for its authors to move on to greater heights. The function of the small press is discovery. If one of our authors, some poet we were the first to publish, gets an offer from a New York publisher, we don't try to stop them, we encourage them." In fact, it was Ferlinghetti who first negotiated a contract for Ginsberg with Knopf. Only because Knopf wouldn't commit to more than a single collected-poems volume did Ginsberg hire an agent to negotiate a larger, six-book contract.

Ginsberg himself says that he rejected earlier offers from trade presses because the close relationship with City Lights brought both practical and personal advantages any larger, impersonal trade press couldn't possibly equal. Besides giving him royalty advances whenever he needed money through the late fifties and the sixties, City Lights served as a San Francisco center for Ginsberg's personal and literary business, and Shig's apartment was a place to stay whenever he was in town.

"I liked keeping my 'amateur status,'" Ginsberg said recently, "or avant-garde, or marginal. We had a very good arrangement. If he [Ferlinghetti] needed more money one year I would give him a larger percentage. We didn't even have a contract for *Howl* until the very end. It turned out nobody could even find a contract. We had a friendship arrangement, and it worked out practically thirty years."

When I ask Ferlinghetti what he thinks now of Ginsberg's work, whether he agrees with critics who say his early work was his best, he hesitates a moment.

"I think it's definitely true that the poem 'Howl' has greater poetic content than anything else, except 'Kaddish.' "

He goes on to talk about the influence of Buddhism on Ginsberg's work.

"There's a poem of Allen's called 'The Change.' He wrote it on the Tokyo–Kyoto express evidently. I've never discussed this with him, but the way I interpret the poem, before 'The Change' he had this enormous obsession with death and death imagery. I remember his journals from South America; we were in Chile in 1959, and he stayed down there much longer than I did. They're full of death's-head drawings in the margins, death-head symbols. It was drug-related symbolism, heavy drugs being really a death trip.

"Then when he went to India and Japan, he went through this change where he rejected the death symbolism. When he came back to this country it was like a different Allen Ginsberg. It was a different person than the young fiery radical. It wasn't that he wasn't radical anymore— but he had become more 'mellow' as they say. The whole message of the Great Paramita Sutra had sunk into his consciousness—no suffering because no sensation. He became more and more benign. Instead of having this antagonistic stance of 'Howl,' aggressively attacking the status quo, or attacking America, or the military, or whatever is the point of attack, he's saying if you counter aggression with aggression, you just get more. It builds and builds. Allen [believes in] absorbing the enemy's territory into your own consciousness rather than projecting hostility. A poem may be a detailed condemnation of the activity of the CIA for drug trafficking, but it treats the actual members of the CIA as poor and befuddled human beings who are wandering around in darkness and need to be led to the light."

Whether or not the later work may be as powerful as "Howl," Ferlinghetti still firmly believes that the body of Ginsberg's work has made him the most important living poet in America.

"But the best new writers now are prose writers—Eduardo Galeano, Márquez, Kundera perhaps are the most important. On the growing edge today, I think it's the Latin Americans who are dominating in fiction and journalism. But among poets, I don't know who would be writing greater poetry these days."

He elaborates on his enthusiasm for Latin American writers and talks about the current political and literary landscape.

"Contemporary reality has bypassed the surrealists. It becomes increasingly difficult for an intellectual to come up with any new synthesis on account of the absolutely overpowering quantity of information which is poured out today in the mass media—in print, in the visual, audio, whatever medium it is. The daily mass of information that the individual is called upon to process in his one little head becomes much more difficult—impossible—to synthesize. That's why writers seem to be so attracted to word processors and computers. Because they help them to synthesize this mass of information which is reality.

"That's why I think 'language poets' in the end are really nowhere in any such attempt to give meaning, to make a new synthesis. They're essentially minimalists, and what is required is a maximalist. The greatest writers today are the maximalists, such as Márquez in *One Hundred Years of Solitude* or *Autumn of the Patriarch*, which is a maximalist reinterpretation of history. Eduardo Galeano is doing this also, and Carlos Fuentes, and Isabel Allende.

"*The Autumn of the Patriarch* is so maximalist you get universal, archetypal situations and figures. The wonderful description of the Patriarch in his last years—of course he's always in his last years—he's in his palace, he's propped up on his throne with his loving children playing around his feet and his wife lovingly circling her arm around his shoulders. And this is on television in the book to show the populace their ruler is still in control and still able to rule the government, and everything is fine, everything is under control, peace will reign, no reason to worry about anything. But at the same time at the foot of the Patriarch, not seen by the television eye, there are cracks in the palace floor with the weeds creeping through and up onto the legs of the throne.

"It's the same thing that was on television just before Marcos abdicated, or before he was thrown out of the Philippines. He was shown on the television in the great armchair with his loving wife and his grandchildren playing at his feet. A *New York Times* article even mentioned that there were cracks in the floor."

When I ask what he thinks about the current poetry scene with its proliferation of published young poets, none of whom seem to make much of a splash outside of their own small pool, he is quick to say that he can't think of any new poets who have particularly impressed him. But he doesn't take the absence of any startling, preeminent new voice as a sign of poetry's permanent decline as a vital force.

"All it awaits is some new Young Turk to spring up and write another masterpiece. Before 'Howl' was published there was a state of doldrums in American poetry. Everything was very academic, much like today—like the language poets today writing poetry about poetry, writing poetry about language. This is just what was going on in poetry before 'Howl' was published in the 1950s. Very academic, very dull, everyone mumbling in their beards and contemplating their navels. Well, everyone always says, everything has been said, nothing new can be said, then along comes some new great voice. It's bound to happen again. It could happen tomorrow. When something like 'Howl' is published, everyone says, well, this was just waiting to be said, why hasn't anyone said this before? If it's a great masterpiece, they think, God, I've never seen the world like that before. Why hasn't anyone said this before? It was just waiting to happen. And the same thing today. There's nothing but a low mumble now. And if I could think of what it is that's just waiting to happen, I would articulate it myself."

Perhaps it is his sense that he hasn't thought of it yet that has fed his deep engagement in painting. For the last five years Ferlinghetti has shared a studio, first with two, now with one other artist, in the old converted naval administration building at Hunter's Point. But during the half-hour drive from his apartment there, he doesn't talk much about painting. Instead, he points out occasional landmarks—not the usual tourist attractions, but places that have more personal meaning, and that have fueled the political passions which are never far from the surface. Stopped at a traffic light near a stretch of green, he glances at a handful of seedier-looking natives who lounge about the park benches.

"Last year they put up signs in Washington Square," he says, referring to the block-square park near City Lights. "No sleeping between ten P.M. and six A.M. I wrote letters to the editor, and other people did, about how if they had that kind of rule, a lot of people from Jack London to Jack Kerouac wouldn't have had a place to sleep. And so they took the signs down, by God. They're all gone. There's about a dozen bums who sleep in Washington Square. There's no reason they couldn't sleep there. It's not doing any harm."

Driving down the Embarcadero, the wide drive skirting the waterfront along the city's north and east perimeters, he points to an elevated freeway on our right that just ends at a temporary barricade.

"See that freeway that blocks the view of the waterfront?" he says. "There was a big fight over it. It was supposed to continue all the way along the waterfront. But they had a revolt about twenty years ago, and it's been like that ever since. Last year it was on the ballot to tear it down, but it lost. People won't walk. They gotta have their cars. They thought they wouldn't be able to get across town fast enough without this fuckin' freeway."

When we get to Hunter's Point, he shows a pass to get into the parking area. The buildings housing the studio are part of the "largest visual artists community in the nation," according to the *San Francisco Bay Guardian*. Begun in 1976 through the instigation of Jacques Terzian, a local artist who makes large installations out of old industrial patterns, studios now occupy five buildings housing over 350 artists.

He drives in and parks, then we walk up the short flight of stairs and down the dim hallway to his studio. The large room, some seventeen hundred square feet, is roughly divided into two work areas, but without any partitions. Though he shares the space with another artist, their respective work habits are such that Ferlinghetti has it to himself almost all the time. Set in a corner, three sides of the room have windows, and against the back wall, another door leads onto a catwalk over the water. With long, quick strides, he walks to the back and leads me out the door. He sweeps his hand past the hills in the background, the ship docked a couple of hundred yards away, the Bay everywhere in front.

"Look out here," he says. "I was one of the first ones out here, so I got one of the best locations. Try to find a studio like this in New York."

Back inside, he flips on the small cassette player to a symphony and begins showing canvases.

"On two weekends a year they open up these studios, everyone puts out wine and stuff. And we have a model on Mondays."

There must be a hundred or more paintings and drawings here, including a number from the fifties when he worked under the spell of Franz Kline and abstract expressionism. Almost all of the paintings he has done since he took it up again in 1977, however, are dominated by figurative elements. He shows a painting called *The Tomb of the Unknown Poet*, one of a series of four. In the center of an abstract blend of dark, gray-blue colors, an image of the Eiffel Tower dominates.

"Always there's a battle between the objective and nonobjective," he says, "where it starts out as a nonobjective painting and I'm determined that it's going to be a nonobjective painting. At the last minute, some figure will show up. This one began as nonobjective, but then the Eiffel Tower showed up. When you see a group of broken images, your eye, your mind, wants to make something of it."

He shows another called *Pocahontas*. On the right half of the canvas, a woman faces a collection of buildings on the left. Below her, toward the corner, an Indian's head faces right.

"You know, Pocahontas was taken by Captain John Smith to London when she was only like fourteen or fifteen years old. She probably got syphilis. She was exhibited in London in a cage, and she died very young.

"But it's funny what happens. I was painting these buildings, and suddenly I saw these figures emerge. And that's very strange, it happens quite often. I don't know where they come from. Like this one, this figure shows up. Of course it wasn't as well defined, and then I start delineating, and then I say, well, who's that? Where did she come from? And then I see this Indian over in the corner skulking about. And I say, that must be Pocahontas. It sounds pretty absurd, but quite quite often it seems like there are these figures that have been waiting through all time to spring upon the canvas. It's like a mysterious force."

This formulation of the mystery in his composition echoes that phrasing of Henri Michaux that Ferlinghetti had first quoted in his 1953 *Art Digest* review of a Michaux exhibit at the Oakland Art Museum.

"Scrawl unconsciously, there practically always appear faces on the paper," Michaux had written. "As soon as I take a pencil, a brush, one after the other they come to me on the paper. . . . From what depths do they come?"

He pulls out a painting of a faceless woman against a purple-white background. At her feet is a bird, perhaps a dove; draped over her arms, which meet at her waist, is an American flag, the blue stripe missing.

"This is *Martha Washington Crossing the Delaware*," he says. He explains that the blue stripe is missing because no American flag existed until after the revolution. "She was probably back on the old plantation while he was here. I consider it a feminist painting."

He shows another painting that also has a feminist theme.

"I call this one *Before the Revolution*. These guys are leering at this woman. The woman as sexual object." Despite his insistence that his painting and his poetry are entirely separate, there are some similarities. Both are frequently narrative, and both often carry overt, didactic content. There are paintings of the sea, of men alone, of nude women, all elements which are in many of his poems. And there are words on several paintings, adding direction to the image.

In both his writing and painting, his style of composition shows some similarity as well.

"*Coney Island* was written practically all at once," he says, "without any revision, over a matter of a few weeks or a few months, I forget how long a time. But there was practically no revision at all. Some of the longer poems, like 'Autobiography' or 'Junkman's Obbligato,' were long poems I cut down. A discursive poem like 'Populist Manifesto' went through maybe six or seven revisions, and generally the poem kept getting shorter."

Though in his painting he doesn't shorten or cut in any way, he also works very quickly, and only over time has he come to spend more hours reworking some canvases. He walks over to the painting he's been working on currently, called *Autogeddon*, apparently inspired by a long poem with the same title by British playwright Heathcoat Williams, part of which Ferlinghetti excerpted in the second *City Lights Review*. The poem, as the title suggests, is about the destructive domination of the automobile in our lives, and the painting provides a corresponding image—a woman, naked, superimposed against the front bumper of a black and white automobile.

Ferlinghetti studies it, then hurries over to the table with his brushes and oils and begins mixing. Working quickly, he adds some shadow to the woman's body. The car's lights are on, the front grille dominating the canvas, and though the detail, characteristically, isn't sharp, the skeletal outlines of the car, the black lines over the eerily shining white that seems to glow from its interior, give the whole foggy gray-black-white scene a ghostly, charged, otherworldly atmosphere.

He stands back to look at the canvas, which is large, like most of his—five feet long by six feet high—then mixes more paint and returns to outline, then cover the woman in gold. Picking up a rag, he outlines her face, blending the new color with the darker grays and reddish tones that had been there. With the rag over his right index finger, he goes on to work the outline down the rest of her body, then picks up the canvas, rests it against the legs of the easel, and steps back. After a moment he lays it on the floor, bends over, and works another half minute with the rag before switching to the brush he's been holding in his left hand. Another minute and he stands over the painting for a few more seconds. He gets some new paint and goes to work on the dark fender of the car where it arcs around the white peeking up from wheel well. All his movements are quick, as he moves from brush to rag to brush, from easel to floor and back. He puts the painting back up on the easel, pauses for another moment, then with the same quickness goes over and changes the cassette tape, which has ended.

"I have a painting called *The Death of Neal Cassady at San Miguel de Allende*," he says, talking again about his revision process. "I finished it once and had it photographed on a four-by-five color slide. A year later I pulled it out and did it again. I thought it was terrible. Then I had it photographed again, and I thought, that's it, now it's finished. Just a few weeks ago, I pulled it out and completely redid it."

The painting views the bare-chested Cassady from underneath, from the ground, through the railroad ties which cross his knees, waist, and cover his face. His arms slightly askew, it is almost as if the tracks themselves were a sort of cross bearing him up. The words "Ferrocarril Mexicana" are written across his chest, though they will be removed in yet a later version.

"Well," Ferlinghetti says, "I think he's really finished this time."

* * *

Another bright, cool San Francisco day. In front of City Lights Bookstore, a few people wait for the bus to take them farther downtown, a few more browse in the front window, a few wait, perhaps for the afternoon's festivities to begin; a few more just wait. It's Sunday, October 2, 1988, and the celebration commemorating City Lights' thirty-fifth anniversary will begin in an hour. But on Columbus Avenue it's any afternoon, nearly any day in the last thirty years. A woman with long white hair ambles around the corner into the alley between the store and Vesuvio's bar. A half dozen men sit in the tavern's gloom, and when a blonde with a camera walks in for a moment, they all look up. A little disconcerted, not finding whatever she was looking for, she quickly backs out. The faces on the street are young and old, oriental, black, Hispanic, white; no one is too well dressed, no one in much hurry.

The smaller window of City Lights, to the left of the entry, displays books by the authors who are being honored today, along with a couple by others connected with the event. Ferlinghetti's proposal to rename San Francisco streets after authors who were born or had lived here finally passed the city's Board of Supervisors the last January, and this week, new signs were installed to mark the twelve renamed streets. Right now, the one next to the store, which used to read Adler's Alley, and the one marking the cul-de-sac across the street are draped in blankets, waiting for the unveiling.

The store's larger window to the right of the door, however, offers no evidence of this milestone. The two dozen or so books behind the glass are not necessarily titles that might be most popular, but those the booksellers think most important. Paul Yamazaki, who worked here in 1970 and 1971, and steadily since 1980, is the chief buyer, but other staff members buy books in their area of expertise. Ferlinghetti's newly published novel, *Love in the Days of Rage*, is one of them, but it gets no special attention, flanked by Edmund White's *Nocturnes for the King of Naples* and *Imagining Argentina*, by Lawrence Thornton.

Ferlinghetti and his exceedingly loyal staff have worked hard to maintain the intellectual, anarchist, bohemian tone that has distinguished the store since its opening. The door still opens into the same tiny room it did in 1953, but now the floor space beyond is four or five times what it was thirty-five years ago, and the downstairs space equals it. There are a few shelves of hardbacks now, just beyond the counter, but none are best-sellers. The rest of the store is filled with paperback books.

To the right, the small room opens to what was the Italian travel agency, which City Lights took over in 1978. The large, open space with room to walk and browse is the main upstairs room now. Beyond is the smaller poetry reading room, opened in June 1987. Now there's actually room for occasional poets and others to sit down for a piece, in one of the chairs set by the two round tables, next to the books of poetry, the dozens of literary magazines, below the blown-up photos and posters, and read or just gaze out the window. There are photos of Corso, Ginsberg naked to the crotch, Walt Whitman, Kerouac, and Cassady, announcements of past City Lights Poets Theater readings by Voznesensky, Yevtushenko, Bukowski, the 1972 benefit for the Greek Resistance. And there's a framed painting: a yellow-green abstract field with a few red streaks, over which is the printed message "Printer's Ink is the Greater Explosive."

At a quarter to three that afternoon, the dark-haired Peters stands beneath the arch to the poetry room in jeans and the black "City Lights 35" T-shirt that was made for the anniversary bash. She's going over the order for the coming events with Karen Larsen, the publicist who did most of the research for the street-renaming proposal. When Peters is done with the rundown, she hands Larsen the clipboard, then excuses herself to go the few blocks to her apartment and change clothes.

Larsen is already decked out for the event in business suit over a white blouse. Tall, her brown hair mixing with gray, she makes a striking figure in more formal dress than is generally seen here. She heads her own publicity agency and got involved in the streets project three years earlier when she and Ferlinghetti were keeping steady company. In 1983 she had been working in an office upstairs from the Caffe Roma, a restaurant and coffeehouse just a block from City Lights, as talent coordinator and publicist for a radio station's fund-raising telethon. She kept running into Ferlinghetti on Columbus Avenue and finally asked him if he'd like to do a volunteer stint answering phones for the telethon.

When he said yes, Larsen remembers, "no one could believe it. I mean you'd get people like Paul Krassner, people who are aligned with him politically, but they're practically comedians, they love to do it. But people who heard would say, is this really Lawrence Ferlinghetti answering telephones?

"That's when I realized he sort of liked me, or he wouldn't have done that."

Those who have known Ferlinghetti well also know that his willingness to participate in such a project is entirely in keeping with his populist values and unpretentious manner.

Ethel Guttman was particularly struck by that part of him.

"I've had people come to class who are artists," she says, "and they look down on the other students, and they're contemptuous. He is a man of position, and he came to class, and he didn't spread his wings, and he participated as a student, and he talked to the other students. As a person, he is one of the most considerate. He's sensitive, and he really puts himself out."

Larsen also was attracted by his unpretentiousness and by their mutual disinterest in anything too fancy or expensive.

"I've often said, no matter how much money I'd ever make I'd live exactly the same," she says, "and I get that feeling about him—an old bohemian style, whatever you want to call it."

She goes on to talk about his sharp sense of humor, so much a part of his poems, which is also so evident in his personal style.

"He's seventy years old," she says, "and he's still goofy. He likes to be silly and use funny voices. And you should see him dance. He dances like a Sufi dancer—he's like floating around, his arms out. He doesn't care what anyone thinks."

When they took a vacation together, it was not to an exotic resort, or to any resort at all. Instead, in November 1985 they drove down the east coast of the Baja Peninsula, spending a few nights in a hotel outside the tiny village of San Felipe, then camping on a desert beach near there. But as important as any political or aesthetic values they shared was their emotional fit.

"I think he has a very vulnerable and sensitive core. I mean, he seems real secure, but there's an emotional vulnerability. He's very delicate there, which is why you can't tease him. And I think a lot of it comes from that early life—not having a mother, not being able to trace his family."

Though he is a highly public poet, and eager to talk about politics, ideas, issues, Ferlinghetti is intensely private in his personal relations; he never discusses his emotional life with anyone. Though Larsen says she herself is not one to discuss her personal life with others, it was that refusal on his part which from her point of view led to the end of any real romance.

"He's a romantic person, but he's not earthy about love and romance; he doesn't want to deal with it. He doesn't want to talk about it. He actually said to me once, if you have to work at a relationship, then who needs it? If it doesn't work out naturally, then I don't want to do it."

They stopped seeing each other regularly in the fall of 1986, but just as he has remained friendly with Paula Lillevand, so Larsen and Ferlinghetti have continued to be friends and to meet occasionally. At three-fifteen on this Sunday, she stands behind the store's front counter, next to the phone, talking with a local producer for NBC. A crew from the network's *Today* show has been in town to profile Ferlinghetti for a segment they will broadcast later in the month, and they will be shooting the afternoon's events. They need some space, and Larsen is telling the producer where the event will be, where the audience will stand, what choices they might have about positioning.

Ferlinghetti himself is in the offices upstairs, where a reporter from the *San Francisco Examiner* is interviewing him. Larsen picks up the phone and buzzes him: can the *Today* people come up and talk to him? She hangs up, then walks out with the producer and his partner to show them to the office where Ferlinghetti is waiting. In the large room where the crowd will gather, the bookshelves are being pushed toward the walls to make room. The posters over the arch to the poetry room where the speakers will stand proclaim familiar sympathies: an Alice Walker broadside, an "Against Apartheid" event. Taped to the side of the balcony on the other wall are the names of the dozen new streets printed on 8″ by 10″ cards: Jack London Alley, Isadora Duncan Street, Jack Kerouac Alley, William Saroyan Place, Ambrose Bierce Street, Frank Norris Street, Via Bufano, Mark Twain Place, Bob Kaufman Alley, Richard Henry Dana Place, Dashiell Hammett Street, Kenneth Rexroth Place. In the corner of the room diagonally across from the arch, a table covered with a maroon paper tablecloth and gold napkins is out to hold the wine and plastic cups.

The program is scheduled to begin at four, and by ten to four, when Dr. James Hart, the head of the Bancroft Library at Berkeley, walks in and asks for Ferlinghetti and Peters, the room is crowded. Though only a handful of speakers wear coats or ties or dresses, almost everyone is dressed neatly, a far distance from the beatnik or hippie costuming of previous decades.

The *Today* producer and his partner have come back into the store, leaving Ferlinghetti by himself. The anticipation swells with the crowd, and the volume rises. Someone points at a woman and asks if that's Nancy Peters (it's not). A half dozen people wear cameras. Two young local poets discuss Dukakis's chances in next month's election. By four, when Ferlinghetti walks into the front room, it's nearly impossible to move.

He's wearing a navy-blue corduroy jacket, blue shirt, and green corduroy pants, and he's immediately surrounded by people who know him. He talks with some members of the Frank Norris Society, who are here to celebrate the naming of a street after that novelist. Others crowd close. After a few minutes he makes his way through the close-packed crowd to the archway at the other end of the filled room, where he takes his place next to Peters, who has returned in a gold and black dress. He takes the small bell she hands him and begins ringing it. When the room is almost quiet enough to hear to the back, Peters briefly welcomes everyone to City Lights' thirty-fifth anniversary celebration.

"In 1953, when City Lights opened," she says, "it began as a pocket book shop, occupying the space just that side of the door." She goes on, summarizing its history. When she recounts that "Lawrence Ferlinghetti here announced that it would carry every paperback book in print," there is a round of laughter.

She announces that Mayor Agnos has proclaimed the day "City Lights Bookstore Day," drawing a round of enthusiastic applause, then launches into an anecdote Gent Sturgeon, one of the booksellers, told her about a man who wandered in, spent some time browsing, and came up to him, bewildered. "He seemed to be the sort of person who might have been born in a mall," she says, "lost here by some awful cosmic error." The audience howls. The man, she goes on, found his way back to Sturgeon and challenged him, asking, "What the hell kind of books are these?"

" 'Books for smart people,' he answered."

The crowd roars its solidarity.

She goes on to announce the official street renaming, then presents "the man whose idea it was—Lawrence Ferlinghetti."

After the prolonged cheers and applause quiet, Ferlinghetti begins. "I feel like Christopher Columbus himself when he landed in North Beach"—he pauses for more laughter and applause—"and said I hereby in the name of the Queen name this Columbus Avenue."

When the laughter dies again, he goes on to mention other projects he proposed: tilting Coit Tower ("Think what it did for Pisa"); giving Alcatraz back to the Indians; then suggests, "Gorbachev for President." Each one is greeted by another round of laughter.

He lists the first six streets, explaining roughly where they are, and their original names. When he says, "Jack Kerouac Alley, right here," pointing toward the door, there is a huge burst of cheers and applause. After mentioning "Mark Twain Place," he steps aside, and Peters describes the others with short explanations and anecdotes about the streets and writers, then introduces Dr. Hart.

Besides heading the Bancroft library, Hart is an expert on California literature and history, professor emeritus at the University of California–

Berkeley, and author of a biography of Richard Henry Dana, for whom one of the streets is renamed. He tells of the dubious distinctions of the men for which some well-known existing San Francisco streets are named. Green Street, he tells us, was named after a political hustler and embezzler who changed his name to Green only after he fled his wife and four children on the East Coast. Once in San Francisco, his real identity was finally discovered much later. The story brings another round of laughter and applause.

After a half hour or so of more speeches, Peters directs the crowd outside, where a ladder is set up next to the street sign at the end of the alley. Ferlinghetti makes his way over to it through the crowd. The sign is draped with a blanket; when Ferlinghetti reaches it, he puts his palms together and makes a slight bow from the waist, then sweeps the blanket away in a single motion to reveal the large green sign proclaiming Jack Kerouac Alley. The onlookers spilling into Columbus Avenue applaud. He climbs down and the whole scene is repeated across the street as he unveils William Saroyan Place, the new name for the little cul-de-sac between Tosca's Cafe and Spec's bar.

By now the crowd is spread along both sides of the street, and the celebration has gone into the bars and restaurants. Ferlinghetti walks into Tosca's, greeting people on the way, spends a few minutes talking to acquaintances in back, and comes out with daughter Julie. The two head up the block and across the street, where Ferlinghetti meets George Williamson, a reporter for the *San Francisco Chronicle*. Dressed in broad-brimmed, light-colored hat, tweed coat, jeans, and boots, almost as tall as Ferlinghetti and much heavier, Williamson cuts a prominent figure as he follows Ferlinghetti in the door to the City Lights office where he will get an interview for the next morning's editions.

Peters and Larsen walk down Columbus in front of City Lights, talking to people, making arrangements. Gregory Corso, in old pants and unshaven, congratulates a family in a mini-van for being the first to drive down Jack Kerouac Alley. A white-haired woman carrying a video recorder comes down the street and asks a bystander to "tell me about money—you know—money. What do you think about it?" A thin, elderly man in jeans, blue T-shirt, and beads, his white hair flowing down his back, brags that he's eighty-two and a hippie forever. Ferlinghetti joins Larsen at Vesuvio's, where they sit at a table next to the door with George Cleve, their mutual friend who is the conductor of the San Jose Symphony Orchestra. They chat for a while—the place isn't too crowded or too loud to talk—while the poets, the writers, the celebrants, carry on up and down Columbus. Local poet Jack Micheline is talking at the bar at Tosca's; poet and activist Jack Hirschman ducks into the bookstore to see someone; a couple in their late thirties or more pushes a carriage with a wide-eyed four-month-old slowly down the street. Kerouac's biographer, Gerry Nicosia, talks about his new book on the history of the Vietnam Veterans' movement; a Chicago filmmaker working on a documentary about Nelson Algren is here for the goings-on and bemoans Chicago's insensitivity in changing a street name there to honor Algren for only a few weeks, then quietly restoring its original name.

Little by little, the twilight descends, and the party goes on. By seven Ferlinghetti has had enough. He will rise early to go swimming again tomorrow morning, to have coffee and read the *New York Times* at the small Puccini café, to do some business at City Lights, to paint. As he has a thousand times, he walks up Columbus Avenue, by himself, nodding his good-byes on the way, headed home.

At the City Lights office the next morning, Ferlinghetti is frustrated at the article in the *Chronicle*. Williamson has chosen to focus on the outlandish side of the crowd, featuring the account of Corso, "legendary Beat poet and wild man," who "launched into an ecstatic North Beach dance," then "howled in the manner of his good pal and mentor, Allen Ginsberg, while blocking the path of a mini-van."

"He had a story written before he came over here," Ferlinghetti says. "You know, we're going to do 'beatniks,' and that was it. It was disgusting. All these dignified people, these important people, and they were excluded."

Coming into the back office where Ferlinghetti is sitting at his rolltop desk, Peters agrees. "Changing the streets honors San Francisco. That's quite an accomplishment in any city, and to treat the celebration as though it's just a bunch of weird people—" She shakes her head.

A little later Peters returns, this time with a copy of the afternoon *Examiner*, where the event is given much more dignity, featured on the back of the first section in a half page with picture. Neither Beats nor beatniks nor any wild dances are mentioned here, the account instead emphasizing the speakers, the streets, and the significance of their new names.

When the phone buzzes to signal a call, Peters goes back into the other room to answer it while Ferlinghetti turns to the one manuscript on his desk. His office here is brighter and cleaner than any room in his apartment. The books are shelved neatly, the posters shine, even the stuffed unicorn seems carefully arranged on its cushion under the table. Left by a film crew, the animal sits on the bed that had belonged to Ferlinghetti's "Pooch," the constant, valued companion who died the previous winter.

There seems little pressing business here this morning; the latest *City Lights Review* was sent to press last week, and with the anniversary over, things are decidedly slow. In the other room there's still plenty to do— Peters's corner desk is crowded, the baskets on the table behind her are filled with business, she talks on the phone. That room is larger, but not at all cluttered. There's a tape casette player, an electronic typewriter, a long table against each wall, Peters's desk, a few shelves, another chair.

A little after noon, Ferlinghetti walks into the other room and grabs his jacket. After a quick good-bye to Peters, he's off down the hall, on the way to his apartment, where he will get his car and drive to his studio to spend the afternoon painting.

The Work, The Life: Poets and Critics on Ferlinghetti

CLICKETY-CLACK

(for Lawrence Ferlinghetti)

> *I took*
> *a coney island of the mind*
>
> *to the coney*
> *island of the flesh*
> *the brighton local*
>
> *riding*
> *past church avenue, beverly, cortelyou, past*
> *avenues h & j*
> *king's highway, neck road, sheepshead bay,*
> *brighton, all the way to stillwell*
> *avenue*
> *that hotbed of assignation*
> *clickety-clack*
> *I started reading when I got on*
> *and somewhere down past newkirk reached*
> *number 29 and read aloud*
> *The crowd*
> *in the train*
> *looked startled at first but settled down*
> *to enjoy the bit*
> *even if they did think I*

was insane or something
and when I reached the line: "the cock
of flesh at last cries out and has his glory
                    moment God"
some girl sitting opposite me with golden hair
fresh from the bottle began to stare dis-
approving and wiggle as tho she had ants
somewhere where it counted
                    And sorry to say
5 lines later the poem finished   and I
started to laugh like hell   Aware
of the dirty look I was getting I
stared back at her thighs imagining
what she had inside those toreador pants beside
                    her bathing suit and, well
                    we both got off at Stillwell
Watching her high backside sway and swish down that
street of tattoo artists, franks 12 inches long, past
                    the wax museum and a soft-drink
                    stand with its white inside,
I stepped beside her and said: "Let's
fling that old garment of repentance, baby!"
                    smitten, I
hadn't noticed her 2 brothers were behind me

                    clickety-clack

                    Horseman, pass by

                    —PAUL BLACKBURN

   Paul Blackburn's homage, written more than fifteen years ago, reminds us again how long a shadow Ferlinghetti's poetry has cast in our times. Unparalleled in popularity, it has been read by more people, in more countries, than that of any living American poet. Countless numbers who may have read no other contemporary poetry—and maybe no poetry at all besides what was forced on them in school—have read Ferlinghetti. And just as remarkably, in an age when advertising is king, his success has had nothing to do with marketing; certainly his longtime publisher, New Directions, never mounted any great national campaign to promote his work.

Bookseller, enabler, novelist, painter, playwright, poet, publisher, spokesman—his roles have been so many, his position is hard to assess except alphabetically. His two novels, and the third he is writing, have much less "public surface" than his poems, and are much less well known; but in the long run, it may be that work which will be best appreciated by future generations. *Her*, particularly, offers in the rich images of its dense prose "a book demanding great attentiveness," in the words of critic Larry Smith, "engendering multiple readings . . . [and] is ultimately rewarding for its insight and its bold evolution of form." Vincent McHugh called it, simply, a "great triumph of narrative."

His recent novel, *Love in the Days of Rage*, also received much positive notice and sold very well; and though his relatively brief engagement in theater never attracted anything like the kind of critical attention or popular audience of his poetry, it too has adherents, and the plays are still occasionally produced. Then there is the painting, which work, "long after we are all dead," as one curator put it, may turn out to be more important than everything else.

Nonetheless, it is the poetry and the publishing that made his reputation and continue to have the greatest impact, having raised him in the sixties to a level of celebrity rarely achieved in America by any except sports heroes and media stars. If his popularity has faded somewhat in the last twenty years, his is still a name hundreds of thousands, probably millions, know. Is such prominence, then, another phenomenon of the time, another case of a media figure pumped up by the extended adolescent rebellion of the baby boom generation, or is it due to something more, something that will last, something with fundamental value that future generations will name as a vital part, not just of an era, but of a whole way of seeing—the characteristic that makes us call it great art?

"He made a major social contribution as a publisher," says Allen Ginsberg. "It was I think the best poetry-publishing venture of its time, and maybe still, for all I know. Certainly during the late fifties and early sixties he had some of the best poets in America and sold them the best, his packaging was the best. Then, City Lights was the first poetry bookstore in America, which was also an innovation, and a great step forward, and a classical step forward since it was modeled on European- and French-style books. So it brought continental sophistication into publishing. And then he's been a supporter of poetry and a father figure of poetry and a pillar of San Francisco society—one who newspapers could call up and whose word meant something. He had a tremendous role in helping other poets. So it's certainly a monumental job.

"But it'll be the poetry, naturally, that lasts."

If Ginsberg is right, it's not an assessment most critics have shared, though there are significant exceptions. But both his supporters and his detractors seem to agree on the main qualities that make the poetry appeal to such a wide audience. And a number of well-known poets and critics who have known him, and a few who haven't, go on to explain.

First and foremost, all agree, it's accessible. In an age when poetry is most often some kind of hermetic language that can only be deciphered by specialists, Ferlinghetti offers a straightforwardness of grammar and style that makes the poems immediately clear to the nonspecialist. It must be much more than simple clarity, however, that has led to such success; there are other poets who are just as clear, but who have never, can never, hope to reach so many.

"There is certainly a sense of romantic nostalgia, and heart yearning, and bohemian idealism, and populist social aspiration and declamation and proclamation," Ginsberg says. "There's a kind of ideal responsiveness to everyday events, political events, yearly political events. And a kind of down-home melancholy for local situations. I guess the greatest thing in his poetry is his affectionateness. As a popular poet, he deserves the kind of affection he gets from audiences."

Poet Robert Creeley, who has also known Ferlinghetti since the fifties, elaborates on some of the same themes. "To me," Creeley says, "his poetry is in some respect what Frost always claims to have written, but in my mind never managed in the least. It's an absolutely common tone, and yet it's not like 'have a nice day' or something; it isn't that banality at all. It's a very subtle commonness of address, that makes everyone feel that they're not threatened by what he has to say. He goes through all the range of common human feelings and response, what people care about, and me too, and has kept that tone flexible and specific for years and years and years. He's also capable of an extraordinarily warm and terrific humor. He's one of the great poets of that authority."

Nearly everyone who has read his work, no matter how different from their own, agrees about the achievement of that distinctive and inclusive Ferlinghetti tone, that invites everyone into his way of seeing, with genuine warmth.

Michael McClure explains it by saying simply, "The poetry entertains. It has so little challenge that it can reach so many people. And there's a great tightwire-walking wit that goes with it."

Honed to a fine satiric edge that cuts away insistently at the most sacred icons of the culture—religion, government, authority in all its forms—it is that wit which is perhaps most distinctive and characteristic. When it first emerged in the mid-fifties, it was both a content and a voice that was completely new in poetry, and so drew immediate attention. Paul Carroll, the poet and editor who was one of the early publishers of Ferlinghetti and other Beats, remembers especially that freshness:

"I liked the freedom and the wit," he remembers. "I like the form that he was using, too, those line breaks. It's a very oral poetry. But I liked most of all the kind of healthy irreverence he had for the kind of poetry that he and I and Allen [Ginsberg] and everyone else had grown up with. And the subject matter also was news, frequently. You didn't have to, on the one hand, expect from one of his poems a rather brokenhearted, shy poem about the closing of the cabin on Fire Island, while the little cats climbed over the rooftop, all rather sad in a Grail of moonlight, in *The New Yorker* or *The Partisan Review*. On the other hand, you got this kind of extremely civilized, sophisticated, and well-crafted, and boring poetry. You were supposed to have an ironical little poem about seeing Goya's prints of the disasters of war in a fancy London gallery, see, and you were supposed to sign it—there's a whole bunch of guys when I was growing up, they're all interchangeable, and they used to bore the hell out of me.

"Lawrence's poetry had more heart, it had more balls, and also talked about attitudes that were taboo among the more museum-type poets. He wasn't afraid to use his head and to talk about his ideas, but he also had a healthy hilarity, and that was news, too. Because funny was supposed to be little ironies. You couldn't just have a real good laugh in poetry, because Eliot wouldn't let you do that. But Lawrence had really good humor, a very positive sense of life. The poems are clear, they're happy poems, they're a celebration of the fact of the sun and of the day, they make fun of all the proper things: our parents and the square world, the eternal targets for all good art.

"He has that great gift of nailing an image or a phrase that everyone really has felt. Kids can understand it as well as poets. *Coney Island* is a book that demands to be read out loud. It's the opposite of most of our experiences with poetry in high school or college where there's usually a Miss Johnson, or in my case a Sister Tomasita, who'll read a poem by Keats, who I think is the most wonderful poet of all time, then she'll breathe heavily in your face and say, 'That was about *beauty.*' "

Ralph Mills, a poet whose major study of contemporary poets, *Cry of the Human*, established his own critical reputation in the sixties, also remembers discovering *Pictures of the Gone World* and *A Coney Island of the Mind* in the late fifties, and "the sudden, exhilarating, even bewildering sense of *openness* that came from his poems on the page—a visual freedom that went along with the directness of speech, especially after the constricted, academic atmosphere that had pervaded so much of the poetry in that decade. These poems of Ferlinghetti's were unashamedly meant to be *heard*," he writes, "to be read aloud—and also to be seen on the page: their layout was a key to the reading of them. This had been true of *The Cantos* to a degree, and of Williams's late work, but William Carlos Williams was still largely a rejected, even a mocked figure at the time. And here, in Ferlinghetti, one found a poet not afraid to address public materials in powerful, eloquent (frequently funny) ways; a poet willing to satirize openly, to use the labels, the name brands, the objects, the politics, the desires and the repressions of American society—and to do so with sharp intelligence and wit, a rich playful sense of language and allusion."

Anne Waldman, whose accessible, oral style first gained her a substantial following in the seventies, remembers especially the force of Ferlinghetti's satire against organized Christianity when she encountered it in high school in the early sixties.

"It was the practice of some of my fellow schoolmates and friends to meet after school at various homes and read poetry and plays aloud," she says. "And I distinctly remember reading aloud 'Christ climbed down. . . .' I was full of the usual questions of that age, seeking answers to the meaning of life, and especially questioning religious and political hypocrisy, and at the same time having spiritual urges. So Ferlinghetti's poem struck home. It had the litany-like cadence of formal church litany, it had a hypnotic quality, it also was outrageous and somewhat brave, and had the potential of speaking to a lot of people and touching some nerves. This is how I perceived it then.

"It also seemed to be addressed to a larger audience. All his work did. But it seemed particularly relevant to the fifties and early sixties. The whole book, *A Coney Island of the Mind*, seemed relevant to my world. As a New Yorker, one made frequent trips on the D train to Coney Island. There was a particular power in that image, 'Coney Island of the Mind.' I felt I knew what that meant."

She goes on to say that the same qualities of availability have applied to his later books as well.

"He's retained that largesse of address throughout his work—having a populist bead on things, challenging in a very accessible way the status quo. That's been a consistent streak in the work."

Diane Wakoski, who has likewise been widely popular for her own brand of sharp-tongued, generally accessible poetry, also elaborates on Ferlinghetti's irreverence and the basis for its appeal.

"He's interested in the hypocrisy of Christian tradition whether you see it in political terms or religious terms," she says. "He's not a religious writer, but he's interested that the Christian aesthetic, or maybe we should call it the Judeo-Christian tradition, has dominated Western civilization, and isn't it ironic that it has dominated us, but we've totally ignored what its principal preaching is. It's sharing, whether you look at that as Marxist economics or democratic politics or the kind of art that the Whitman tradition is about, for the common man. It's the revolution of independence."

The often overt political attitudes in Ferlinghetti's poems to which Wakoski alludes, while contributing to the poems' popularity, are at the same time, some think, partly responsible for the generally poor treatment he's received at the hands of critics. Gary Snyder, in fact, thinks that the political content is one main reason for negative critical attitudes.

"The critical establishment is against political poetry," he says flatly. "That's something Allen [Ginsberg] and I get criticized for also. It's ridiculous," he goes on, "but this is the Reagan era, and in particular in the last seven or eight years of the eighties, critics have become very conservative, and our kind of politics has been used as an excuse to ignore us."

Poet and critic Thomas Parkinson agrees that political content and topical references in current poetry frequently get criticized in the present climate, and he finds such an attitude "curious" in light of the history of great poetry. Discussing Yeats's well-known "The Second Coming," which is part of a new edition of one of Yeats's books that he is editing, he points out that though some commentators have argued differently, it clearly begins with specific reference to the current political situation during the Irish Revolution, when it was written.

"That's the disorder that he's talking about in that poem—the disorder that he saw all around him. After all, the Black and Tan smashed all the doors down in his tower. And there's so many things like that in Yeats's poetry. And if you get to know any poet well—like Wordsworth, or Donne, or Dryden, any of them—they're all very topical poets in many ways. Milton couldn't have been more topical or autobiographical." In fact, he goes on, "The urge toward the political poem is almost inevitable. In a secular world like ours, the overt content of values is likely to be political."

In Ferlinghetti's case, Parkinson says, "I think of another Lawrence— you would never believe that D. H. Lawrence said this: 'the feeling of justice is the most sensuous of all experiences.' I think you could say the same thing about Ferlinghetti's poetry. That the sense of justice is a valid human experience, as valid as any sensuous experience."

That championing of independence which Wakoski emphasizes, and of justice which Parkinson emphasizes—indeed, Ferlinghetti's whole stance of dissent against established conventions, against the cultural icons—has always appealed especially to young people, who are inevitably less invested in the status quo. That smaller investment is probably a large part of the reason that Ferlinghetti's appeal has been greatest among the young, and that his greatest popularity came during the late sixties when the huge baby boom generation were in their late teens and early twenties, and were leading their own cultural revolution.

Nancy Peters has been struck with Ferlinghetti's continuing popularity among that group.

"People come into the store," she says of *A Coney Island of the Mind*, "the third generation, and say, 'My grandmother read this book.' And it continues to have that same appeal year after year. It has a lot of emotional impact, an intuitive spirit that appeals to people. He has a tremendous influence on people when they're very young. Hundreds of people come and say, I loved these poems and realized that poetry didn't have to be hard—it could be fun, it could be almost sentimental, it could have charm. Many poets have found Lawrence to be a tremendous initiator into poetry."

McClure echoes that view. "I would say Lawrence's influence has been primarily in initiating an enormous audience into poetry. The Beat Generation was a surge of rebellious intellect, and he was the most accessible part of it. In other words, a kid in Lincoln, Nebraska, or wherever, could pick up his work and read something by a member of the Beat Generation or San Francisco Renaissance, or whatever you want to call it, and read it, and understand it, and furthermore agree with it."

Philip Lamantia, who has worked in the store for several years, agrees. "Lawrence has been able to actually create an audience for poetry among young people. He seems to have done so now for two decades or more, particularly of the late high school to early college age; and he has a tremendous reputation in that zone. It was especially so in the sixties. When they were twenty or eighteen and looking for poetry, they were no doubt startled by writing which they could feel. He seemed to be tremendously available. He seemed to be intuitive to a need. I'm sure he didn't think of that consciously, but it's there, there's no doubt about it. *A Coney Island of the Mind* remains a milestone of communication."

These themes of warmth and accessibility, of humor, of the oral quality of the poetry, are all particularly evident in Ferlinghetti's public performances, and they have been as successful and popular as anything he's put on the page. Beginning with his first performance at the 1955 Poets' Follies, to his appearances with Rexroth and The Cellar jazz band a couple of years later, to his readings through the sixties and since, Ferlinghetti has continued to charm, delight, and move audiences.

Creeley, in fact, remembers not being especially taken by Ferlinghetti's work until he first heard it.

"I hadn't been that moved by reading him myself. I'd been respectful, but not really 'turned on,' " he says. "But hearing him read, I saw and heard what that's all about. It was extremely effective. It's very hard to qualify Lawrence's rapport with an audience. It's immensely familial. It isn't that he's working the crowd in some awful disposition. But he projects a very simple and clear order of real person. And his humor and the pace of his humor is absolutely comfortable. And the wit is very relaxed and human. It's immensely reassuring humor that Lawrence is the master of. So I heard him read that first time, and I remember being extraordinarily moved."

Such warmth and accessibility have much to do also with the "common language" which Ferlinghetti has crafted in his poems. The idea that poetry should speak the "language really used by men" was first articulated by Wordsworth in his preface to *Lyrical Ballads* at the beginning of the nineteenth century, then re-formed in America by Whitman more than half a century later. Ferlinghetti has many times emphasized his belief in the importance of "public surface," so that the poem is accessible to any reader. He writes, he has said, for the man or woman in the street. It is a claim that has led to the poems which are so popular, but at the same time to some of the aspects of his poetics which critics deprecate.

"I've committed the sin of too much clarity," Ferlinghetti said in trying to explain the critical neglect, if not outright disapproval, in which his work is held by much of that establishment. There have been a couple of attempts to make a place for him in academic canons, but it does seem true that the very surface simplicity of the poems works against such efforts. After all, if the ambiguities and complications that fuel the academic engine aren't thick, the machine stalls. There's not enough to study, they think; it's all there for anyone, and no special training or perception is needed to understand it. Literary criticism being as subject to fashion as anything else, that may change, and there are a few rumblings from time to time; there certainly are poets and critics who feel that neglect is unjust.

But as Snyder points out, "It's in the nature of academic criticism for the work of the academic critic to give luster to the critical author. He has to show his own ingenuity, and Lawrence's work, being accessible, does not provide employment for academic critics. So there has to be a public aesthetic that understands and appreciates accessibility and the subtleties that are within that, rather than this Anglo-American hangover from New Criticism days that wants ambiguity and tension and irony and complexity."

Wakoski agrees. "Critics are going to gravitate to the poet who has the most complicated surface, and seems to be the most difficult," she says, "because it gives the critic a function." She goes on to say that this is seriously misleading, however, and is no index to real depth or importance, illustrating with a comparison to painting.

Someone without any particular education in art history "can look at a painting with an obvious human figure in it, or an obvious landscape, and say I like that, whereas he can't look at the Jackson Pollock because he doesn't know how to look at the fragmented figure. On the other hand, if the painter is really working with the myth of Odysseus, that is not what the average person is looking at. He's not looking at what is really the literary, artistic, or aesthetic components of the painting, he's only looking at the surface. This is too easy. The painting couldn't possibly have any value if it didn't have all those things behind it. Portrait painting has traditionally been dismissed because it's just rich people's paintings, whereas if you get far enough away from the portrait you see that even when the painter isn't trying specifically to portray the woman as Venus or specifically trying to portray the burgher as Zeus or somebody else, and specifically getting the irony of this woman who has a very high position actually having won it by her whorelike activities or whatever, that isn't what people are looking at on the surface.

"It's what we all look at when we start looking at art as art and not just as beautiful entertainment. And there are certain kinds of artists who prefer to have the easy surface because they're still trying to get a wider audience. So what poets like Ferlinghetti always have to do is a hundred years later win the attention of the critics because they've had the popular audience, and maybe sometimes in their own lifetime lost it, because the popular audience goes someplace else.

"What Ferlinghetti's trying to put together is the same thing I'm trying to put together, what Whitman, Ginsberg, a lot of people try to put together—the common speech with somebody who is not a common man. It's very Wordsworthian. The poet has to speak the language of the common man. The common man really unites us all, whether you're a factory worker or a college professor, insurance salesman or whatever. I think that comes through content. Sex, religion, and politics—you get one of those subjects started at a dinner table, I don't care how different the people are, you can have a conversation, a dialogue, a dialectic, and you can probably have art. And critics are afraid of this."

At the same time, however, Wakoski, like many others, has doubts about the existence of this "common" man or woman. Referring to the early fifties and the birth of the Beat Generation, she says, "It's that idealistic, post–World War II interest in—whatever you want to call it—socialism, Marxism, some kind of communal democratic politics . . . that made Ferlinghetti decide that he wanted these pocket books with the, to me, hilariously idealistic idea that they were small enough that a workman, a factory worker, could stick them in his pockets so he could be reading them in between work on the line at Boeing or wherever.

"The feeling was that World War II should have created a situation where there was so much wealth that everyone could share it, and while it did in some ways, in other ways it didn't succeed. And the idealistic poets were still interested in this idea of the common man and what was he getting out of all this. And Ferlinghetti is the one who was most politically articulate about all of this. So the ideology behind City Lights and the Pocket Poets is that these people were speaking the common language.

"We're right back to Whitman. Whitman thinks he's doing it even if he's not doing it, and these poets think they're doing it even though they're not doing it. Factory workers in fact are going to hate the Beats more than they would hate something that's more elitist. And Ferlinghetti is right there in the center of it."

Parkinson voices a similar view, but offers qualification. "The one paradox in Lawrence's work," he says, "is that he writes for the man in the street, but the man in the street has a junior college degree; he's taken a survey course in English literature and knows some of the famous lines from Yeats and Eliot, and Lawrence plays on them almost shamelessly."

On the other hand, Parkinson says, "It's surprising how literary Lawrence's poetry really is."

Critic Michael Skau, in his recently published study of Ferlinghetti's work, also points out that though many of the references are of the most known variety ("The Norton Anthology School of Allusions," another critic, Robert Peters, writes somewhat scornfully), many others are much more wide-ranging and even academic. Phrases from Djuna Barnes, Gertrude Stein, Pietro di Donato, Apollinaire, and many, many more who are not nearly so familiar, all crop up to inform different poems, Skau notes.

It may well be that it is the combination that adds to the appeal—the ease of recognition of many of the allusions reminds readers that they know more than they perhaps thought, that they are smarter than they knew. It's a subtle affirmation we all appreciate. At the same time, the less obvious references don't put off readers who are not familiar with them, first, because they are invariably used so that the phrase is clearly understandable in the context of the poem, and second, because those others that are well known keep the reader from feeling excluded by the more subtle ones.

So in a poem like the second of *Coney Island*, he describes "Sailing thru the straits of Demos," and says after some pretty obviously parodic, surrealistic descriptions, "we lashed ourselves to masts and stopt our ears . . . ," quoting almost directly the well-known lines from Pound's version of *The Odyssey*, and which most readers with even a casual literary education will recognize. When he ends the poem with an arrival in the suburbs, to find us looking "at each other / with a mild surprise / silent upon a peak / in Darien," which is a town in Connecticut, few beyond the specialists are likely to know the phrase plays on Keats's poem "On First Looking into Chapman's Homer," at whose conclusion Cortéz's men "Looked at each other with a *wild surmise* [emphasis mine] / silent on a peak in Darien"—in this case the Isthmus of Panama, where Balboa (not Cortéz, as Keats mistakenly had it) first saw the Pacific.

The meaning is nonetheless absolutely clear because of the context, as is the satire, even if its final sharpness is missed by those who don't recognize the parody of Keats. It's a conscious strategy on Ferlinghetti's part, enhancing the sense of inclusion that widens the audience.

Obscure or not in his poetic references, his popularity clearly testifies to the poems' widespread availability. And if he is not generally admitted to some approved canon of literary convention—and many, even among his admirers, believe his poems fall short in important ways—plenty of others think his poetry has indeed made a substantial contribution to the literary landscape.

"The one thing that I've kept after him about over the years," Ginsberg says, "was that it seemed he didn't have sufficient minute particular details of observation line by line and verse by verse of his poems, and that they were made up too much of generalization—nostalgic generalization—or paraphrase, or puns." Ginsberg goes on to explain with reference to the Greek terms Pound used to describe the three ways of charging language poetically with meaning.

"A lot of it," he says, "depended on the logopoeia rather than on phanopoeia—witty references, the paraphrases and puns, and a sort of melodic cello feeling—melopoeia—but not enough pictorial phanopoeia. So I wished he would crowd more detail into the poems, in the tradition of Charles Reznikoff or William Carlos Williams, or even T. S. Eliot. Ferlinghetti very often will include some sort of dying fall or archaic inversion of language for the sort of cello or violin sound of it. So that it's more dreamy than iron-hard realistic.

"Of course," Ginsberg adds, "that's his specialty. That sort of dreamy bohemian tone. Though that may be too strong a way of putting it. Because as a writer, as a novelist, he has great powers of observation, and when he does pick up the detail, like in Mike's pool hall or 'The Dog,' it's got a great deal of power."

In his critical memoir *Whitman's Wild Children*, poet Neeli Cherkovski enlarges on that tone, describing "the haunting, opaque quality to Ferlinghetti's poems, as if the speaker is looking at the world from a distance, over an unbridgeable gulf. The poems are direct gateways to a rare world of angelic and satanic impulses that gently merge, sometimes so subtly that it might take two or three readings before one says, 'That is a damn good poem.' "

Another part of Ferlinghetti's poetic strength, Cherkovski says, "is his ability to deal with metaphysics in a direct manner, cutting away excess and complexity while never sacrificing his poetic instincts."

But Cherkovski is taken most of all with Ferlinghetti's lyricism, and has even considered editing a "Lyrical Ferlinghetti" anthology. The language of his lyrical poems, Cherkovski writes, "suggests notions of insurmountable loss, magical landscapes, and the unanswerable questions evoked by love and death. They are a sweet admixture of himself and such older writers as W. B. Yeats and Jacques Prévert [with] strains of e. e. cummings as well."

Ginsberg also readily points out Ferlinghetti's contribution. "What Ferlinghetti did," he says, "was adapt the French loose verse—that you get out of Prévert and Cendrars and a few other poets—to the American style, and that was a great contribution. An ongoing Apollinaire, long, discursive thought sequence in short lines."

Mills echoes this sense of Ferlinghetti's contribution.

"Ferlinghetti once called himself a 'semi-surrealist,' and he has surely brought into American poetry through his own work the influence of Apollinaire, Cendrars, and Prévert (whom he has beautifully translated), among others; but he has used such poetic ingredients in his own fashion and made from American speech his unique style." Lamantia, Wakoski, and Snyder likewise agree about the importance of the European flavor he's brought into his poetry.

"I think there is a thread in all of his poems which I would definitely see influenced by the surrealist movement," Lamantia says, "though not any kind of stereotype of the idea. Because there was no such thing as a standard surrealist poem. That is a mistake made by the academics in discussing it. But the sort of poems called conversational poems, which were some of the most powerful influences on the young French poets in the First World War period, or a little later.... The dialectic, the dynamism of surrealism is based on, not a synthesis—an absurd idea, a synthesis—and it isn't a denial of consciousness, it isn't a denial of the rational, but it's a way of positioning yourself between the rational and irrational—between the temporal and the eternal, the subjective and the objective, and never choosing one over the other, but allowing free movement of unconscious action, poetically, to determine what's going on. It's a give-and-take between the inner and the outer, to put it almost too bluntly."

Noting Whitman's warm reception in France, and Apollinaire's admiration of Poe as well as Whitman among other examples, Lamantia sees Ferlinghetti as clearly a part of the tradition relating the two countries' poetics.

"Valéry Larbaud and all the French poets of the pre-Dada period were great admirers of Whitman," he says. "There's a kind of interesting relation all the time between poets and poetry in America going to France," he says, "then undergoing a transformation, and then coming back to us in the forties and fifties, and then the other way. The American poets of the Beat Generation influenced a whole crop of people in Paris—huge anthologies of this sort of blue-jean poetry, or what they call electric poetry, that they had in the sixties."

As for Ferlinghetti himself, Lamantia says, "It isn't that he is Francophile, it doesn't come from that; it comes from something that has to do with this exchange that's going on between the two countries from the beginning. If Apollinaire said, somewhere around 1912, 'Paris is the center of the poetic world,' then you could say after 'Howl' and Lawrence and that whole movement, that the U.S. became the center of the poetic world for a time."

Wakoski also talks about Ferlinghetti's particular joining of European and American poetics.

"What Ferlinghetti does," she says, "is put together—for lack of a better word—the linguistic crudeness or obviousness, the 'barbaric yawp' of Whitman, that we can see in Ginsberg, with the subtle irony of that European tradition that comes out of Aristotle and winds up in somebody like Prévert. Maybe we have no other poet than Ferlinghetti putting that together. So the critics who like the subtlety that comes through the European are going to reject Ferlinghetti, and the ones who accept the barbaric yawp are not going to see it in Ferlinghetti because it's linguistically not there. He has made an amalgam that so far there's no other critical model for. A groundbreaker," she goes on, "is somebody who puts things together from the past in a way they have never been put together, and that is so attractive that it sets its own tradition." In that way, she says, "he may be more of a groundbreaker than, for instance, Ginsberg, who is [directly] carrying on the Whitman tradition."

In emphasizing the European aspects of Ferlinghetti's work, Snyder also points out the political components of that influence. "His uniqueness," he says, "has been a kind of almost European intellectual, political, direct engagement in a vernacular mode, with maybe a little more lightness and a little more humor than Ginsberg has. So when I think of Lawrence's work and I think of his contribution, I think of a witty, high-toned, European-style intellectual, poetic engagement. And not only European, but you find it also in South America. I think of Neruda, for example, or in some cases, some poems of Octavio Paz. The Europeanness of Lawrence, or the non-Americanness, is in his role as a political man of letters, which very few American poets are willing to take on."

One aspect of those politics that some feminists have criticized is the attitude toward women that some of his poems seem to evince, as in early published versions of "In a Time of Revolution for Instance," or more generally the view of woman as some kind of aesthetic-sexual object, rather than a coequal being endowed with the same human complexity as men.

But Waldman, discussing that criticism, disagrees that Ferlinghetti is in any real sense sexist and argues that the attitudes toward women in his work have a different origin.

"He's decidedly part of his generation," she acknowledges, "which was centered on a male point of view and reflected the particular economic and social situation of the times. And in that tradition [he is] adoring of women and appreciative of women—in fact, can't do without them. Woman is still the muse, woman is the virgin, the angel, the ingenue, and also the bitch, the vampire, the mother.... It's interesting looking at writing of that period, particularly Kerouac, say, and how the female is manifested in her many forms and guises, and maybe is manifested most, for them, as a kind of threat, or something to be controlled. But I see it more from a mythological, mytho-poetic point of view, I think, than maybe some of the hard-core feminists.

"In looking back over his poetry, it seems to be addressed beyond male-female issues, and more toward the larger public. The things he concentrates on, the context of his work, seem to go beyond that. I never feel he's intentionally putting women in their place or putting them down."

It is a view she says is reinforced directly by her own experience with him and other poets of the Beat Generation.

"Personally I've always been treated very decently, and with respect, particularly by these writers of the Beat Generation whom I admire, and I have very interesting and heart-to-heart friendships with Robert Creeley and Phil Whalen, and William Burroughs, Allen [Ginsberg] of course, and Michael McClure.

"I think if I'd been a member of their generation it might have been different, but I was meeting them after they were established, after they'd fought and won some battles. Perhaps they were mellowed or more relaxed and generous. Certainly times have changed, women writers have come into their own."

As to Ferlinghetti's development over the years, another measure of a poet's achievement, Ginsberg thinks his recent work certainly demonstrates such growth. "He's getting older and more wise. Realizing that each poem has to have some kind of special artfulness to it, and putting an effort into the verse form a little more."

McClure feels even more strongly. "He's probably grown the most of any poet I can think of," he says. "Take one of his early poems—I published 'Constantly risking absurdity . . .' in *Ark II-Moby I*, and I realize that a million people greatly admired that poem and bought the book, but I didn't think it was one of the great poems I'd read. I thought it was a really fine poem, in the sense that it has much grace and finesse, but not the masterfulness that you get into in *Over All the Obscene Boundaries*, which I think is absolutely tremendous.

"You go to a poem in that book, like 'The Rebel,' I mean that's a great poem. And I pick it because it's in the same style as 'Constantly risking absurdity. . . .' It's got the same rhythm, it's laid out on the page the same way, only he's not talking about looking for beauty, he has achieved beauty. And he's not using his little Charlie Chaplin man image anymore. And the echoes of Prévert and e. e. cummings, if there are any, they're inconsequential."

Whether or not his poetry is appreciated by his contemporaries, however, or acknowledged to have some distinction, or is popular with a large public, or is thought by others to demonstrate growth and development, one of the major tests of a poet's real importance is often the extent of his influence on other poets. It is again a question that can't be answered except after many years, but it's certainly true, as Ferlinghetti himself noted, that Eliot, for example, was widely imitated in his own time, as were the original surrealists, as is, to a lesser extent, Ginsberg, in his poetics of extreme personal confession. And though Ginsberg's style of accumulating minute, personal detail isn't necessarily imitated specifically by most, the confessional urge at its root is certainly the current dominant mode, and has been for thirty years.

Clearly Ferlinghetti hasn't had anything like that influence, certainly not to the extent that Eliot did, or probably that Ginsberg has, at least not yet. Many poets of his own generation, and slightly younger, have been known in fact to criticize Ferlinghetti as little more than pop vaudeville fare for a not very well educated audience. But some of that of course comes from common jealousy. And there is no question that he has influenced not only younger, beginning poets to imitate him but some older, better-known poets as well.

Paul Blackburn's poem, one of his *Early Selected y Más*, clearly demonstrates Ferlinghetti's stamp, though this singular example is not necessarily typical of Blackburn's work. Robert Bly, however, has said that it was reading Ferlinghetti's "Tentative Description of a Dinner to Promote the Impeachment of President Eisenhower" in the fifties that made him see the possibilities for an effective political poetry. And in writing and performing his own political poetry during the height of the Vietnam era, Bly went on to garner huge audiences and the kind of respect and attention that helped him win the 1967 National Book Award.

Ginsberg himself acknowledges a larger debt, talking about Ferlinghetti's influence both as editor and as literary friend.

"His whole way of publishing and of approaching poetry is an influence," Ginsberg says. "The attitude as Whitmanic, open, popular. And French.

"The poem 'America,'" he goes on, "I don't think I would have published unless Ferlinghetti had liked it. I thought it was just silly, shallow. It was more his style—kind of puns and joking. It is apparently pretty good, but I never understood that. I thought 'Howl' was good, there's some quite amazing phrasing in 'Howl'; but in 'America' you just have slogans. Very witty slogans sometimes, but just slogans and tones, changes of tones. So it's mostly tone rather than poetry. So he influenced me on that one. I probably wouldn't have published it in a book unless he liked it.

"It's a whole style that I got into, one specialized form of public poetry which I have a lot of. Some of it's successful, some of it's just like journal writings. So I would say that was an influence—political and social commentary poetry."

But perhaps even more important is a particular, enlarged sense of the mind from which Ginsberg says he writes, crediting Ferlinghetti with helping shape the very vision through which he sees in his poems.

"I always have him in mind as I write," he says, "as I have a lot of people. I think of Burroughs, I think of Kerouac, I think of Lionel Trilling, Peter [Orlovsky]—and Ferlinghetti. I'm very conscious of what he would like and what he wouldn't like. Of his mind and his abilities."

He is quick to say that it's not that he thinks of Ferlinghetti as an "audience," which, he says, is a "vulgarized way of saying, and anybody who reads it who is a poet will get the wrong idea; and not only will get the wrong idea, but will mess up. It's not that they're the audience, it's that you look through their eyes. They're you. You become them. Bad poets write for them as an audience, good poets become them and look through their eyes, and expand their own intelligence and imagination to include theirs.

"One reads through someone else's brain. It's a very good trick and all poets should know it and most don't. It's psychedelic. You expand your own intelligence by including others. It's not hard to do. Like the guru leaves an imprint on your mind. They say even when the guru dies, his mind becomes the world, or the sky. It's because you have so much internalized his intelligence and his reactions by the imprinting of it. Like you've internalized your mother's and your father's. It's just part of your nature finally.

"If I read things through Larry's eyes, I see what becomes too literary and what becomes charming, and what becomes engaging, and what becomes sentimentally right—right in sentiment. So his mind, his nature, becomes part of my nature, and I'm sure a good deal of my nature is part of his at this point. I think all good poets do that."

What is Ferlinghetti's place, then, in the literary landscape of his time? Considered separately as a novelist, or playwright, or painter, or even as publisher or poet, his accomplishments may not seem major in the current age of specialists. But as some suggest, our whole model for such assessment doesn't fit. No matter how contemporary he has been, and continues to be, Ferlinghetti's achievement seems to belong to an older idea. He is "a man of letters," to use Parkinson's term; a literary "amicus curiae," as Creeley once described him.

Waldman says, "He's been a statesman, an international statesman. He's been important in bringing a political point of view as a poet and a publisher everywhere he goes. I think that work in the world is as important as the real work.

"What I always got from him was that public, political voice, that witness voice, wanting to communicate, from his heart, questioning establishment values—which is what that whole [Beat] generation was doing. Certainly Allen [Ginsberg] needed a publisher like Lawrence. Certainly Allen's career would have been very different without Lawrence.

"It's hard to look back and say well, if this had been that, if this hadn't been this—who's to say about what is going to last? He's been important as who he's been, a force in contemporary American poetry."

Creeley similarly speaks of the larger context of Ferlinghetti's importance.

"His intentions and feeling of and toward the world have always impressed me as being absolutely decent and true," he says. "Though that's an almost saccharine way to put it, it is for me the emphatic point of the way he's conducted his life. He's an immensely responsible man, to his friends. He's been awfully good to the people he's befriended and helped.

"I think there are people, and occasionally poets—Neruda was one, Dylan Thomas was one in spite of himself, in spite of his social vulnerabilities, Yevtushenko was one, no matter that the younger Russians feel he's simply a businessman, et cetera—there are those who are able to make an extraordinary social place of the world, and reassure others that this is after all its occasion and its possibility.

"It has nothing at all to do with being a bon vivant or with being hip. But Lawrence's world is always, primarily, the given social material of the community, in this case, literally San Francisco. And he feels a commitment to it, a conviction of its significance. He is a community person. He's always had the extreme wit and intelligence to know what he wanted in a circumstance, and when therefore it was time to quit. So he's never been plagued with many of the ills of our dear generation—excessive uses of drugs, love, or any other damn thing. He's an immensely healthy man. He supplies the spirit, and common access, as they say. Lawrence is like a terrific public park. He really gives you a place to sit down."

When asked whether he thinks Ferlinghetti's work might have claim to some ineffable immortality, Parkinson puts it even more simply.

"Will it last?" he says. "It's a question I don't think of. If the poem has an attractive surface and gives a richer quality to my life, I accept it. I like it."

As to his overall contribution, Parkinson echoes nearly everyone Ferlinghetti and his work have touched.

"I've always given this definition of Lawrence for myself," he says. "There are people who make civilization possible, and Lawrence is one of them. I think this comes through in the poetry, it comes through in the publishing, it comes through in his presence."

Afterword

When we walk outside the City Lights office, that day after the thirty-fifth anniversary celebration, the sky has cleared, and the bright light etches shadows into the asphalt and concrete of Columbus Avenue.

"It's all here!" Ferlinghetti exults, gesturing about the street, at the cafés, the huge mural wrapped around the corner of Columbus and Broadway. He waves at the artist who has been working on it for months, and is just now crossing Columbus.

"I'm in it, right over there." He points to a spot in the mural above Broadway, where a flat, simple portrait of Ferlinghetti and his dog gaze down at the traffic.

"Remember the poem about the morning light?" he says as we cross Columbus Avenue, then walk down Stockton toward Union Square. He's referring to number 5 of his "Paris Transformations":

> *The white sun of Paris*
> *softens sidewalks*
> *sketches white shadows on skylights*
> *traps a black cat*
> *on a distant balcony*
> *And the whole city sleeping drifts*
> *through white space*
> *like a lost dirigible*
> *unconscious of*
> *the immense mystery*

273

"People talk about Paris light," he says, "but the light here is just as special."

The fog's blowing off has created an intensity about the light, making everything seem sharper, more brilliant, with an early morning freshness, though the morning is already over. We walk past the square where a few idlers sit on benches, a few more hurry by, the streets of North Beach much less crowded than yesterday when the Sunday tourist crowds filled them. The smells of fresh bread, of Italian and Chinese cooking drift through the air as we pass open storefronts, a produce truck unloading, a Chinese woman sweeping a landing.

"Just look at it!" he bursts out again, his long strides suddenly even longer. At the top of the hill on the corner of Lombard, a trim, clean-shaven man dressed in T-shirt and shorts comes up. Around forty, he looks on the way to—or from—his daily jog, or whatever athletic regimen, perhaps before going to work in the financial district. Whoever he is, there's no seedy "bohemian" trace anywhere about him; nothing of the atmosphere with which both national and local press have surrounded City Lights and Ferlinghetti for years, and which the morning *Chronicle* article about yesterday's events repeated. He wants to congratulate Ferlinghetti on the anniversary. Ferlinghetti thanks him, and the man is on his way again. We pause one more instant, the blue water of the Bay, and Mount Tamalpais, glistening at the end of Stockton Street, beyond the city.

Ferlinghetti crosses the street, and in an instant he's gone, down the hill, into the San Francisco light.

A Selected Bibliography

BY FERLINGHETTI

Poetry

Pictures of the Gone World. City Lights Books, 1955.
A Coney Island of the Mind. New Directions, 1958.
Starting from San Francisco. New Directions, 1961.
The Secret Meaning of Things. New Directions, 1969.
Open Eye, Open Heart. New Directions, 1973.
Who Are We Now? New Directions, 1976.
Northwest Ecologue. City Lights, 1978.
Landscapes of Living and Dying. New Directions, 1979.
Endless Life: Selected Poems. New Directions, 1981.
The Populist Manifestos. Grey Fox Press, 1981.
Over All the Obscene Boundaries. New Directions, 1984.

Novels

Her. New Directions, 1960.
Love in the Days of Rage. E. P. Dutton, 1988.

Plays

Unfair Arguments with Existence. New Directions, 1963.
Routines. New Directions, 1964.

Translations

Paroles. Jacques Prévert. City Lights, 1958.
Roman Poems (trans. with Francesca Valente). Pier Paolo Pasolini. City Lights, 1986.

Travel Journals

The Mexican Night. New Directions, 1970.
Seven Days in Nicaragua Libre. City Lights, 1984.

Other

Tyrannus Nix. New Directions, 1969.
Back Roads to Far Places. New Directions, 1970.
The Illustrated Wilfred Funk. City Lights, 1971.
Literary San Francisco, with Nancy Peters. City Lights and Harper & Row, 1980.
Inside the Trojan Horse. Don't Call It Frisco Press, 1988.
Leaves of Life: Fifty Drawings from the Model. City Lights, 1983.

ON FERLINGHETTI

Cherkovski, Neeli. *Ferlinghetti: A Biography.* Doubleday, 1979.
Skau, Michael. *Constantly Risking Absurdity.* Whitson Publishing Company, 1989.
Smith, Larry. *Lawrence Ferlinghetti: Poet-at-Large.* Southern Illinois University Press, 1983.

SELECTED BOOKS PUBLISHED BY CITY LIGHTS

Angulo, Jaime. *Indians in Overalls.* 1989.
Antler. *Factory.* 1980.
Artaud, Antonin. *Artaud Anthology.* 1965.
Baudelaire, Charles. *Intimate Journals.* 1983.
————. *Twenty Prose Poems.* 1988.
Beach, Mary, ed. *Journal for the Protection of All Beings, No. 2: On the Barricades.* 1968.
Beck, Julian. *The Life of the Theater.* 1972.
Bowles, Paul. *One Hundred Camels in the Courtyard.* 1962.
Broughton, James. *Seeing the Light.* 1976.
Bukowski, Charles. *Erections, Ejaculations & Tales of Ordinary Madness.* 1972.
————. *Notes of a Dirty Old Man.* 1973.
————. *Shakespeare Never Did This.* 1979.
Burroughs, William S., *Roosevelt After Inauguration.* 1980.
————. *The Burroughs File.* 1984.
Burroughs, William S., and Allen Ginsberg. *The Yage Letters.* 1963.
Cardenal, Ernesto. *From Nicaragua with Love.* 1987.
Cassady, Neal. *The First Third.* 1971.
Codrescu, Andrei. *In America's Shoes.* 1983.
Corrie and Stein, eds. *Journal for the Protection of All Beings, No. 3: Green Flag.* 1969.
Corso, Gregory. *Gasoline.* 1958.
————. *Vestal Lady on Brattle.* 1968.
Cossery, Albert. *Men God Forgot.* 1961.

Doolittle, Hilda (H.D.). *Notes on Thought & Vision.* 1983.

DiPrima, Diane. *Revolutionary Letters.* 1971.

―――. *In My Time: Selected Poems.* 1989.

Duncan, Isadora. *Isadora Speaks.* 1981.

Duncan, Robert. *Selected Poems.* 1959.

Ferlinghetti, Lawrence, ed. *Beatitude Anthology.* 1960.

―――. *City Lights Journal,* No. 1–4. 1961, 1964, 1966, 1978.

―――. *City Lights Anthology.* 1974.

Ferlinghetti, Lawrence, Michael McClure, and David Meltzer, eds. *Journal for the Protection of All Beings, No.1: Love Shot.* 1961.

Ferlinghetti, Lawrence, and Peters, eds. *City Lights Review,* No.1–3. 1988–1990.

García Lorca, Federico. *Ode to Walt Whitman & Other Poems.* 1988.

―――. *Poem of the Deep Song.* 1988.

Ginsberg, Allen. *Howl and Other Poems.* 1956.

―――. *Kaddish and Other Poems.* 1961.

―――. *Reality Sandwiches.* 1963.

―――. *Airplane Dreams.* 1968.

―――. *Planet News.* 1968.

―――. *Indian Journals.* 1970.

―――. *The Fall of America.* 1972.

―――. *Iron Horse.* 1974.

―――. *Mind Breaths.* 1977.

―――. *Plutonian Ode & Other Poems.* 1981.

Ginsberg, Allen, and Ann Charters. *Scenes Along the Road.* 1970.

Hemingway, Ernest. *Collected Poems.* 1960.

Hirschman, Jack. *Lyripol.* 1976.

Joyce, James. *Pomes Penyeach.* 1966.

Kaufman, Bob. *Golden Sardine.* 1967.

Kerouac, Jack. *Book of Dreams.* 1961.

―――. *Scattered Poems.* 1971.

Kovic, Ron. *Around the World in Eight Days.* 1984.

Lamantia, Philip. *Selected Poems.* 1967.

―――. *Becoming Visible.* 1981.

―――. *Meadowlark West.* 1986.

Laughlin, James. *In Another Country.* 1977.

―――. *Selected Poems,* 1986.

Levertov, Denise. *Here and Now.* 1956.

Lowry, Malcolm. *Selected Poems.* 1962.

McClure, Michael. *Meat Science Essays.* 1963.

Michaux, Henri. *Miserable Miracle.* 1963.

Norse, Harold. *Hotel Nirvana.* 1973.

O'Hara, Frank. *Lunch Poems.* 1964.

Olson, Charles. *Call Me Ishmael.* 1967.

Orlovsky, Peter. *Clean Asshole Poems & Smiling Vegetable Songs.* 1978.

Parra, Nicanor. *Anti Poems.* 1960.

Patchen, Kenneth. *Poems of Humor and Protest.* 1956.

―――. *Love Poems.* 1960.

Pessoa, Fernando. *Always Astonished: Selected Prose.* 1988.
Ponsot, Marie. *True Minds.* 1956.
Purdy, James. *In a Shallow Grave.* 1988.
Rexroth, Kenneth. *Thirty Spanish Poems of Love & Exile.* 1956.
Sanders, Ed. *Investigative Poetry.* 1976.
Shepard, Sam. *Fool for Love.* 1983.
———. *Motel Chronicles.* 1983.
Snyder, Gary. *The Old Ways.* 1977.
Solomon, Carl. *Mishaps Perhaps.* 1966.
———. *More Mishaps.* 1968.
Voznesensky, Andrei. *Dogalypse.* 1972.
Waldman, Anne. *Fast Speaking Woman.* 1975.
Watts, Alan. *Beat Zen, Square Zen.* 1959.
Whitman, Walt. *An American Primer.* 1969.
Williams, William Carlos. *Kora in Hell.* 1957.
Yevtushenko, Voznesensky & Kirsanov. *Red Cats.* 1962.

RELATED WORKS

Allen, Donald, ed. *The New American Poetry 1945–1960.* Grove Press, 1960.
Allen, Donald, and Warren Tallman, eds. *The Poetics of the New American Poets.* Grove Press, 1973.
Buchwald, Art. "The Upbeat Beatnik," *Evergreen Review*, ed. Barney Rosset. Vol. 4, No. 14. Grove Press, 1960.
Charters, Ann. *Kerouac.* Straight Arrow Books, 1973.
Cherkovski, Neeli. *Whitman's Wild Children.* Lapis Press, 1988.
Chicago Review. Ed. Paul Carroll and Irving Rosenthal. Vol. 12, No. 1. Spring, 1958.
Dana, Robert. *Against the Grain: Interviews with Maverick American Publishers.* University of Iowa Press, 1986.
Duncan, Robert. "On Kenneth Rexroth (an interview with Linda Hamalian)," *Conjunctions* 4, 1983, pp. 85–96.
Eberhart, Richard. "West Coast Rhythms," *New York Times Book Review.* September 2, 1956, pp. 7, 18.
Evergreen Review Reader. Ed. Barney Rosset. Grove Press, 1979.
Ginsberg, Allen, *Howl: Original Draft Facsimile, Transcript & Variant Versions, Fully Annotated by Author with Contemporaneous Correspondence, Account of First Public Reading, Legal Skirmishes, Precursor Texts & Bibliography.* Ed. Barry Miles. Harper & Row, 1986.
Kherdian, David. *Six San Francisco Poets.* Gilgia Press, 1969.
Kramer, Jane. *Allen Ginsberg in America.* Random House, 1969.
Manchester, William. *The Glory and the Dream: A Narrative History of America, 1932–1972.* Little Brown & Co., 1974.
Meltzer, David. *The San Francisco Poets.* Ballantine, 1971.
McClure, Michael. *Scratching the Beat Surface.* North Point Press, 1982.
Miles, Barry. *Ginsberg.* Simon and Schuster, 1989.
Nicosia, Gerald. *Memory Babe.* Grove Press, 1983.

Patchen, Kenneth. *Collected Poems*. New Directions, 1968.
———. *The Journal of Albion Moonlight*. New Directions, 1941.
Phelps, Robert, and Peter Deane. *The Literary Life: A Scrapbook Almanac of the Anglo-American Literary Scene from 1900 to 1950*. Farrar, Straus, and Giroux, 1968.
Read, Herbert. *Poetry and Anarchism*. Faber & Faber, 1938.
———. *Existentialism, Marxism and Anarchism*. Faber & Faber, 1956.
Rexroth, Kenneth. "Excerpts from the Unpublished Autobiography," *Conjunctions*, No 4, 1983, pp. 97–114.
———. *The Alternative Society: Essays from the Other World*. Herder and Herder, 1972.
Richards, Janet. *Common Soldiers*. Archer Press, 1979.
Rigney, Francis J., and L. Douglas Smith. *The Real Bohemia*. Basic Books, Inc., 1961.
Rorabaugh, W. J. *Berkeley at War: the 1960's*. Oxford University Press, 1989.
Roszak, Theodore. *The Making of a Counter Culture*. Doubleday & Co., 1969.
Sawyer-Laucanno, Christopher. *An Invisible Spectator: A Biography of Paul Bowles*. Weidenfeld & Nicholson, 1989.
Wholly Communion: International Poetry Reading at the Albert Hall. Grove Press, 1965.

¶Index